Educational Technology in the 21st Century

Educational Technology in the 21st Century

Edited by
Dmitri Ivazov

WILLFORD PRESS
www.willfordpress.com

Published by Willford Press,
118-35 Queens Blvd., Suite 400,
Forest Hills, NY 11375, USA

ISBN: 978-1-68285-670-3

Cataloging-in-Publication Data

Educational technology in the 21st century / edited by Dmitri Ivazov.
p. cm.
Includes bibliographical references and index.
ISBN 978-1-68285-670-3
1. Educational technology. 2. Educational innovations.
3. Teaching--Aids and devices. I. Ivazov, Dmitri.
LB1028.3 .E38 2019
371.33--dc23

For information on all Willford Press publications
visit our website at www.willfordpress.com

Contents

Preface

E-learning refers to the practice of using, managing and creating technological processes to improve performance and facilitate learning. In the present age, it is practiced in four different ways, which are synchronous and asynchronous, computer-supported collaborative learning (CSCL), flipped classroom and computer-based training (CBT). E-learning is a vast field, which uses different platforms to function, such as virtual learning environment (VLE), learning content management system (LCMS), training management system, etc. A significant aspect of educational technology is e-assessment, which enables the use of information technology for educational assessment. Some common examples of e-assessment include e-marking, computerized adaptive testing and computerized classification testing. This book discusses the fundamentals as well as modern approaches of e-learning. The topics covered herein deal with the core aspects of this domain. In this book, using case studies and examples, constant effort has been made to make the understanding of the difficult concepts of e-learning as easy and informative as possible, for the readers.

This book is a comprehensive compilation of works of different researchers from varied parts of the world. It includes valuable experiences of the researchers with the sole objective of providing the readers (learners) with a proper knowledge of the concerned field. This book will be beneficial in evoking inspiration and enhancing the knowledge of the interested readers.

In the end, I would like to extend my heartiest thanks to the authors who worked with great determination on their chapters. I also appreciate the publisher's support in the course of the book. I would also like to deeply acknowledge my family who stood by me as a source of inspiration during the project.

Editor

The Internet Implementation of the Hierarchical Aggregate Assessment Process with the "Cluster" Wi-Fi E-Learning and E-Assessment Application — A Particular Case of Teamwork Assessment

Martin Lesage, Gilles Raîche, Martin Riopel, Frédérick Fortin and Dalila Sebkhi

Additional information is available at the end of the chapter

Abstract

A Wi-Fi e-learning and e-assessment Internet application named "Cluster" was developed in the context of a research project concerning the implementation of a teamwork assessment mobile application able to assess teams with several levels of hierarchy. Usually, teamwork assessment software and Internet applications for several hierarchy level teams are included in the field of Management Information Systems (MIS). However, some assessment tasks in teams with several levels of hierarchy and assessment may be performed in an educational context, and the existing applications for the assessment and evaluation of teams with several levels of hierarchy are not applications dedicated to the assessment of students in an educational context. The "Cluster" application is able to present the course material, to train the students in teams as well as to present individual and team assessment tasks. The application's special functionalities enable it to assess the teams at several levels of hierarchy, which constitute the hierarchical aggregate assessment process. In effect, the members of the teams may have appointments of team member, team leader and team administrator that supervises team leaders. This application can therefore evaluate simultaneously different knowledge and skills in the same assessment task based on the hierarchical position of the team member. The summative evaluation of the application consists of work to submit as well as objective examinations in HTML format, while the formative evaluation is composed of assessment grid computer forms of self-assessment and peer assessment. The application contains two mutually exclusive modes, the assessor mode and the student mode. The assessor mode allows the teacher to create courses, manage students, form the teams and also assess the students and the teams in a summative manner. The student mode allows the students to follow courses, write exams, submit homework, perform in teams and submit self- and peers formative assessment. The theoretical consideration of the project establishes the link between hierarchical aggregate assessment applications and management information systems (MIS). The application is an electronic portfolio (e-portfolio) management system in the competency-based learning and an Internet test administration system in the mastery learning approach. The aim of the chapter is to introduce the reader to the field of hierarchical aggregate assessment and to show how to implement complex assessment tasks with several levels of hierarchy into an Internet software application.

Keywords: E-learning, E-assessment, Teamwork assessment, Hierarchical aggregate assessment

1. Introduction

1.1. General

The current research project is in the assessment field of education. The members of the project has developed an Internet Wi-Fi application that can assess teams with several levels of hierarchy. This application could be considered as an assessment management system (AMS). The application is a complex assessment task in collaborative mode display engine. In fact, during the assessment task, team members can be appointed as team members, team leaders and team administrators that supervise team leaders. These appointments define the hierarchical levels used in the software application. This application is able to process and manage courses, course material, students, teams, hierarchical appointments, assessment tasks, student's curriculums, student's progression in courses and also summative and formative assessments. The application stores all the assessment data to accelerate the organization's assessment process at all hierarchy levels. Hierarchical aggregate assessment of learning in the education domain is a subfield of teamwork assessment where teams have several levels of hierarchy and supervision. Team members are either students or members of any organization that participates in teams in a collaborative mode complex assessment task. In the mastery learning paradigm, this application is a system that presents exams [1] or a system that presents tests to be solved in teams [2] that is a test management system in comparison with the competency-based approach paradigm that defines the application as a collaborative mode complex assessment task display engine [3] and an electronic portfolio (e-portfolio) management system[4] because the application stores all the summative and the formative assessments of presented tests and tasks in its database.

Hierarchical aggregate assessment is a teamwork assessment project that groups students in teams with several levels of hierarchy and assign them a hierarchical position as team member, team leader and team administrator to present them complex assessment tasks in a collaborative mode in an authentic context. When the assessment task is completed, the actual teams are dissolved and the team members are grouped in new teams with new hierarchical positions to perform another assessment task. One of the goals of this chapter is that the term "hierarchical aggregate assessment" to be accepted by the scientific community. This process is shown in Figure 1.

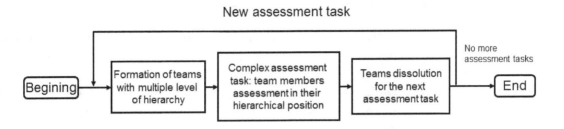

Figure 1. Hierarchical aggregate assessment process

Hierarchical assessment process is applied everywhere teams have several levels of hierarchy. This process could execute itself either manually or automatically with computerized algorithms executed on computer or Internet servers driving Wi-Fi applications. This process finds its origins in the management field where it is applied since human race worked in teams in large organizations. This process surely has been executed by Julius Caesars's generals to assess combat effectiveness of soldiers and their officer's leadership to lead troops in combat.

Hierarchical aggregate assessment includes the standard or the conventional assessment field that provides the same type of assessment for all the students in the class. Hence standard or conventional assessment process is the assessment of the same abilities, performances, knowledge and skills in the same assessment task. So standard or conventional assessment is a particular case of the hierarchical aggregate assessment field. Hierarchical aggregate assessment includes the standard or the conventional assessment and is the assessment of different abilities, performances, knowledge and skills in the same assessment tasks according to the hierarchical position assigned to the team member as shown in figure 2.

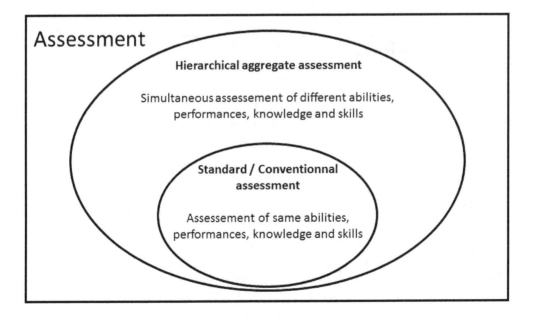

Figure 2. Situation of hierarchical aggregate assessment in the assessment field

1.2. Objectives of the actual research

The objectives of the actual research that is also the subject of a doctoral dissertation is the automation and the computerization of the hierarchical aggregate assessment process with Internet applications and mobile technologies (Wi-Fi). With computer algorithms, Internet applications and mobile technologies, teamwork could be done over the Internet with collaborative work applications used by team members. An Internet application named "Cluster" was developed by researchers of the CDAME [5] laboratory for a PhD project to automate and computerize the hierarchical assessment process with the research and development (R & D) methodology for the development of educative products stated by Harvey and Loiselle [6]. This application currently resides at the following address: http://eval.uqam.ca/cluster/.

1.3. Fields and application domains

The process of hierarchical aggregate assessment has been performed everywhere by mankind throughout the ages. Although the process of hierarchical aggregate assessment was performed through ages, no scientist has considered to define a particular case of teamwork assessment where team members have several levels of hierarchy. The domain of hierarchical aggregate assessment first situates itself in the field of management and its computerization is in the field of computer science. However, the actual research also wants to situate this process in the field of education through complex assessment tasks in collaborative mode with an authentic context, as shown in Figure 3.

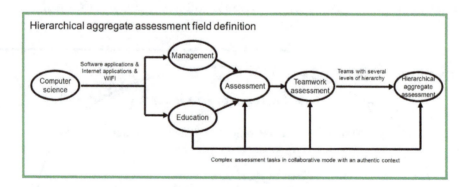

Figure 3. The field of hierarchical aggregate assessment

In effect, in the field of education, it can happen that courses or complex assessment tasks that could be performed in teams can have several hierarchical levels. The authentic context under the hierarchical aggregate assessment occurs when students perform the task in a similar environment to the workplace. This context also applies to the use of mobile technologies (Wi-Fi) in the workplace through which students can perform a complex assessment task in collaborative mode through their cell phone, iPad, iPod or laptop. The use of information technologies in the process of hierarchical aggregate assessment ensures that this process can take place in the field of mobile learning and especially in the mobile assessment field.

The "Cluster" Internet application is a complex assessment task presentation engine in collaborative mode with an authentic context that implements the hierarchical aggregate assessment process. One of the goals of this chapter is to formally define the domain of hierarchical aggregate assessment to be accepted and recognized by the scientific community.

1.4. Chapter structure and organization

This chapter will first define the problematics and the theoretical framework of the hierarchical aggregate assessment field. This chapter will then describe the computerized implementation of the hierarchical aggregate assessment process in the field of education. This process is actually implemented with the research and development (R & D) methodology of educational products defined by Harvey and Loiselle [6] using the "Cluster" Internet application. This chapter will finally present and discuss the results of testing of the "Cluster" application by high school students of the school board of Montreal in the study of geology and by army cadets for the learning of cartography by performing navigation patrols in teams.

2. Problematics

2.1. General

None of the teamwork assessment authors in the education domain as Sugrue, Seger, Kerridge, Sloane and Deane [7], Volkov and Volkov [8] and Baker and Salas [9] have specifically studied the field of teamwork assessment where teams have several levels of hierarchy. Usually, the assessment of organizations with several levels of hierarchy and supervision is part of the Management Information Systems (MIS) field. However, some teamwork assessment tasks in the field of education can have several levels of hierarchy. So, it is important to explore this domain to add new research and theories into the education and assessment field. This new field of research could develop interesting Internet software application as assessment management systems in competency-based learning (AMS) and test assessment systems (TAS) in mastery learning.

Until now, no scientist and no domain expert in the fields of management, information technology, education and assessment has studied and defined hierarchical aggregate assessment. No scientist has yet found a name to define an assessment process with several levels of hierarchy that has always been applied everywhere and has always existed. This process executes itself when individuals are grouped in teams with several hierarchy levels in order to accomplish a task. The research described in this chapter will cause changes and provide a name of this complex process that will be "hierarchical aggregate assessment". This definition will eventually be recognized by the scientific community.

2.2. Teamwork assessment

The problematics that is at the base of the process automation foundations of the assessment process of teams with several hierarchy levels resides in the development of a procedure or a computer application. According to Loiselle [10], the research and development methodology (R & D) of educational products is at the origin of the creation of educational products and the induction of theories produced by researchers throughout the development cycles of educational product development. In the case of the actual research, an Internet application implementing the hierarchical aggregate assessment process has been developed by researchers of the CDAME laboratory according to the research and development methodology (R & D) of educational products. The process of hierarchical aggregate assessment is the theory induced by the process of research and development for the implementation of an Internet application able to process the assessment of teams with several levels of hierarchy, as shown in Figure 4.

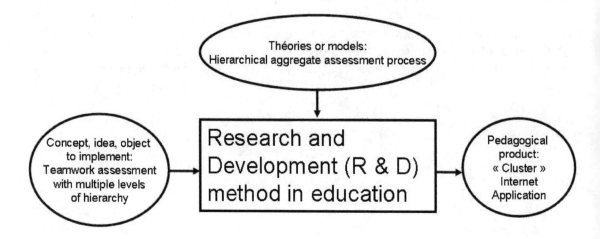

Figure 4. Hierarchical aggregate assessment in the field of education

The hierarchical aggregate field defines itself as a subfield of teamwork assessment. Teamwork assessment is part of both management and education domain. So the hierarchical aggregate assessment field is a common field of education and business administration domains. This states the problematics origin of the hierarchical aggregate assessment where the assessment of teams with several levels of hierarchy has been mostly studied by management and information systems researchers while very few work has been done on several levels of hierarchy teamwork assessment in the education field even if complex assessment tasks with several levels of hierarchy could be performed in a classroom of professional training, as shown in Figure 5.

A large amount of work and research have been done in the assessment field regarding teamwork assessment. Throughout the research and the produced literature, authors such as Sugrue, Seger, Kerridge, Sloane and Deane [7]; Volkov and Volkov [8]; Baker and Salas [9]; Zaccaro, Mumford, Connelly, Marks and Gilbert [11]; MacMillan, Paley, Entin and Entin [12]; Furnham, Pendelton and Steele [13]; Freeman and McKenzie [14, 15]; Ritchie and Cameron [16]; and Lurie, Schultz and Lamanna [17] performed researches and developed theories and assessment grids regarding the dynamics of teamwork with a single level of hierarchy that includes a single leader who runs one or more team members. So far, very few authors, scientists and researchers in the field of assessment teams produced research or theories

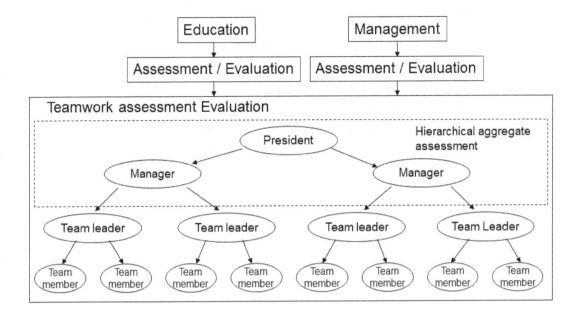

Figure 5. Problematics origin of hierarchical aggregate assessment

regarding the assessment of teams with several hierarchy levels (Lesage, Raîche, Riopel & Sebkhi [18]; Lesage, Raîche, Riopel, Fortin & Sebkhi [19, 20]; Sebkhi, Raîche Riopel & Lesage, [21]). This problematic funnel is described in Figure 6.

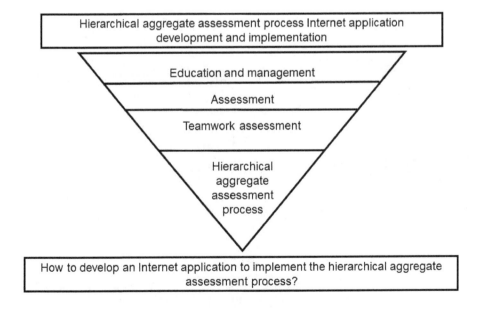

Figure 6. Problematics funnel of hierarchical aggregate assessment

The process of hierarchical aggregate assessment brings together team members into teams that include multiple levels of hierarchy where these people can occupy the hierarchical positions of president, team manager, team leader as well as team member, as shown in Figure 7. The structure of the team is in the form of a pyramid or an inverted tree representing an organizational chart in which each branch is a team which is a team member aggregate. The process of hierarchical aggregate assessment is the action of grouping team members together in a hierarchical organizational structure on several levels and then make an assessment process for each member of the team that is a leaf of the tree or a node of the organizational structure. The Internet application "Cluster" has implemented this data structure located in its MySQL [22] database, and its complex assessment task presentation engine in collaborative mode can perform assessment procedures for each team member or each node of the tree. So in one assessment task, the application can assess different objectives, skills, abilities and knowledge. This feature has not been implemented completely in other distance learning applications such as Moodle [23], Blackboard [24] and WebCT [24], and this statement defines the fundamentals of the problematics of this research.

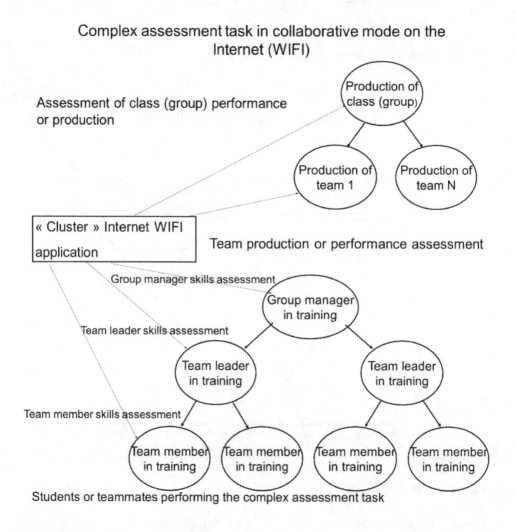

Figure 7. Hierarchical aggregate assessment process capabilities for simultaneous assessment of multiple skills

2.3. Available internet teamwork assessment applications

Online learning software (e-learning) and online assessment software (e-assessment) commercially available are Moodle [23], Blackboard [24] and WebCT [24]. These applications can implement collaborative learning via the Internet by the formation of virtual classrooms where a student may be a member of one or more working groups and may attend one or more classes. They have basic assessment features such as homework submission in electronic format by uploading files to be given to the teacher as well as possessing database repositories of many multiple-choice questions that are part of HTML autocorrecting tests. However, none of these applications have the data structure and software architecture to group or aggregate groups of individuals or teams of students to several hierarchical levels in order to achieve complex assessment tasks in collaborative mode as the "Cluster" application does.

Few of the applications mentioned in the literature is capable of simultaneous assessment of different skills and knowledge according to the hierarchical status of the learner in the same assessment task. The following authors studied peer assessment, but only for the assessment of the same skills and knowledge of team members having the same hierarchical status: Sugrue, Seger, Kerridge, Sloane and Deane [7]; Volkov and Volkov [8]; Baker and Salas [9]; Zaccaro, Mumford, Connelly, Marks and Gilbert [11]; MacMillan, Paley, Entin and Entin [12]; Furnham, Pendelton and Steele [13]; Freeman and McKenzie [14, 15]; Ritchie and Cameron [16]; and Lurie, Schultz and Lamanna [17]. The "Cluster" application data structure is designed to record the group organizational tree structure that contains the hierarchical levels, linking the team members together, while the Moodle [23], Blackboard [24] and WebCT [24] Internet application only allows them to record virtual classes without several levels of hierarchy.

3. Theoretical framework

3.1. General

The theories and research produced by the actual project are an extension of previous work made by Nance [25] that is using a similar aggregation process as the "Cluster" application to form teams with several levels of hierarchy for educational purposes to manage project teams in software engineering courses and also the work of Freeman and McKenzie [14, 15] on the development of the "SPARK" software application that is an Internet distance assessment system managing self-assessment and peer assessment made with assessment grids. Peer assessment is in level 5 of Krathwohl's affective domain taxonomy (Legendre [1]; Lavallée [26]; Krathwohl, Bloom and Masia [27]). Competency assessment in the field of hierarchical aggregate assessment can be made with observation grids or competencies assessment grids (Hubert & Denis [28]; Jeunesse [29]) and also with portfolio (Allal [4]) that usually contains self-assessments (Endrizzi and Ray [30]).

The actual research is based on the development of the "Cluster" Internet application which implements the process of hierarchical aggregate assessment. This application is a presentation engine of collaborative mode complex assessment tasks in an authentic context. The development of the "Cluster" Internet application finds its theoretical foundations in (1) the complex assessment tasks (Louis & Bernard [31]; Tardif [32]), (2) authentic context assessment (Palm

[33], p. 6; Louis & Bernard [31]; Wiggins [34, 35]; Hart [36]; Allal [4]; Rennert-Ariev [37]), (3) teamwork assessment (Baker & Salas [9]; Marin-Garcia & Lloret [38]), (4) collaborative work assessment (Swan, Shen & Hiltz [39]; Volkov & Volkov [8]; Boud, Cohen & Sampson [40]; MacDonald [41]; Swan, Shen & Hiltz [39]; Worcester Polytechnic Institute[42]), and (5) assessment grids (Durham, Knight & Locke [43]; Marin-Gracia & Lloret [38]) as well as self-assessment and peer assessment (Lingard [44]; Goldfinch [45]; Goldfinch & Raeside [46]; Northrup & Northrup [47]).

3.2. Definition of hierarchical aggregate assessment process in general terms

The hierarchical aggregate assessment is defined in general terms as a process that groups teams as well as a subfield of teamwork assessment in which teams have several levels of hierarchy and supervision (Lesage, Raîche Riopel & Sebkhi [18]; Lesage, Raîche Riopel, Fortin & Sebkhi [19, 20]; Sebkhi, Raîche Riopel & Lesage [21]). This assessment process with several levels of hierarchy and supervision in the field of education, that is one of the main theoretical contributions of this research project, has been named "hierarchical aggregate assessment". This process includes the formation of teams with several levels of hierarchy, the display of exams or complex assessment tasks to the teams and also the dismantling of the teams for the next assessment task in teams, as shown in Figure 1.

3.3. Definition of hierarchical aggregate assessment process in education

In the education field, the process of hierarchical aggregate assessment is defined as a team grouping process and a teamwork assessment subfield. In this subfield, teams have several levels of hierarchy and supervision where team leaders that could be students are assessed by one or many group managers that could be other students, teachers or professors (Lesage, Raîche, Riopel & Sebkhi [18]; Lesage, Raîche, Riopel, Fortin & Sebkhi [19, 20]; Sebkhi, Raîche, Riopel & Lesage [21]).

3.4. Situation of the field of hierarchical aggregate assessment process in the mastery learning paradigm

The assessment process in the mastery learning paradigm wants to determine the level at which the educational objectives are mastered or attained (Legendre [1]). Bloom's [48] cognitive level taxonomy of educational objectives allows to determine educational objectives by a statement describing knowledge, skill or performance and a description concerning the application of this knowledge, skill or performance. Bloom's cognitive level taxonomy of comprehension, application, analysis and synthesis is considered to represent the most important goals of the education field. This constatation has provided a foundation to raise the complexity level of tests and teaching programs towards educational objectives that could be in the higher levels of Bloom's taxonomy (Krathwohl [49]). According to some authors as Wiggins [34], traditional tests based on educational objectives are using out-of-context rote learning or open questions needing a few words for answers as an exam on multiplication tables. Those type of tests or exams are verifying if the students meet the criteria mentioned in the course curriculum.

The hierarchical assessment process is based on teamwork assessment. According to the mastery learning paradigm, the assessment process is realized by tests or exams that could contain items [49], questions and tests (De Ketele & Gérard [2]) and also work to accomplish [48]. As stated by the mastery learning paradigm, an exam or a test done in teams needs an accurate work or performance accomplished by a team at the end of a course or a study program [1]. Exam questions and learning objectives, concerning work or team performances, are included in the levels of Bloom's cognitive level taxonomy. In the hierarchical assessment process, the tests and exams are done in teams, so the persons taking part in the team exam can assess quantitatively and qualitatively the work done in teams to determine if the production or the performance meets the determined criteria; this type of assessment being part of level 6 of Bloom's [48] cognitive level taxonomy is named "evaluation". In some exams taken in teams, the persons taking part in the exam could do self-assessment and peer assessment. The peers' assessment process is part of level 5 of Krathwohl's [27] affective level taxonomy which interprets value or belief system classification [01, 26, 27].

3.5. Situation of the field of hierarchical aggregate assessment process in the competency-based approach paradigm

In the competency-based paradigm, the execution of a competency is based on resource mobilization to solve a complex situation (Van Kempen [3]). Competencies include the grouping of skills, attitudes and knowledge allowing a person to perform tasks (Bastiaens [50]). The competency-based approach paradigm replaces classical tests based on objectives by assessment tasks or situations that include social interaction (Allal [4]). Assessment tasks are evaluation tools that use or mobilize resources to solve a problematic situation or to perform a complex task. These tools are used to develop competencies with complex tasks allowing knowledge synthesis (Saskatchewan Professional Development Unit [51]; Olivier [52]; Louis and Bernard [31]; Tardif [32]; Van Kempen [3]; De Ketele & Gérard [2]).

The objectives of learning and assessment situations are to develop disciplinary and transversal competencies and to assess all students that must prove that they can resolve a problematic situation with their knowledge and skills (Bibeau [53]). The aim of competency assessment is to verify if the student has well used all available resources to accomplish a task successfully. During this process, students should be involved in their own assessment and perform their self-assessment (Jeunesse [29]). The competency formative assessment process is based on interactive regulation that comes with student-teacher interaction, interactions with peers and learning tools. The learner can imply himself in the assessment process with self-assessment, peer assessment and co-evaluation (Allal [4]). The hierarchical assessment process in the competency-based approach paradigm is the implementation of complex assessment tasks in teams. These tasks could include summative assessment that are performance or tasks to accomplish either individually or in teams and also includes formative assessment that is produced by self-assessment and peer assessment of team members. The competency-based approach in the hierarchical aggregate assessment field could be performed with observation grids or competency assessment grids as shown in Figures 21, 22 and 23 (Hubert & Denis [28];

Jeunesse [29]) and also with portfolio assessment (Allal [4]) that usually contains self-assessment (Endrizzi & Ray [30]).

3.6. Previous work and similar available existing internet applications

The current research project finds its origins and its theoretical framework in other previous research and through other distance assessment Internet applications that have been developed with a research and development methodology (R & D). These applications are SPARK developed by Freeman and McKenzie [14, 15] and Willey and Freeman [54, 55]; MLE developed by Marshall-Mies, Fleischman, Martin, Zaccaro, Baughman and McGee [56]; Mega Code developed by Kaye and Mancini [57]; and the application that is most similar to the current research project is a collaborative work management Internet application developed by Nance [25].

SPARK [14, 15, 54, 55] is a remote rating system that calculates the results of self-assessment and peer assessment grids to determine the final grade of engineering students on projects during practical work in engineering. This primarily detects the team members who have not done their fair share of work by giving poor performance in their team by letting others do their work for them.

MLE [56] is an application that predicts and assesses the leadership potential of high-level military managers such as colonels and generals with complex assessment tasks that are case studies and resolution of war scenarios.

Mega Code [57] is a software application used in the field of medicine and that is a cardiac arrest simulator. This application is used to assess the performance of resident doctors and nurses when they hold the role of leader of a resuscitation team who treated the case of patients who suffered a cardiac arrest according to the five main roles that are (1) the doctor who is in charge of the team, (2) the controller of respiration, (3) the head of the defibrillator, (4) the head of chest compressions and (5) the head of injections and intravenous infusions. The assessment of the team leader is made using an assessment grid that checks the two main aspects of cardiac resuscitation that are the team effort and the process and directions given to the members of the team by the team leader to resuscitate the patient.

The collaborative work management Web application developed by Nance [25] is used by students of engineering and computer science faculties. This application uses a multiple-level aggregation process for the grouping of teams that is similar to the aggregation process implemented in this research and in the "Cluster" Internet application. Nance's research [25] consists of the implementation of an Internet-based collaborative work application that is used to manage and assess the projects and the productions of engineering and computer science students. This application has the features needed to group students in teams that have multiple levels of hierarchy and supervision including team leaders and project managers (bosses) and project administrators (bosses of bosses (BOB)) supervising several project managers in the field of engineering and computer science. Nance's application collaborative work implementation is based on electronic mail (E-mail) and a discussion forum website.

3.7. Link between hierarchical aggregate assessment applications and Management Information Systems (MIS)

A management information system (MIS) software application "uses computer equipment and software, databases, manual procedures, models for analysis, planning, control and decision-making" (Davis, Olson, Ajenstat & Peaucelle [58]). These systems may contain information about the function, department and the hierarchical position of the members of the organization that are stored in hierarchical databases (Burch & Grudnitski [59]; Davis & Olson [60]; Davis, Olson, Ajenstat & Peaucelle [58]; Laudon & Laudon [61]; Laudon, Laudon & Brabston [62]). Some authors such as Kanter [63] indicate that the employee file can be sorted by order of position or assignment to identify employees who have the same hierarchical position. A database diagram illustrating an employee's position is shown in Figure 8. A hierarchical aggregate assessment software application is therefore a management information system where the employees to manage are students who have a hierarchical position.

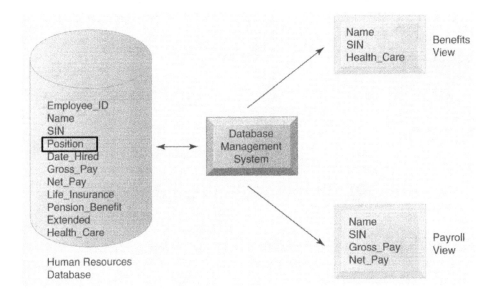

Figure 8. The record of an employee in a management information system database [62]

In the actual paradigm, there is a major difference between distance assessment systems and management information system software applications. A distance assessment system software application is a question bank repository stored in a database that usually presents the same questions or the same assessment tasks to all the students to assess the same skills and knowledge and there is no hierarchical relationship or hierarchy levels between the students. A management information system (MIS) is a software application that stores and processes management data and information on employees to produce information used for decision-making. The assessment data that a management information system produces and computes for the employees are usually sales data and production performance. Management information systems are able to record the hierarchical relations and positions of the employees, while distance assessment applications cannot.

In the hierarchical aggregate assessment paradigm, there is only a slight difference between hierarchical aggregate assessment applications and management information systems because both records the hierarchical relations and positions of the employees. The only difference is that the management information system processes management data, while the hierarchical aggregate assessment software application processes assessment data, course material, question banks and complex assessment tasks with several levels of hierarchy. Hence, any management information system could be modified to record course material and question banks to present complex assessment tasks with several levels of hierarchy. So the modified management information system has now been added hierarchical aggregate assessment capability and is equally now a hierarchical aggregate assessment software application, as shown in Figure 9.

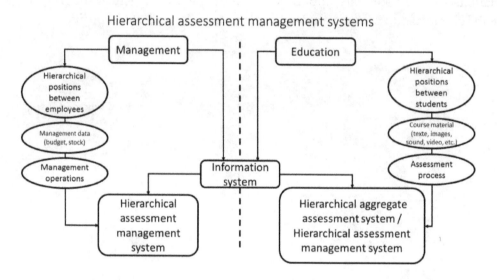

Figure 9. Link between hierarchical aggregate assessment applications and management information systems (MIS)

4. Methodology

4.1. Choice of methodology and software application design process

The implementation of teamwork complex assessment tasks with several levels of hierarchy is the implementation concept that was at the beginning of the research and development process (R & D) used to develop an Internet software application named "Cluster" that will be an educational product. The educational research and development model used is the one implemented by the authors Harvey and Loiselle [6]. The research project's objectives are to develop an Internet multilevel teamwork assessment application in accordance with the Harvey and Loiselle [6] model and to test the application with high school students and Canadian army cadets that will assess his usability with the Questionnaire for User Interaction Satisfaction ("QUIS") [64]. The Harvey and Loiselle [6] research and development process used in the present research project will give two results, the first result will be the "Cluster" Internet application and the second result will be the theoretical statement of the hierarchical aggregate assessment process for his acceptance by the scientific community.

The actual research project is the development of an educational tool that implements the hierarchical aggregate assessment process. Richey and Nelson [65] states that the development of a software application that will be used as an educational tool is part of the research and development (R & D) methodology for educational products. The development of the "Cluster" Internet application and its use by students and teachers will place this research in the paradigm of the research and development (R & D) methodology with mixed data analysis using qualitative and quantitative methods. The qualitative aspect is in the field of the interpretivist epistemology paradigm [66, 67] and used primarily to determine if users like to use the software, resistance-to-change factors as well as the assessment of the proper functioning of the software. The quantitative aspect of the research project, for its consideration, is in the field of the positivist epistemology paradigm [66, 67] and used to assess the increase in knowledge and the course success and dropout rate of students.

Regarding the choice of a research and development model, several authors have proposed models or developed research approaches such as Borg and Gall [68], Nonnon [69], Cervera [70], Van der Maren [71] and Harvey and Loiselle [6]. In all cases, these models include the phases of (1) problem analysis, (2) project planning, (3) production or development, (4) testing, (5) evaluation and (6) review [10]. The model chosen is the one developed by Harvey and Loiselle [6] because it is newer than Nonnon's model [69, 72], and it summarizes all stages of the research and development models of the previously cited authors. The research and development model used in the current research project is the model of Harvey and Loiselle [6] which includes five phases: (1) determination of the cause of the research, (2) determination of the theoretical background, (3) determination of methodology, (4) implementation or development of the educational product and (5) production of the results, as shown in Figure 10.

Figure 10. The research and development model of Harvey and Loiselle [6]

The research and development methodology is similar to the technical development of durable and consumable products used in engineering. Loiselle [10] defined the research and development methodology as an iterative process that involves seven steps that are (1) the preliminary analysis; (2) the prototype design and evaluation; (3) testing phase; (4) evaluation, revision and correction phase; (5) publication of results phase; (6) distribution phase; and (7) marketing phase. If the developed product has some lacks, failures or defects in the final stages of the development process such as evaluation, revision and correction, publication of results, distribution and marketing phases, the process returns to the analysis phase to find a solution to correct the defects of the product, as shown in Figure 11. The first functional tests or alpha tests were conducted by the authors of this chapter to ensure that the "Cluster" Internet application was ready to use by teachers and students. Once the functional tests were completed, the second series of tests or beta tests were performed by Mrs. Dalila Sebkhi's high school students [18, 19, 20, 21] during her third education bachelor internship where she taught geology for high school students of the Montreal School Board (CSDM). Then after, other beta tests were made by the authors through the distance learning implementation of map using for Canadian army cadets with navigation patrols in teams [18, 19, 21]

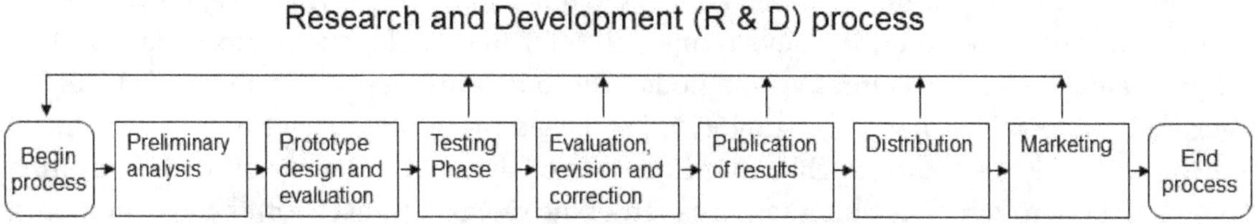

Research and Development (R & D) process

Figure 11. General research and development process (R & D) [10]

4.2. The testing of the "Cluster" internet application with high school students

The "Cluster" Internet application has first been tested with high school students during teaching assignments III and IV of Mrs. Dalila Sebkhi [18, 19, 20, 21]. These teaching assignments are part of the Université du Québec à Montréal's bachelor in education curriculum. This application has been used during Mrs. Dalila Sebkhi's teaching assignment III as an educational tool used as a teaching aid to support the learning of high school students for science and technology classes in the "La Voie" high school of the "Commission Scolaire de Montréal (CSDM)".

The experimental subjects were 113 (N = 113) 9th grade high school students divided into four classes. The course studied was a geology course that included sections on the solar system, the relief and also the rocks and minerals. The course content has been converted to electronic format and placed in the database of the "Cluster" Internet application so that students could access the course material at home outside school hours. This experiment only used qualitative methods and was based on the analysis of the testimonies of students and school officials who used the application. Mrs. Sebkhi would also have wanted to use the "Cluster" Internet application during her teaching assignment IV that included 118 11th grade high school students of the « St-Luc » high school divided into four classes which also belong to the "Commission Scolaire de Montréal (CSDM)". The course studied was thermodynamics. However, this experiment did not take place due to resistance to change because Mrs. Sebkhi's teaching assignment IV directors felt that too much time would be needed for students to learn to use the "Cluster" Internet application effectively.

4.3. The testing of the "Cluster" internet application with canadian army cadets

The "Cluster" Internet application was also experimented by the Royal Canadian Army Cadets with an experimental group of 27 young army cadets (N = 27) and with a control group of 12 cadets (N = 12) [18, 19, 20, 21]. All experimentation subjects came from two cadet corps of the Quebec province in Canada and had an average of 14 years of age. The current study was a military map-using course entitled "PO 122 – Identify a location using a map". The theoretical content of the course is found in the book *"A-CR-CCP-701/PF-001, Green Star, Instructional guides"* published by the staff of the Royal Canadian Army Cadets [73].

Both groups used in the experimentation had to study topography and map using to perform navigation patrols in teams. The experimentation group had to use the "Cluster" Internet application to study map using, while the control group has also to study map using but in a classroom with traditional teaching methods that are Canadian force instructional techniques. Subjects in the experimentation group were from the cadet corps "2567 Dunkerque" from the city of Laval, while subjects in the control group were part of the cadet corps "2595 St-Jean" from the city of Saint-Jean-sur-Richelieu. The cadet corps "2595 St-Jean" resides in the buildings of the Royal Military College Saint-Jean.

The classes given were part of a topography and map-using course that included five theoretical lessons that were (1) the different types of maps, (2) marginal information found on a map, (3) map symbols and conventional signs, (4) map contour lines and (5) four-, six- and eight-digit coordinates. The course material has been converted to electronic format and placed in the "Cluster" Internet application database. The topography and map-using course was divided into two parts: a first theoretical part where the experimentation subjects were studying the course material and a second practical part where the subjects were patrolling in the training area between two eight-digit coordinates given by the experimenter. Subjects or students in the control group had to study with traditional teaching manners the theoretical part in a classroom with a teacher, who in the military is called an instructor. Subjects in the experimental group, for their part, had to study the theoretical part of the group at home using the "Cluster" Internet application. However, both groups had to do the practical part of the course that consisted in navigation patrols in teams in training areas to prove the validity of the learning in presence and the distance learning on the Internet.

The validity of the experimentation was conducted using mixed methodology grouping tools of quantitative and qualitative methods. The experiment used qualitative research methods such as observation, interview and post-exercise report analysis. This is to determine whether the application was easy to use, the accuracy of training and if the test subjects had enjoyed using the "Cluster" Internet application. Usability and user interface conviviality factors are crucial to mitigate the effect of resistance to change during the implementation of software that will be used to make a transition from traditional education in class to e-learning.

Quantitative research methods used in the experiment were used to determine the levels of user interface conviviality and the influence of the "Cluster" Internet application on student learning rates. Quantitative instruments used in the experiment were (1) initial knowledge exam, (2) HTML auto-correcting objective exams, (3) work to submit by upload in electronic format, (4) final knowledge exam, (5) electronic self-assessment forms, (6) electronic peer assessment forms, (7) course module confirmation examinations and (8) QUIS questionnaire (Questionnaire for User Interaction Satisfaction) [64, 74]. Formative assessment is given by the students of the course using electronic forms of self-assessment and peer assessment, while summative assessment is provided by HTML questionnaires, homework to submit and course module confirmation examinations and also by the mark given by the teacher or evaluator for the practical part of the course consisting of navigation patrols in teams. These complex assessment tasks in collaborative mode consist of navigation patrols in teams using a topographic map. The results of the initial and final knowledge tests are not included in the course final result. The results of the initial and final knowledge tests are only used for the purpose of establishing research findings and conclusions regarding the increase of knowledge for both experimental and control groups. The QUIS questionnaire is used to quantitatively assess the levels of user interface conviviality of the computer application and the satisfaction level of the users, as shown in Figure 12.

The curriculum or course progression for a student is (1) to take the initial knowledge exam, (2) to achieve the five course modules performed in class for the control group and at distance with the "Cluster" Internet application for the experimental group that include a test based on a HTML objective exam at the end of each module that accounts for 50 % of the final mark, (3) to participate in at least three navigation patrols that will count for the other 50 % of the final grade in which the student successively held the team member, team leader and group administrator assignments and (4) to complete the self-assessment and peers evaluation forms after each patrol and (5) the teacher or the assessor is responsible for assessing the patrol team and will assign each student a mark for all the work he did during patrols and that will count for the other 50 % of the final grade and (6) the student will write the final or end-of-course knowledge exam.

5. Results

5.1. General

The "Cluster" application is now fully functional and resides at the address http://eval.uqam.ca/cluster/. The application is relatively easy to use and constitutes a software-programmable shell to implement courses. To create courses in assessor mode, the teacher needs the course material, the course schedule, the assessment tasks definition, the student's names and the team's organogram. The teacher has to enter all these data in the application's database to implement a course. Once the course is started, the teacher can form the students in teams and assess individual and teamwork tasks. To follow a course, the student has to login into the application. After the login, the student has to select the course he wants to follow. Once entered in the course, the student can study the course material, write exams, submit homework, participate in assessment tasks and submit self-assessment and peer assessment. The "Cluster" Internet application experimentation results with high school students and army cadets stated resistance to change by the users and the need to implement some software modifications to the application that were the addition of (1) a field identifying the name of the student group or class to the database, (2) return buttons to avoid the students to get stuck in the interface and course modules and (3) a course progression matrix for each student group or class.

OVERALL REACTION TO THE SOFTWARE		0	1	2	3	4	5	6	7	8	9		NA
1. 🗩	terrible	○	○	○	○	○	○	○	○	○	○	wonderful	○
2. 🗩	difficult	○	○	○	○	○	○	○	○	○	○	easy	○
3. 🗩	frustrating	○	○	○	○	○	○	○	○	○	○	satisfying	○
4. 🗩	inadequate power	○	○	○	○	○	○	○	○	○	○	adequate power	○
5. 🗩	dull	○	○	○	○	○	○	○	○	○	○	stimulating	○
6. 🗩	rigid	○	○	○	○	○	○	○	○	○	○	flexible	○
SCREEN		0	1	2	3	4	5	6	7	8	9		NA
7. Reading characters on the screen 🗩	hard	○	○	○	○	○	○	○	○	○	○	easy	○
8. Highlighting simplifies task 🗩	not at all	○	○	○	○	○	○	○	○	○	○	very much	○
9. Organization of information 🗩	confusing	○	○	○	○	○	○	○	○	○	○	very clear	○
10. Sequence of screens 🗩	confusing	○	○	○	○	○	○	○	○	○	○	very clear	○

Figure 12. A section of the QUIS questionnaire [64, 74]

The actual doctoral project aims to computerize the assessment of teams on several hierarchical levels using a research and development methodology of educational products. Since the process of research and development in education not only gives educational products, but also theories, this research will produce the following results: (1) the definition of the hierarchical aggregate assessment process, (2) the "Cluster" Internet application, (3) considerations and changes caused by an experiment on high school students and (4) considerations caused by experimentation on army cadets.

5.2. Hierarchical aggregate assessment process

The process of grouping students into teams with several hierarchical levels that is implemented in the "Cluster" Internet application was the object of theoretical considerations of the research and development process that led to the statement of its definition. The actual doctoral project researchers would like that the term hierarchical aggregate assessment be accepted and recognized by the scientific community as a whole because this process has always existed and occurred in large organizations.

5.3. The "Cluster" internet distance assessment application

The "Cluster" distance assessment Internet application (e-assessment) is a collaborative mode presentation engine in authentic context. This computer application is developed in PHP and supported by a MySQL database. Phases of preliminary analysis and functional analysis of the software development process of the "Cluster" Internet application were done by the CDAME software analysts. The application development with the PHP programming language and also the software application database management system (DBMS) modelling and design in MySQL [22] were done by Frédérick Fortin [19, 20], information systems analyst and a programmer for the "LabMECAS (Laboratoire mobile pour l'étude des cheminements d'apprentissage en sciences (FCI))"   [75]. The software architecture of the "Cluster" Internet application is shown in Figure 13.

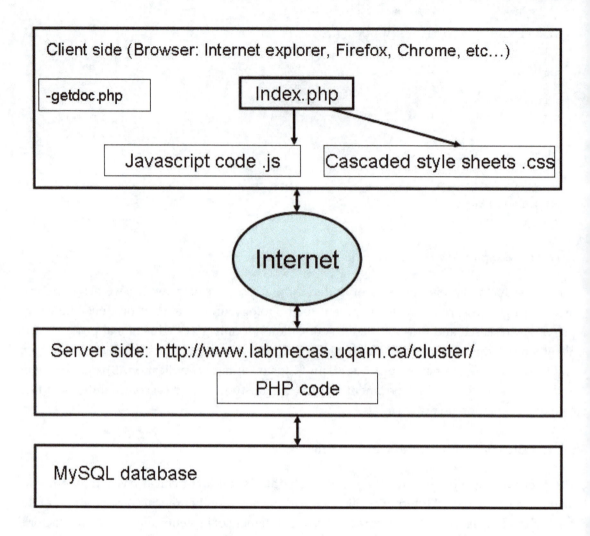

Figure 13. "Cluster" Internet application software architecture

The database management system of the "Cluster" Internet application is able to manage (1) student data, (2) course material, (3) team formation, (4) courses, (5) formative and summative assessments and (6) hierarchical relationships between team members who may have several levels. In the data structure, a course is broken down into modules, and modules include tasks that may have assessment or not. This assessment can be individual or in teams. Individual assessment consists of either HTML objective questionnaire examinations or homework to submit in electronic format with the system's upload functionality. Assessment tasks in teams include formative assessments that are self-assessment and peer assessment and also summative assessment that is the mark given to the team by the assessor for a production, task or performance. The database architecture of the "Cluster" Internet application is shown in Figure 14.

The application has two mutually exclusive operating modes: student mode and the administrator or assessor mode. In fact, the system does not allow an individual with an administrator

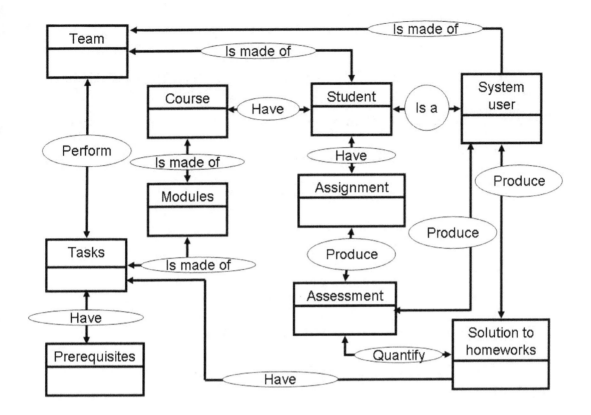

Figure 14. "Cluster" Internet application database architecture

or assessor status to study the course material as well as to participate in an assessment task as a team member. Furthermore, the system does not allow an individual with student status to change over the databases and students or to execute some system administrator commands. In the student mode, a user cannot give summative assessments and assess homework as well as team tasks. The mode of application is determined when connecting to the system with the login page when the system recognizes if the username belongs to a student, an assessor or an administrator. The home page contains the login parameters entry fields for username and password and is shown in Figure 15.

The student mode is only used by students or candidates on distance courses given with the "Cluster" Internet application. Student mode allows candidates on courses to (1) study the course material; (2) check out the curriculum record sheet to know what course modules are done and their progression through course modules; (3) perform HTML examinations; (4) submit homework; (5) be part of a team to perform a complex evaluation task in teams; (6) occupy a hierarchical position in the team as a team member, team leader and group administrator; and (7) fill in forms of self-assessment and peer assessment. Once the students have begun a session in the application, they can choose the course they want to study if they are registered in several courses with the form shown in Figure 16.

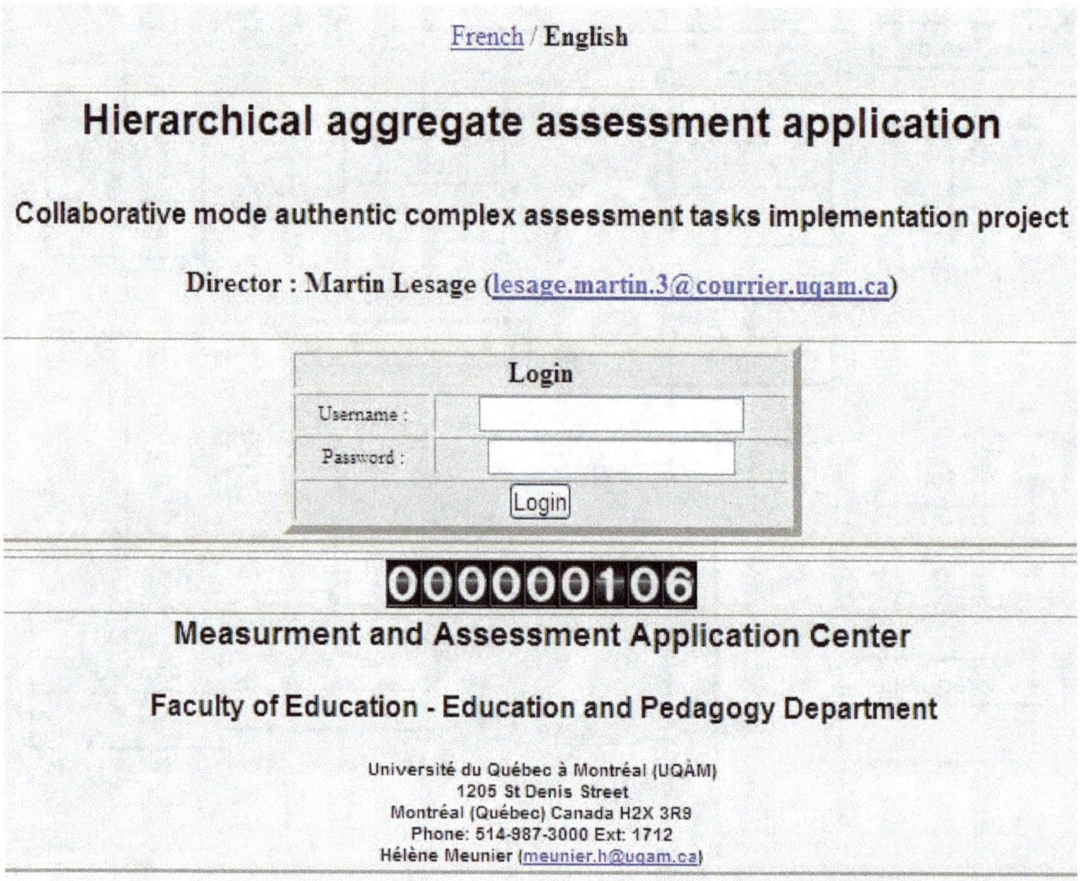

French / **English**

Hierarchical aggregate assessment application

Collaborative mode authentic complex assessment tasks implementation project

Director : Martin Lesage (lesage.martin.3@courrier.uqam.ca)

Login	
Username :	
Password :	
	Login

000000106

Measurment and Assessment Application Center

Faculty of Education - Education and Pedagogy Department

Université du Québec à Montréal (UQÀM)
1205 St Denis Street
Montréal (Québec) Canada H2X 3R9
Phone: 514-987-3000 Ext: 1712
Hélène Meunier (meunier.h@uqam.ca)

Figure 15. « Cluster » Internet application login page

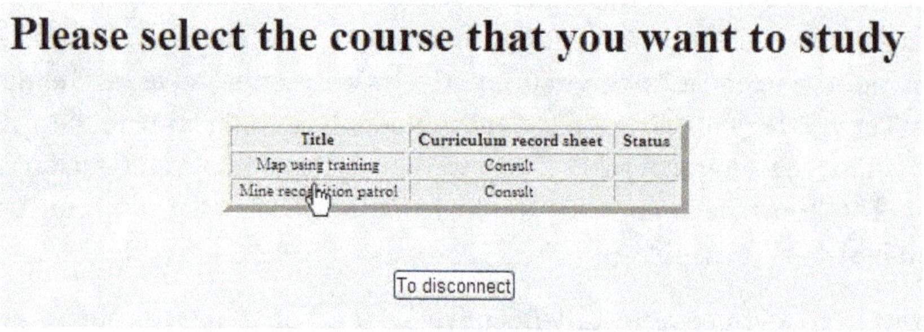

Please select the course that you want to study

Title	Curriculum record sheet	Status
Map using training	Consult	
Mine recognition patrol	Consult	

To disconnect

Figure 16. Course selection screen

Once the student has chosen the course he wants to study, the user interface drop-down menu allows access to the modules of the course. The course module selection menu is shown in Figure 17.

The menu allows the student to study the course material sequentially from the first module to the last. An application functionality prevents the student from browsing or to navigate randomly in the course modules. The student is only allowed to study the course material in

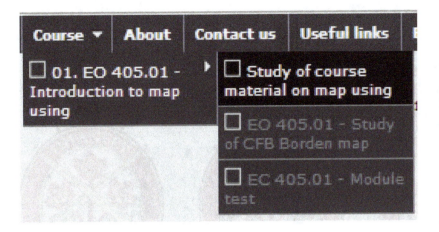

Figure 17. Course module selection menu

course modules from the first to the last, the last module being the end of the course. The application displays the course material for the student to be able to read it on the screen. When displaying the course material, a pop-up menu allows the student to save or print the displayed course material for future revisions. The course material is displayed using the computer screen shown in Figure 18.

The student can consult at any time the curriculum record sheet that shows the progress of students in the course modules and tasks. The computer screen representing the curriculum record sheet is shown in Figure 19.

Status	Student		Designation/rank	Mcpl.		Name	Smith		First name	Peter	

Curriculum record sheet   Course ▾   About   Contact us   Useful links   Exit course

Map using training
Curriculum record sheet

01. EO 405.01 - Introduction to map using ✎	
Study of course material on map using	Completed
EO 405.01 - Study of CFB Borden map	Completed
EC 405.01 - Module test	Completed 80% 8/10
02. EO 405.02 - The meaning of map conventional signs ✎	
EO 405.02 - Meaning of conventional signs	Completed
EC 405.02 - Module test	Completed 100% 10/10
03. EO 405.03 - Four and six figures grid references ✎	
EO 405.03 - Four and six figures coordionates determination on the map	Completed
EC 405.03 - Four and six figures grid references	Completed 75% 15/20
04. EO 405.04 - Route determination with the map ✎	
EO 405.04 - Course notes on route determination on the map	Completed
EO 405.04 - Map and Compass handout	Completed
EC 405.04 - Route determination with two six (6) figures coordinates	Completed 80% 16/20
05. PC 405 - Performance check - Route determination with map ✎	
PC 405 - Performance test - The conduct of a patrol	Completed 81% 32.4/40
	Total : 81.4 / 100

Figure 19. Curriculum record sheet display screen

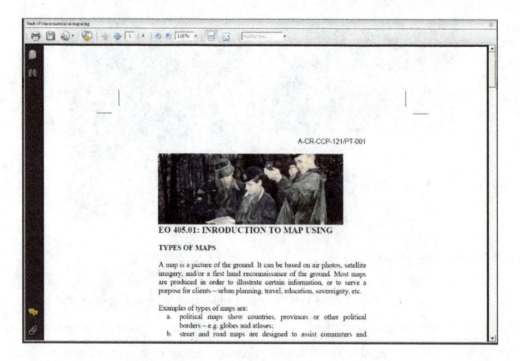

Figure 18. Course material display screen

PO 122.01 Test

Identify the type of maps
Weight: 5% of final score

Question 1 - What is a topographic map?
(Choose only one answer)

- A contour lines representation
- A document that shows roads emplacement
- A reprsentation of the ground
- A document that locates political boundaries of countries, states and cities
- An electronic document that could by downloaded in a GPS

Question 2 - What detail or information is not shown on a topographic map?
(Choose only one answer)

- Rivers
- Forests
- Elevations
- Roads
- Production data for mines and petroleum troughout the country

Question 3 - What is to avoid when a map is used?
(Choose only one answer)

- Write on it with a pen
- Plastify or laminate the map
- Put the map in a plastic bag
- Spread or expand the map when it is wet to dry it
- Fold the map

Question 4 - Which type of map is similar to orientation maps?
(Choose only one answer)

- Road maps
- Statistical maps
- Political maps
- Topographic maps
- Nautical maps

Question 5 - What data, document or information is used to produce topographic maps?
(Choose only one answer)

- Street emplacements
- Tourist guides
- Mundial atlas
- Landscape sketches
- Aerial photos

Submit your answers

Figure 20. HTML objective questionnaire

The "Cluster" Internet application has two assessment modes: the individual assessment and the assessment in teams or teamwork assessment. The individual assessment will be processed with HTML objective exams and homework submission in electronic format by an upload function, while the teamwork assessment is done by the teacher and the assessor that can observe the team or assess a performance or a production with a mark. The HTML objective questionnaire is shown in Figure 20.

Performances, work and productions of the students will be submitted using a standard upload computer screen shown in Figure 21.

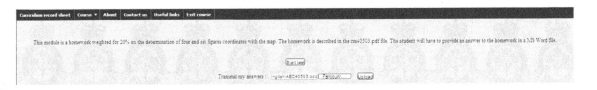

Figure 21. Standard upload computer screen

The "Cluster" Internet application is able to assess different knowledge, skills, productions and performances simultaneously in the same assessment task in teams. Hence, a student participating in an assessment task in teams can occupy team member, team leader and group administrator hierarchical positions. When the student completes an assessment task, he must complete the self-assessment and the peer assessment forms. It is therefore necessary that the self-assessment and peer assessment forms have different assessment criteria based on the hierarchical position of the assessed student that could be a team member, team leader or group administrator. The team member assessment form is shown in Figure 22.

The team leader assessment form is shown in Figure 23.

The group manager assessment form is shown in Figure 24.

The administrator or assessor mode is the operating mode used by system administrators, teachers, assessors as well as distance learning courses developers on the Internet (e-learning) to (1) manage and modify the student database, (2) manage and modify the course material database, (3) mark the students' homework submitted in electronic format, (4) assess the performance of the students in teams, (5) group students into teams and (6) assign team members hierarchical positions as team member, team leader and group manager in order to implement the tree structure made by the hierarchical aggregation of team members. The student management computer screen is shown in Figure 25 and allows the teacher or the assessor to create a new student as well as to modify or delete the record of an existing student.

The course task management form is shown in Figure 26 and allows the teacher or the evaluator to create a new course task as well as modify or destroy an existing task from the course material database.

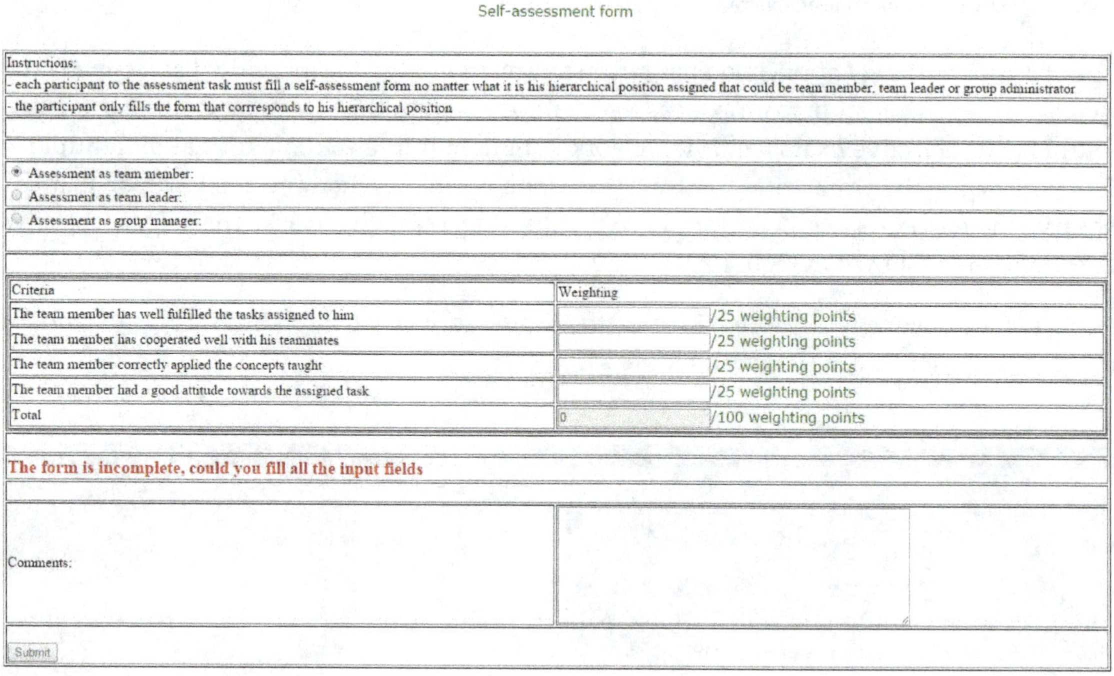

Self-assessment form

Instructions:
- each participant to the assessment task must fill a self-assessment form no matter what it is his hierarchical position assigned that could be team member, team leader or group administrator
- the participant only fills the form that corresponds to his hierarchical position

⦿ Assessment as team member:
○ Assessment as team leader:
○ Assessment as group manager:

Criteria	Weighting
The team member has well fulfilled the tasks assigned to him	/25 weighting points
The team member has cooperated well with his teammates	/25 weighting points
The team member correctly applied the concepts taught	/25 weighting points
The team member had a good attitude towards the assigned task	/25 weighting points
Total	0 /100 weighting points

The form is incomplete, could you fill all the input fields

Comments:

Submit

Figure 22. Team member assessment form

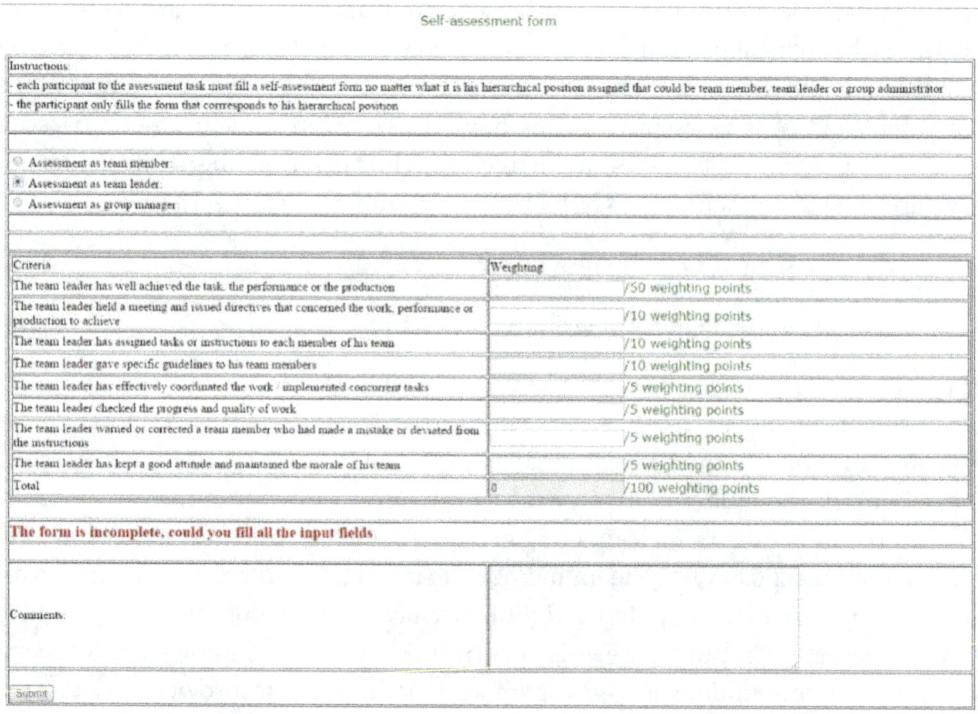

Self-assessment form

Instructions:
- each participant to the assessment task must fill a self-assessment form no matter what it is his hierarchical position assigned that could be team member, team leader or group administrator
- the participant only fills the form that corresponds to his hierarchical position

○ Assessment as team member:
⦿ Assessment as team leader:
○ Assessment as group manager:

Criteria	Weighting
The team leader has well achieved the task, the performance or the production	/50 weighting points
The team leader held a meeting and issued directives that concerned the work, performance or production to achieve	/10 weighting points
The team leader has assigned tasks or instructions to each member of his team	/10 weighting points
The team leader gave specific guidelines to his team members	/10 weighting points
The team leader has effectively coordinated the work / implemented concurrent tasks	/5 weighting points
The team leader checked the progress and quality of work	/5 weighting points
The team leader warned or corrected a team member who had made a mistake or deviated from the instructions	/5 weighting points
The team leader has kept a good attitude and maintained the morale of his team	/5 weighting points
Total	0 /100 weighting points

The form is incomplete, could you fill all the input fields

Comments:

Submit

Figure 23. Team leader assessment form

Self-assessment form

Instructions:
- each participant to the assessment task must fill a self-assessment form no matter what it is his hierarchical position assigned that could be team member, team leader or group administrator
- the participant only fills the form that corresponds to his hierarchical position

○ Assessment as team member:
○ Assessment as team leader:
● Assessment as group manager:

Criteria		Weighting
The group manager has ensured that the group well achieved the task, performance or production		/50 weighting points
The group manager held a meeting and issued directives to the team leaders concerning the work, performance or production to achieve		/10 weighting points
The group manager has assigned tasks or instructions to each member of his team		/10 weighting points
The group manager gave specific guidelines to his team leaders		/10 weighting points
The group manager has effectively coordinated the work implemented concurrent tasks		/5 weighting points
The group manager checked the progress and quality of work		/5 weighting points
The group manager warned or corrected a team manager or a team member who had made a mistake or deviated from the instructions		/5 weighting points
The group manager has kept a good attitude and maintained the morale of his team		/5 weighting points
Total	0	/100 weighting points

The form is incomplete, could you fill all the input fields

Comments

Submit

Figure 24. Group manager assessment form

Students team management
User creation

* Username		* Password		* Confirm	
* Access Student ▼		* E-Mail			
First name		Name		Designation rank ▼	
GPA %		Seniority		Gender ▼	
Academic program		School/Academic year		Ethnicity	
Date of birth		Age		Name of academic institution	
Street number		Street name		Appartment	
City		Province/State		Country	
Postal / Zip code		Residence phone number		Work phone number	
Cell phone		Fax		Preferred language English ▼	
Function		Group		☐ Banned user	

Back Restart Save

Figure 25. Student management form

The teacher or assessor may mark individual homework or assignments submitted in electronic format and write comments about a student's performance with the work or performance assessment form shown in Figure 27. This form is only used by the teacher or assessor for summative assessment purposes to give marks to work uploaded by students.

Figure 28 is a computer form that allows the teacher or the assessor to perform teamwork assessment. In fact, during a teamwork assessment task, each student is assessed twice: the student first receives marks or assessment data that is a formative assessment concerning his individual performance as team member, team leader and team or group manager. The student

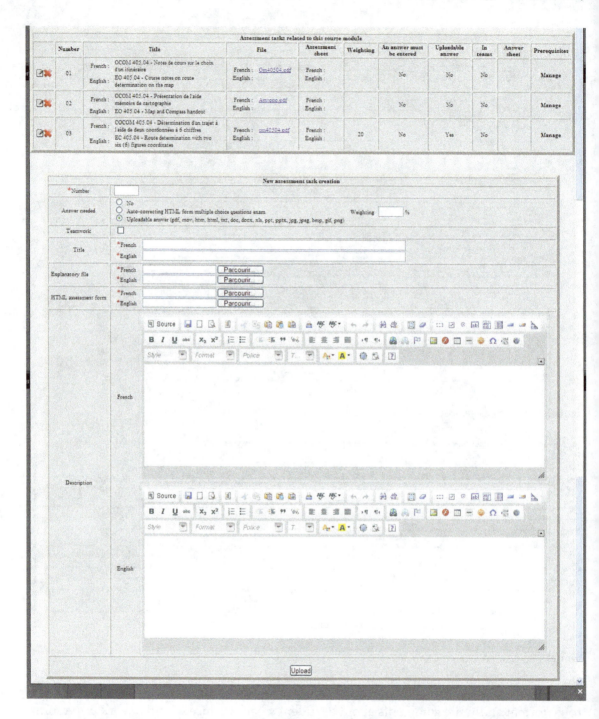

Figure 26. Course task management form

also receives a score that is a summative assessment for the performance he gives during the teamwork assessment tasks and for his individual performances that are homework submitted in electronic format and HTML exams. The teacher or assessor can assess each student performance during a teamwork task with the team member assessment form shown in Figure

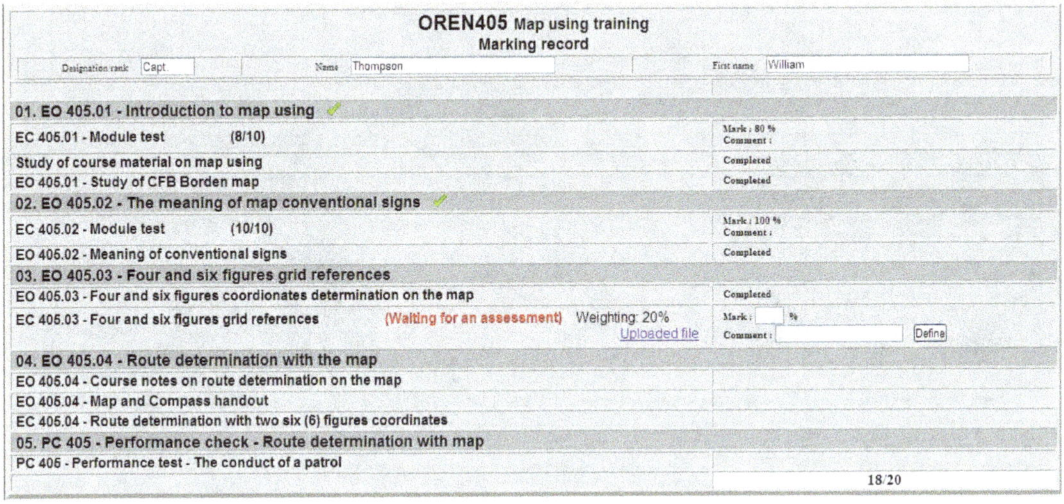
OREN405 Map using training
Marking record

Designation rank: Capt. | Name: Thompson | First name: William

01. EO 405.01 - Introduction to map using	
EC 405.01 - Module test (8/10)	Mark : 80 % Comment :
Study of course material on map using	Completed
EO 405.01 - Study of CFB Borden map	Completed
02. EO 405.02 - The meaning of map conventional signs	
EC 405.02 - Module test (10/10)	Mark : 100 % Comment :
EO 405.02 - Meaning of conventional signs	Completed
03. EO 405.03 - Four and six figures grid references	
EO 405.03 - Four and six figures coordionates determination on the map	Completed
EC 405.03 - Four and six figures grid references (Waiting for an assessment) Weighting: 20% Uploaded file	Mark: % Comment: Define
04. EO 405.04 - Route determination with the map	
EO 405.04 - Course notes on route determination on the map	
EO 405.04 - Map and Compass handout	
EC 405.04 - Route determination with two six (6) figures coordinates	
05. PC 405 - Performance check - Route determination with map	
PC 405 - Performance test - The conduct of a patrol	
	18/20

Figure 27. Student's individual work or performance assessment form

28, which is the same form used by students to give self-assessment and peer assessment previously shown in Figure 22. This assessment form then has two functions: first, it is used for formative assessment by students who use them for self-assessment and peer assessment. Secondly, it is used to make summative assessment by teachers or assessors to mark the individual performance of the student in his team.

The software application team member individual assessment screen is shown in Figure 29.

Once all individual formative assessment is done by team members with the completion of self-assessment and peer assessment forms, a data entry form shown in Figure 30 is presented to the assessor to enter the mark or the score for the assessment of the task done in a team.

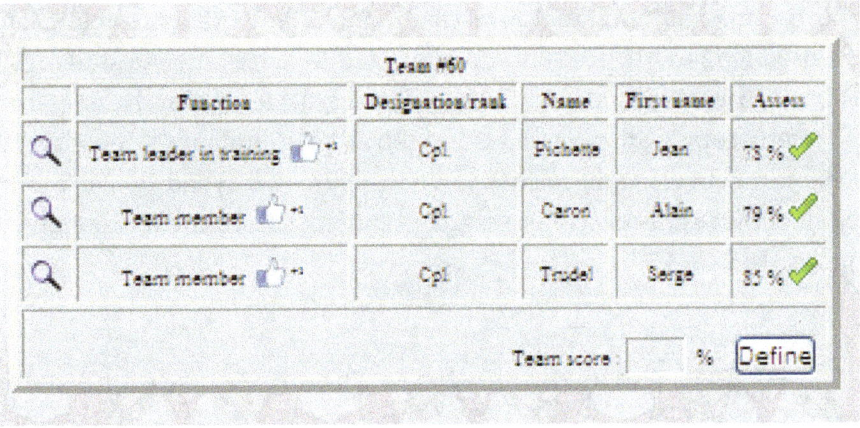
Team #60

	Function	Designation/rank	Name	First name	Assess
	Team leader in training +1	Cpl	Pichette	Jean	78 %
	Team member +1	Cpl	Caron	Alain	79 %
	Team member +1	Cpl	Trudel	Serge	85 %

Team score: % Define

Figure 30. Screen for the assessment of a task in a team

The teacher or the assessor gives summative assessment to the student by observing his team performance based on his hierarchical position, which can be either as team member, team

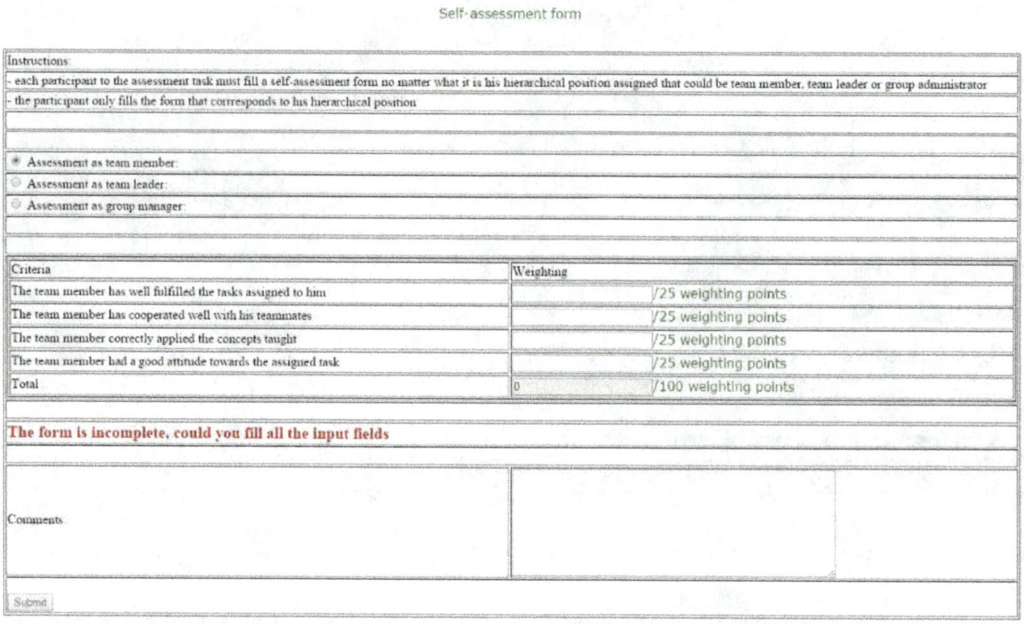

Self-assessment form

Instructions	
- each participant to the assessment task must fill a self-assessment form no matter what it is his hierarchical position assigned that could be team member, team leader or group administrator	
- the participant only fills the form that corresponds to his hierarchical position	

* Assessment as team member:
  Assessment as team leader:
  Assessment as group manager:

Criteria	Weighting	
The team member has well fulfilled the tasks assigned to him		/25 weighting points
The team member has cooperated well with his teammates		/25 weighting points
The team member correctly applied the concepts taught		/25 weighting points
The team member had a good attitude towards the assigned task		/25 weighting points
Total	0	/100 weighting points

The form is incomplete, could you fill all the input fields

Comments

Submit

Figure 28. Team member assessment form

leader or group manager. The assessment criteria on the assessment forms are different depending on the hierarchical position occupied by the student, as shown by Figures 22, 23 and 24. This feature is a direct implementation of the problematics of teamwork assessment with several hierarchical levels. This functionality is currently only implemented in the "Cluster" Internet application and is not found in any other e-learning and e-assessment Internet applications such as Moodle, WebCT and Blackboard.

During the teamwork assessment process, the teacher or the assessor has to produce both formative and summative individual assessment and teamwork assessment. These assessments will be used to mark the team productions and to determine the student's final grade for a given course. To assess a student and assign grades, the teacher or the assessor can consult the "Cluster" Internet application database and retrieve the student's self-assessments as well as all the peer assessment using the forms shown in Figures 22, 23 and 24. The computer screen that displays all of the results of self-assessments and peer assessments for a given student is shown in Figure 31.

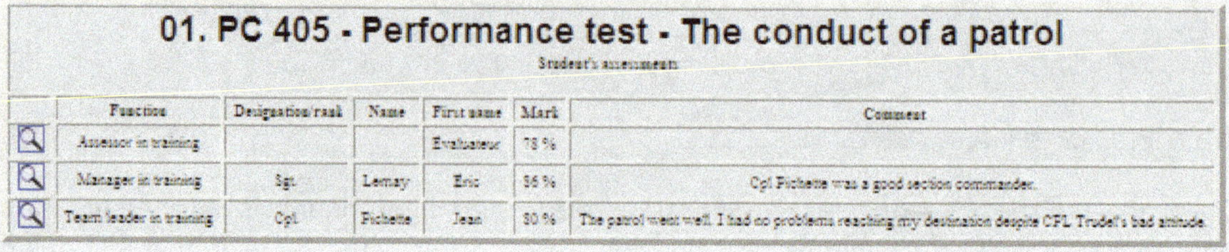

01. PC 405 - Performance test - The conduct of a patrol

Student's assessment

	Function	Designation/rank	Name	First name	Mark	Comment
🔍	Assessor in training			Evaluateur	78 %	
🔍	Manager in training	Sgt	Lemay	Eric	86 %	Cpl Pichette was a good section commander.
🔍	Team leader in training	Cpl	Pichette	Jean	80 %	The patrol went well. I had no problems reaching my destination despite CPL Trudel's bad attitude.

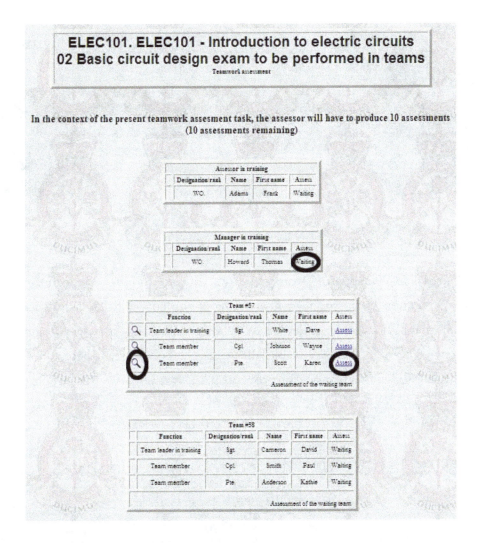

Figure 29. Team member individual assessment screen

Figure 31. Self-assessment and peer assessment display screen

The course final grade is computed by (1) the sum of all the individual scores that includes HTML exams and homework to submit in the course modules and (2) the sum of all scores assigned by the teacher or the assessor to the student for the tasks he performed as a team member. Finally, the main innovation of the "Cluster" Internet application at the origin of current doctoral project is the aggregation function whose tree data structure is implemented into the application's database and thereby allows the grouping of students into teams with multiple hierarchical levels. This feature allows the system to assign the student hierarchical functions such as team member, team leader and group manager. The aggregation function is accessible from the main menu of the application that is shown in Figure 32.

The aggregation functionality implemented in the "Cluster" Internet application provides a solution to the problem of the current research project concerning the implementation of an assessment process for the teams with several hierarchical levels that is less implemented in

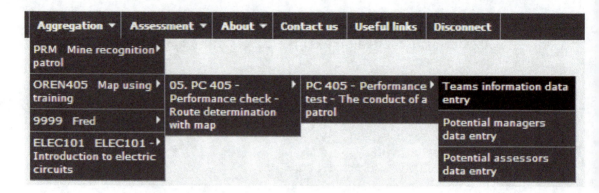

Figure 32. Aggregation menu for team formation

Moodle, WebCT and Blackboard. The form of the "Cluster" Internet application that implements the aggregation process that groups teams of students with levels of hierarchy and assigns team members as team leader, team member and group manager is the computer screen shown in Figure 33. The form enables the teacher or the assessor to begin the aggregation process to group students in teams. This process builds the multilevel tree structure stored in the MySQL database application.

ELEC101. ELEC101 - Introduction to electric circuits

Aggregation
Team formation

Number	Designation/rank	Name	First name	GPA	Seniority	Age	Gender	Ethnicity	Language	
216	WO.	Adams	Frank	0 %	11	27	M	Caucasian	En	☐
217	WO.	Howard	Thomas	0 %	10	28	M	Black	En	☐
218	Sgt.	White	Dave	0 %	9	30	M	Caucasian	En	☑
219	Sgt.	Cameron	David	0 %	8	41	M	Caucasian	En	☐
220	Cpl.	Johnson	Wayne	0 %	6	35	M	Caucasian	En	☑
221	Cpl.	Smith	Paul	0 %	5	42	M	Black	En	☐
222	Pte.	Scott	Karen	0 %	3	25	M	Caucasian	En	☑
223	Pte.	Anderson	Kathie	0 %	1	29	M	Black	En	☐

* To sort, please select one or more columns

Team leader	White, Dave ▾
	White, Dave
	Johnson, Wayne
	Scott, Karen

Reset the sorting process   Form the team

Figure 33. Aggregation process and team formation screen

5.4. Experimentation with high school students

The testing of the "Cluster" Internet application performed on high school students by Mrs. Dalila Sebkhi [18, 19, 20, 21] were the first beta tests used to experiment the application on a large population of over 100 students (N > 100). Alpha tests were done before Mrs. Dalila Sebkhi's experimentation by the CDAME researchers [18, 19, 20, 21]. In this experiment, the "Cluster" Internet application was used by high school students of the province of Quebec as an alternative method to teach geology courses. The results of the experiment were purely qualitative and were based on Mrs. Sebkhi's observations during the experiment where students used the application in their geology classes. Several students who used the application "Cluster" and some directors of the Montreal School Board argued that the application user interface was too rigid and not friendly enough for students who were teenagers from 12 to 16 years of age.

The high school students wanted the applications' user interface to make more use of multimedia elements such as videos and animated graphics so that the course would be more like a video game with avatars as in the "Mecanika" application implemented by François Boucher-Genesse [76] rather than the actual "Cluster" Internet application's basic drop-down menus user interface. However, for some students, learning to use the "Cluster" Internet application was simple and easy. These students did not had any problem to study the course material, review all the course modules and take the geology course exams placed at the end of course modules while the less talented students had experienced various problems when using the "Cluster" Internet application such as (1) resistance to change, (2) losses of usernames and passwords, (3) errors while filling the HTML exams, (4) being lost in navigation when studying the course material, (5) impossibility to go back in the user interface navigation if the course material is not understood or saved and that the student wants to regain access to the course materials or to the previous sections and (6) difficulty for teachers or course assessors to keep track of progress while performing modules and examinations for groups or classes having a large number of students.

Mrs. Sebkhi's high school students faced the described problems; she therefore requested that four modifications could be made to the "Cluster" Internet application user interface [18, 19, 20, 21]. These changes were implemented a few months after the end of his teaching assignment III so that Mrs. Sebkhi could use the new functionalities of the application to the start of her teaching assignment IV. The first modification shown in Figure 34 was the addition of a field in the database to identify the group or the student's class so that all students in the database are divided into classes or groups.

The second modification is the implementation of a back button allowing the student to be able to return to the previous module or chapter, as shown in Figure 35.

The third modification shown in Figure 36 is the implementation of a form to access the curriculum record sheet of all the students registered in the "Cluster" Internet application database. This form will allow the teacher or the assessor to access the curriculum record sheet of a given student to know his progression into the course modules without having to open a session (login) into the account of the student.

The fourth modification shown in Figure 37 is the implementation of a form that displays a matrix that shows the progress in the course modules for all students in a class or a group.

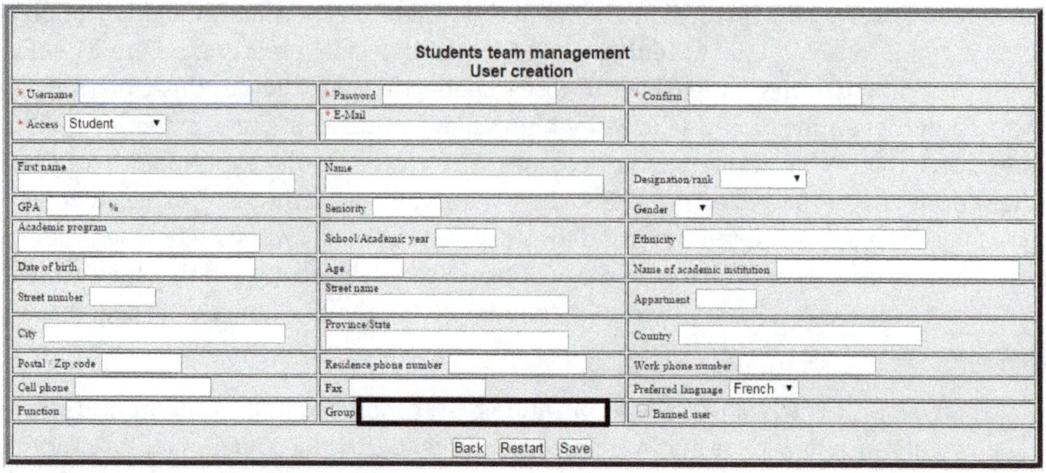

Figure 34. Addition of a field for the group or the class of the student

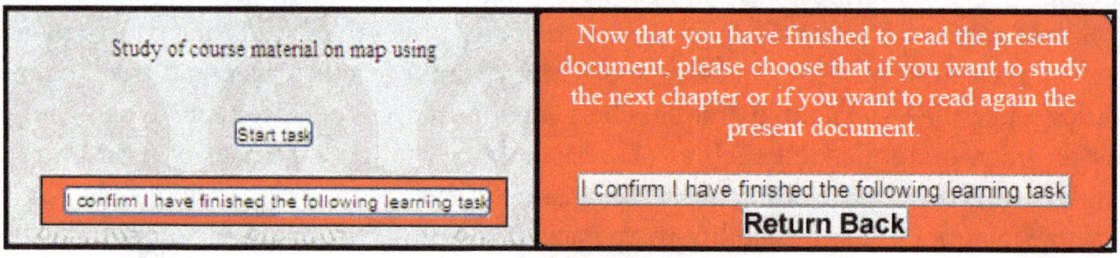

Figure 35. Implementation of a button to return to the previous module

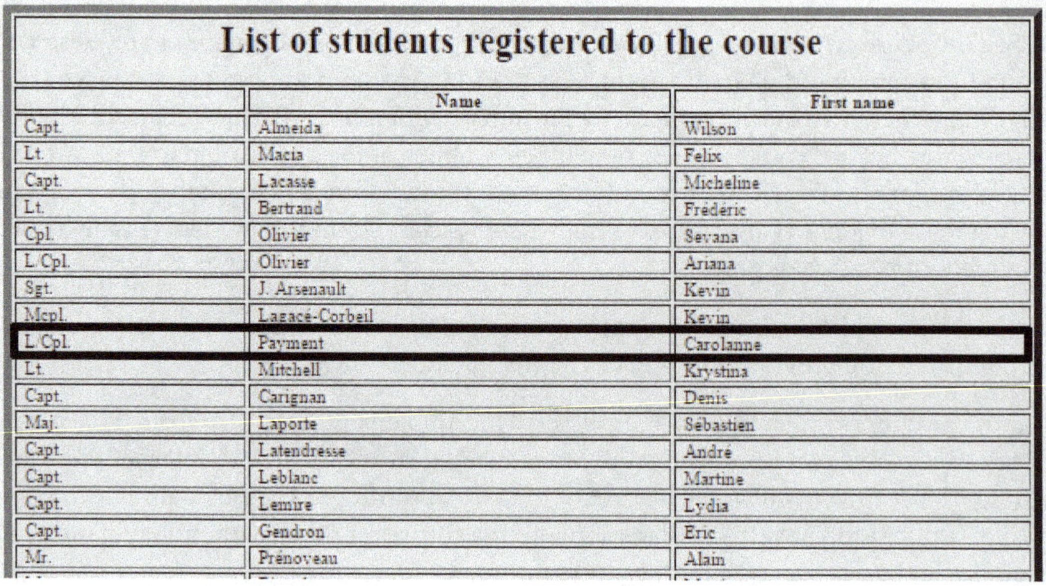

List of students registered to the course

	Name	First name
Capt.	Almeida	Wilson
Lt.	Macia	Felix
Capt.	Lacasse	Micheline
Lt.	Bertrand	Frédéric
Cpl.	Olivier	Sevana
L/Cpl.	Olivier	Ariana
Sgt.	J. Arsenault	Kevin
Mcpl.	Lagacé-Corbeil	Kevin
L/Cpl.	Payment	Carolanne
Lt.	Mitchell	Krystina
Capt.	Carignan	Denis
Maj.	Laporte	Sébastien
Capt.	Latendresse	André
Capt.	Leblanc	Martine
Capt.	Lemire	Lydia
Capt.	Gendron	Eric
Mr.	Prénoveau	Alain

Figure 36. Curriculum record sheet access screen

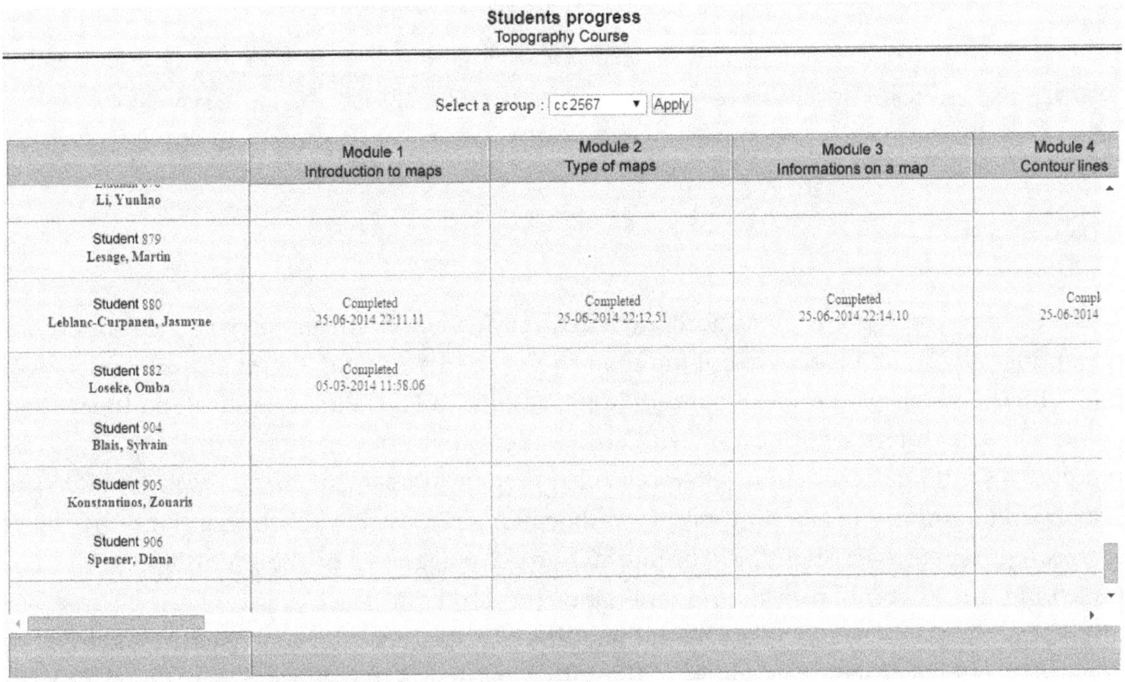

Figure 37. Student progress matrix screen

5.5. Experimentation with Canadian army cadets

The results of the experiment of the "Cluster" Internet application with Canadian army cadets are shown in Table 1 [18, 19, 20, 21].

	Experimentation group	Control group
Population (N)	27	12
Topography course pretest	12.81 %	7 %
Topography course post-test	63.40 %	55 %
Topography course overall score	83.45 %	66.15 %
Knowledge increase rate	50.59 %	48 %
Number of candidates that has succeeded the course	6	10
Course abandon (dropout)	21	2
Success rate	22 %	83 %
User interface satisfaction rate (QUIS)	- Liked : user friendliness - Disliked :	Not applicable

	Experimentation group	Control group
	Feedback, terminology and resistance to change	

Table 1. Experimentation of the "Cluster" on Canadian army cadets for navigation courses in teams using the map

6. Discussion

The current research project produced three main results under the research and development methodology: (1) the theory describing the process of hierarchical aggregate assessment, (2) the "Cluster" Internet application and (3) data, results and conclusions regarding the testing of the "Cluster" Internet application with army cadets during navigation patrols in teams. The theories describing the process of hierarchical aggregate assessment are now submitted to the scientific community through numerous publications [18, 19, 20, 21] so that the term "hierarchical aggregate assessment" will be internationally recognized by the scientific community. Following a first iteration in the research and development process, the "Cluster" Internet application has undergone a first set of amendments that has been proposed by Mrs. Dalila Sebkhi during her teaching assignment III at the Université du Québec à Montréal (UQAM). These results were presented and discussed in the « Results » section of this chapter, and the « Cluster » Internet application is now fully operational. Although the experiment is over, the organization of the army cadet has found useful "Cluster" Internet application in the cadet movement to provide distance learning and help for cadets with learning disabilities and to help late entry cadets of 15 to 18 years of age to progress faster in their career. This application is now used by the cadets to provide distance courses on topography, navigation patrols, instructional techniques and general military knowledge. The results for the testing of the application "Cluster" by the army cadets demonstrate that the increase of knowledge produced with the "Cluster" Internet application is 50.59 %, an increase which is almost identical to that produced by the traditional classroom teaching methods that is of 48 %. This similarity of percentages for the increase of knowledge in both cases could be explained by the "Clark [77]-Kozma [78] debate" where Clark (Clark, 1983, p 44.) states that "the media are only a vehicle transporting knowledge and do not influence knowledge".

However, the success rate for the learning of topography using the "Cluster" Internet application is only 22 % compared to the control group which is 83 %. The success rate of 22 % produced by distance learning can be explained by the fact that many of the cadets in the experimental group were having learning disabilities. Some of the major drawbacks of distance learning are to leave the student alone in his learning process without being in the classroom and lacking the presence of a teacher or colleagues to help him. Very often, students with learning disabilities registered in distance courses became confused by the lack of classroom dynamics that destroys motivation and desire to learn.

7. Conclusion

The actual research project wants that the term "hierarchical aggregate assessment" will be accepted and recognized by the entire scientific community. The process of hierarchical aggregate assessment has been used everywhere and throughout the ages without any researcher or scientist having the idea to define this process by a name or a term. One of the goals of the present research project is to resolve this issue by proposing the term "hierarchical aggregate assessment". The work done in this research was to implement this process in the areas of education, assessment and information technologies (IT). Further work and future research performed by the CDAME researchers will focus on (1) improving the user interface in the fields mentioned by the "QUIS" questionnaire that are feedback, terminology and resistance to change, (2) the implementation of the process of hierarchical aggregate assessment in the field of management and (3) the determination of the "Cluster" Internet application influence on knowledge increase, user satisfaction and student success rates.

Author details

Martin Lesage*, Gilles Raîche, Martin Riopel, Frédérick Fortin and Dalila Sebkhi

*Address all correspondence to: lesagelm@hotmail.com

Faculty of Education, Education and Pedagogy Department, Université du Québec à Montréal (UQÀM), C.P., Montréal, Canada

References

[1] Legendre, R. (2005). *Dictionnaire actuel de l'éducation* (3rd Edition). Montréal: Guérin.

[2] De Ketele, J. M., & Gérard, F.-M. (2005). La validation des épreuves d'évaluation selon l'approche par les compétences. *Mesures et Évaluation en Éducation, 28* (3), 1-26.

[3] Van Kempen, J. L. (2008). *Pourquoi a-t-on développé les compétences à l'école?* [On Line]. Union des Fédérations d'Associations de Parents de l'Enseignement Catholique (UFAPEC). Access: http://www.ufapec.be/nos-analyses/pourquoi-a-t-on-developpe-les-compétences-a-l-ecole/.

[4] Allal, L. (2002). Acquisition et évaluation des compétences en milieu scolaire. In J., Dolz, & E., Ollagnier (Eds.), *L'énigme de la compétence en éducation* (p. 77-94). Bruxelles: de Boeck.

[5] CDAME. (2013). *Site Internet du Centre CDAME (Collectif pour le Développement et les Applications en Mesure et Évaluation)* [On Line]. Access: http://www.cdame.uqam.ca.

[6]   Harvey, S. & Loiselle, J. (2009). Proposition d'un modèle de recherche développement. *Recherches qualitatives, 28* (2), 95-117.

[7]   Sugrue, M., Seger, M., Kerridge, R., Sloane, D. & Deane, S. (1995). A prospective study of the performance of the trauma team leader. *The Journal of Trauma: Injury, Infection and Critical Care, 38* (1), 79-82.

[8]   Volkov, A. & Volkov, M. (2007). Teamwork and assessment: A critique. *e-Journal of Business Education & Scholarship of Teaching, 1,* 59-64.

[9]   Baker, D. P. & Salas, E. (1992). Principles for measuring teamwork skills. *Human Factors, 34,* 469-475.

[10] Loiselle, J. (2001). La recherche développement en éducation: sa nature et ses caractéristiques. In D. M. Anadón, & M. L'Hostie (Eds), *Nouvelles dynamiques de recherche en éducation* (p. 77-97). Québec: Les Presses de l'Université Laval.

[11] Zaccaro, S. J., Mumford, M. D., Conelly, M. S., Marks, M. A. & Gilbert, J. A. (2000). Assessment of leader problem-solving capabilities. *Leadership Quarterly, 11* (1), 37-64.

[12] MacMillan, J., Paley, M. J., Entin, E. B. & Entin, E. E. (2004). Questionnaires for distributed assessment of team mutual awareness. In N. A. Stanton, A. Hedge, K. Brookhuis, E. Salas, & H. W. Hendrick (Eds.), *Handbook of human factors and ergonomic methods*. Boca Raton: Taylor and Francis.

[13] Furnham, A., Steele, H. & Pendelton, D. (1993). A psychometric assessment of the Belbin Team-Role Self-Perception Inventory. *Journal of Occupational and Organizational Psychology, 66,* 245-257.

[14] Freeman, M. & McKenzie, J. (2000). Self and peer assessment of student teamwork: Designing, implementing and evaluating SPARK, a confidential, web based system [On Line]. In *Flexible learning for a flexible society*. Proceedings of ASET-HERDSA 2000 Conference. Toowoomba, Qld, 2-5 July. ASET and HERDSA. Access: http://www.aset.org.au/confs/aset-herdsa2000/procs/freeman.html.

[15] Freeman, M. & McKenzie, J. (2002). SPARK, a confidential web-based template for self and peer assessment of student teamwork: Benefits of evaluating across different subjects. *British Journal of Educational Technology, 33* (5), 551-569.

[16] Ritchie, P. D. & Cameron, P. A. (1999). An evaluation of trauma team leader performance by video recording. *Australian and New Zealand Journal of Surgery, 69,* 183-186.

[17] Lurie, S. J., Schultz, S. H. & Lamanna, G. (2011). Assessing teamwork: A reliable five-question survey. *Family Medicine, 43* (10), 731-734.

[18] Lesage, M., Raîche, G., Riopel, M. & Sebkhi, D. (2013). *Le développement d'une application Internet d'évaluation hiérarchique des apprentissages (évaluation agrégée) selon une méthodologie de recherche développement (R & D)*. Association Francophone Internationale de Recherche Scientifique en éducation (AFIRSE).

[19] Lesage, M., Raîche, G., Riopel, M., Fortin, F. & Sebkhi, D. (2014). An E-Assessment Website To Implement Hierarchical Aggregate Assessment. *ICCSSE 2014: International Conference on Computer Science and Software Engineering*, Rio de Janeiro, Brazil.

[20] Lesage, M., Raîche, G., Riopel, M., Fortin, F. & Sebkhi, D. (2014). An E-Assessment Website to Implement Hierarchical Aggregate Assessment. *World Academy of Science, Engineering and Technology, International Science Index 86, 8* (2), 925-933.

[21] Sebkhi, D., Raîche, G., Riopel, M. & M. Lesage. (2013). *Une première mise à l'essai d'une application Internet d'évaluation hiérarchique des apprentissages (évaluation agrégée) avec des élèves du secondaire dans le cadre des stages III et IV de l'UQAM en accord avec l'approche par compétence du Ministère de l'Éducation des Loisirs et des Sports du Québec (MELS).* Association Francophone Internationale de Recherche Scientifique en éducation (AFIRSE).

[22] MySQL. (2013). *MySQL Website* [On Line]. Access: http://www.mysql.com.

[23] Moodle. (2013). *Moodle Website* [On Line]. Access: http://www.moodle.org.

[24] Blackboard. (2013). *Blackboard* [On Line]. Access: http://www.blackboard.com.

[25] Nance, W. D. (2000). Improving information systems students' teamwork and project management capabilities: Experiences from an innovative classroom. *Information Technology and Management, 1* (4), 293-306.

[26] Lavallée, M. (1969). *Taxonomie des objectifs pédagogiques. Tome 1: Domaine cognitif.* Québec: Presses de l'Université du Québec (Éducation nouvelle).

[27] Krathwohl, D. R., Bloom, B. S. & Masia, B. B. (Eds.). (1964). *Taxonomy of educational objectives: Handbook II: The affective domain.* New York: McKay.

[28] Hubert, S. & Denis, B. (2000). Des outils pour évaluer les compétences transversales, *Actes du 1er Congrès des chercheurs en Éducation*, 24-25 mai 2000, Bruxelles.

[29] Jeunesse, C. (2007). Évaluer un apprentissage en ligne : éléments théoriques & pistes de réflexion. In J. C. Manderscheid, & C. Jeunesse (Eds.), *L'enseignement en ligne à l'université et dans les formations professionnelles. Pourquoi? Comment?* Louvain-la-Neuve: De Boeck.

[30] Endrizzi, L. & Rey, O. (2008). *L'évaluation au cœur des apprentissages* [On Line]. Dossier d'actualité n°39, Service de veille scientifique et technologique INRP. Access: http://www.scribd.com/doc/8574511/levaluation-au-coeur-des-apprentissages.

[31] Louis, R. & Bernard, H. (2004). *L'évaluation des apprentissages en classe: théorie et pratique.* Montréal: Groupe Beauchemin, éditeur ltée.

[32] Tardif, J. (2006). *L'évaluation des compétences. Documenter le parcours de développement.* Montréal: Chenelière Éducation.

[33] Palm, T. (2008). Performance assessment and authentic assessment: A conceptual analysis of the literature [On Line]. *Practical Assessment, Research & Evaluation, 13* (4). Access: http://pareonline.net/pdf/v13n4.pdf.

[34] Wiggins, G. (1990). The case for authentic assessment [On Line]. *Practical Assessment, Research & Evaluation, 2* (2). Access: http://PAREonline.net/getvn.asp?v=2&n=2.

[35] Wiggins, G. (1993). Assessment: Authenticity, context and validity. *The Phi Delta Kappan, 75* (3), 200-214.

[36] Hart, D. (1994). *Authentic assessment: A handbook for educators.* New York: Addison Wesley.

[37] Rennert-Ariev, P. (2005). A theoretical model for the authentic assessment of teaching [On Line]. *Practical Assessment, Research & Evaluation, 10* (2). Access: http://pareonline.net/pdf/v10n2.pdf.

[38] Marin-Garcia, J. A. & Lloret, J. (2008). Improving teamwork with university engineering students. The effect of an assessment method to prevent shirking. *WSEAS Transactions on Advances in Engineering Education, 1* (5), 1-11.

[39] Swan, K., Shen, J. & Hiltz, R. (2006). Assessment and collaboration in online learning. *Journal of Asynchronous Learning Networks, 10* (1), 45-62.

[40] Boud, D., Cohen, R. & Sampson, J. (1999). Peer learning and assessment. *Assessment & Evaluation in Higher Education, 24* (4), 413-426.

[41] MacDonald, J. (2003). Assessing online collaborative learning: Process and product. *Computer & Education, 40,* 377-391.

[42] Worcester Polytechnic Institute (WPI) (2011). *Teamwork and teamwork assessment* [On Line]. Access: http://www.wpi.edu/Images/CMS/IQP/teamworkandteamworkassessment.doc.

[43] Durham, C. C., Knight, D. & Locke, E. A. (1997). Effects of leader role, team-set goal difficulty, efficacy, and tactics on team effectiveness. *Organizational Behavior and Human Decision Process, 72* (2), 203-231.

[44] Lingard, R. W. (2010). Teaching and assessing teamwork skills in engineering and computer science. *Journal of Systemics, Cybernetics and Informatics, 18* (1), 34-37.

[45] Goldfinch, J. (1994). Further developments in peer assessment of group projects. *Assessment & Evaluation in Higher Education, 19* (1), 29-35.

[46] Goldfinch, J. & Raeside, R. (1990). Development of a peer assessment technique for obtaining individual marks on a group project. *Assessment & Evaluation in Higher Education, 15* (3), 210-231.

[47] Northrup, S. G. & Northrup, D. A. (2006) *Multidisciplinary teamwork assessment: Individual contributions and interdisciplinary interaction*. Communication présentée à la 36ième conférence ASEE/IEEE Frontiers in Education,Octobre 28-31, San Diego.

[48] Bloom, B. S., Engelhart, M. D., Furst, E. J., Hill, W. H. & Krathwohl, D. R. (Eds.). (1956). *Taxonomy of educational objectives: The classification of educational goals. Handbook I: Cognitive domain*. New York: Davis McKay.

[49] Krathwohl, D. R. (2002). A revision of Bloom's taxonomy: An overview. *Theory into Practice, 41* (4), 212-218.

[50] Bastiaens, T. (2007). *Instructional design of authentic E-learning environments*. Oral presentation at E-Learn 2007, Québec, Canada.

[51] Saskatchewan Professional Development Unit (2003). *Performance Assessments: A wealth of possibilities* [On Line]. Access: http://www.sasked.gov.sk.ca/branches/aar/afl/docs/assessment_support/perfassess.pdf.

[52] Olivier, L. (2002). *L'évaluation des apprentissages* [On Line]. Commission Scolaire de Montréal.   Access: http://www.csdm.qc.ca/Csdm/Administration/pdf/reforme_vol1_no2.pdf.

[53] Bibeau, R. (2007). Des situations d'apprentissage et d'évaluation (SAE) sur Internet. *Revue de l'association EPI* [On Line], 91. Access: http://www.epi.asso.fr/revue/articles/a0701a.htm.

[54] Willey, K. & Freeman M. (2006). *Completing the learning cycle: The role of formative feedback when using self and peer assessment to improve teamwork and engagement*. Proceedings of the 17th Annual Conference of the Australasian Association for Engineering Education, 10-13 décembre 2006, Auckland, New Zealand.

[55] Willey, K. & Freeman, M. (2006). Improving teamwork and engagement: The case for self and peer assessment [On Line]. *Australasian Journal of Engineering Education, 02.* Access: http://www.aaee.com.au/journal/2006/willey0106.pdf.

[56] Marshall-Mies, J. C., Fleishman, E. A., Martin, J. A., Zaccaro, S. J., Baughman, W. A. & McGee, M. L. (2000). Development and evaluation of cognitive and metacognitive measures for predicting leadership potential. *Leadership Quarterly, 11* (1), 135-153.

[57] Kaye, W. & Mancini, M. E. (1986). Use of the Mega Code to evaluate team leader performance during advanced cardiac life support. *Critical Care Medicine, 14* (2), 99-104.

[58] Davis, G. B., Olson, M. H., Ajenstat, J. & Peaucelle, J. L. (1986). *Systèmes d'information pour le management. Volume I: Les bases*. Boucherville: Éditions G. vermette Inc.

[59] Burch, J. G. & Grudnitski, G. (1989). *Information systems: Theory and practice* (5th Edition). New York: John Wiley.

[60] Davis, G. B. & Olson, M. H. (1985). *Management information systems: Conceptual foundations, structure, and development*. New York: McGraw-Hill.

[61] Laudon, K. C. & Laudon, J. P. (2000). *Management information systems: Organization and technology in the networked enterprise* (6th Edition). Upper saddle River: Prentice Hall.

[62] Laudon, K. C., Laudon, J. P. & Brabston, M. E. (2011). *Management information systems: Managing the digital firm* (5th édition canadienne). Toronto: Pearson Education Canada Inc.

[63] Kanter, J. (1984). *Management information systems* (3th Edition). New Jersey: Prentice Hall.

[64] Chin, J. P., Diehl, V. A. & Norman, K. L. (1988). *Development of an instrument measuring user satisfaction of the human-computer interface.* Proceedings of SIGCHI '88, p. 213-218, New York. ACM/SIGCHI.

[65] Richey, R. C. & Nelson, W. A. (1996). Developmental research. In D. H. Jonassen (Ed.), *Handbook of research for educational communications and technology* (p. 1213-1245). New-York: Mac Millan.

[66] Savoie-Zajc, L. (2004). La recherche qualitative/interprétative en éducation. In T. Karsenti & L. Savoie-Zajc (Eds.), *La recherche en éducation: étapes et approches* (p. 123-150). Sherbrooke: Éditions du CRP.

[67] Savoie-Zajc, L. & Karsenti, T. (2004). La méthodologie. In T. Karsenti & L. Savoie-Zajc (Eds.), *La recherche en éducation: étapes et approches* (p. 109-121). Sherbrooke: Éditions du CRP.

[68] Borg, W. R. & Gall, M. D. (1983). *Educational research: An introduction* (4th Edition). New York: Longman.

[69] Nonnon, P. (1993). *Proposition d'un modèle de recherche Développement (R&D) technologique en éducation.* Regards sur la robotique pédagogique. Technologies nouvelles et éducation. Publications du service de technologie de l'éducation de l'Université de Liège et de l'Institut nation de recherche pédagogique, Paris, pp. 147-154.

[70] Cervera, D. (1997). *Élaboration d'un environnement d'expérimentation en simulation incluant un cadre théorique pour l'apprentissage de l'énergie des fluides.* Thèse de doctorat inédite, Université de Montréal.

[71] Van der Maren, J. M. (2003). *La recherche appliquée en pédagogie: Des modèles pour l'enseignement* (2ième Édition). Bruxelles: De Boeck.

[72] Nonnon, P. (2002). *La R&D en éducation.* Contribution aux actes du symposium international francophone sur les technologies en éducation de l'INRP sous la direction de Georges Louis Baron & Éric Bruillard, Paris, France (p. 53-59).

[73] Ministère de la défense nationale, Gouvernement du Canada. (2007). *A-CR-CCP-701/PF-002 – Guides pédagogiques de l'étoile verte.* Ottawa, Ministère de la défense nationale, Cadets royaux de l'armée canadienne.

[74] Sittig, D. F., Kuperman, G. J. & Fiskio J. (1999). Evaluating physician satisfaction regarding user interactions with an electronic medical record system. *Proceedings of the American Medical Informatics Association (AMIA) Annual Symposium*, 400-404.

[75] LabMÉCAS. (2013). *Laboratoire mobile pour l'étude des cheminements d'apprentissage en science (LabMÉCAS)* [En ligne]: Access: www.labmecas.uqam.ca/.

[76] Boucher-Genesse, F., Riopel, M. & Potvin, P. (2011). Research results for Mecanika, a game to learn Newtonian concepts. In *Games, learning and society*. Conference proceedings, Madison, Wisconsin.

[77] Clark, R. E. (1983). Reconsidering research on learning from media. *Review of Educational Research, 17* (2), 445-459.

[78] Kozma, R. B. (1994). Will media influence learning: Reframing the debate. *Educational Technology Research and Development (ETR&D), 42* (2), 7-19.

2

Personalization and User Modeling in Adaptive E-Learning Systems for Schools

Todorka Glushkova

Additional information is available at the end of the chapter

Abstract

The manuscript presents a model for the personalization of e-Learning systems in secondary schools. Approaches are discussed about the implementation of this model by the application of the SCORM-standard, ITL (ITL-Interval and temporal logic), policies, etc. Comments on the possibilities for increasing the relevance of e-Learning systems in the real classroom environment schools are also included.

Keywords: E-Learning, User Modelling, Personalization, Adaptation, Interaction, SCORM, ITL

1. Introduction

Dynamically changing realities in modern society require more dynamic and adequate changes in education, which is inherently conservative. Every innovation and change in the traditional school system requires a long time for synchronizing the legal basis, approbation, and implementation in school practice. This generates a continuous delay in the fast increasing requirements to the educational system, which makes it difficult to meet public expectations. The world community sees a way to solve this problem through the application of ICT and e-Learning in the educational process. Environments that offer a variety of teaching materials and services to different user groups, such as students, parents, learners, employees, etc., are created. As a rule, all these systems are developed faster and cost much cheaper than their traditional equivalents. They enable the implementation of new and different approaches from the traditional and provide solutions as well as access to educational materials within the process of learning. The standardization of individual modules and processes bring order to the variety of systems for computer training and make it possible to use them independently because of the software and hardware platform features. All this seemed to solve the problems of didactic theory and practice, but the reality is different. There is a delay in the process of implementation and actual use of these systems despite the rapid development of information and communication technologies. Research groups from different universities and educational communities define the main reason as learning by means of ICT is an innovative process that requires in-depth research by pedagogical science and practice [1]. Psychological attitudes, motivation, and cognitive characteristics of students of different age groups are different in terms of learning processes. The didactic theory and practice for many years examine these processes and provide solutions for the improvement of the traditional forms of training, however, the mechanisms in e-Learning environments of educational portals are still not well investigated and explained. There is a gap between the expectations of developers and real results in the educational practice. The rapid development of computer science and technology for the creation of learning environments requires a high level of qualification and experience of the developers of such systems. These developers are highly qualified and highly specialized IT professionals who create systems in accordance to their abstract vision of the learning process. However, they rarely or never are pedagogical specialists and therefore, do not know the actual in-depth psychological processes of learning. This leads to the fact that institutions have learning environments that have a good software perspective quality but poor quality as a pedagogical tool. To these reasons, we can add the difference in terminology, the desire to maximize profits of software vendors, unclear criteria for evaluation of the learning process, etc. As a result, we see many factors that negatively affect the whole process and can significantly hinder it.

Despite these problems, there are many areas in which the results are very good. Summarizing the results of higher education in the analysis of the Sloan Consortium in [2], successfully use of e-Learning environments in the USA and Canada grew by 20% over the last few years. The indicators are particularly good for students who are trained in a distance form of teaching, as well as with electronic training courses that are similar in nature to the traditional teaching process. Secondary schools also have sectors that experience very good results. Examples are as follows: the using of educational environments in blended learning (classroom training and independent work) and the creation of a portfolio of students who successfully combined with project training [3].

The problem analysis allows us to conclude that the creation of training systems must comply with specifics of the particular educational institution and be developed in direct communication with educational experts as were probed directly in the real learning environment. This publication will present a model for personalizing learning systems for electronic and distance learning in secondary schools by application of didactic methodology, setting of educational goals and objectives, the motivation of the student, and his or her personal goals, plans, and ambitions.

The structure of the manuscript corresponds to the described methodology. In section 2, "Interaction and Adaptation" discusses various aspects of interactivity and adaptability connected with the personalization of the learning process and provides access to educational resources. Here, the adaptive levels of the system in horizontal and vertical plans are reviewed.

Section 3, "Adaptive levels and interaction Student-Learning system", describes the three adaptive levels and some mechanisms for their implementation of the SCORM-based e-learning system.

Section 4, "Personalization and User modelling", are connected with the opportunities for development of the personalization and UM on different adaptive levels according to the described methodology. An algorithm is proposed for the implementation of the model in the e-Learning environment.

The results of the partial implementation of the proposed model of e-Learning in secondary schools are encouraging. Work on the realization of the full adaptive model continues.

2. Interaction and adaptation

According to the definitions in [4], [5], and [6] e-Learning is a computer and an internet-based learning, in which the delivery of electronic learning resources is carried out on the principles of dynamic interaction with the educational system and the other participants in the learning process, according to didactic set goals and objectives and according to the characteristics of the course and the personal characteristics of the student. Based on this definition, the team of University of Plovdiv, together with partners from the Institute of Information Technologies (BG), University of Limerick (Ireland), De Montfort University in Leicester (UK), Humboldt University (Germany), Secondary school in Brezovo (BG), etc., developed a system for electronic and distance training (DeLC[1]). As part of this project, an environment is developed for e-Learning and distance training for secondary schools. In order to minimize the problems mentioned above, we chose a methodology by which, together with pedagogical specialists, creates step by step the different prototypes of the system and tested them directly in the real learning environment (Figure 1).

To create an interactive and adaptive system that meets these requirements, it is necessary to model the different interactive levels and adaptive aspects. We accept the definition in [7] and define it as a dialog between users and the learning system and will view it at the following three levels:

• Standard Experience – the physical structure and hierarchy of the learning content remains unchanged;

• Personal Experience – the hierarchy of content changes and adapts to the user's behaviour and selections;

• Open Experience – an open and live system with continuous engagement between the producer, user, and message.

---

1 DeLC- Distributed eLearning Centre

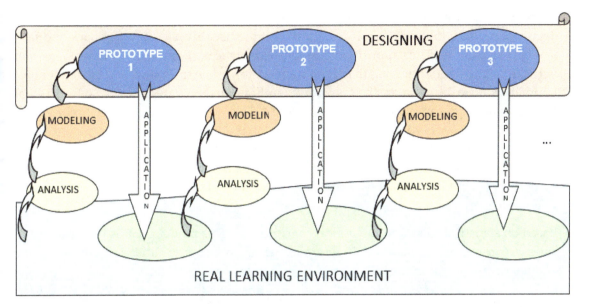

Figure 1. Iterative model of research methodology

Within these levels, there are six categories of interactivity: Feedback; Control; Productivity; Creativity; Communication and Adaptation. Ensuring interactivity for each level and related categories requires the development of a comprehensive adaptive model to provide personalization of the training through: the basic knowledge of the student; his plans and purposes; his cognitive characteristics; his preferences and habits; emotional profile, and so on (see [8]).

According to various aspects of the application and the use of e-Learning systems, the adaptability can be defined differently. We will define adaptability as a feature of the training system to be adapting itself and changed according to the requirements and the characteristics of the users before and during use of it. The main elements of the adaptive model are "condition-action" rules that change the parameters of the environment and realize the adaptation to a user's knowledge, goals, abilities, preferences, etc. The different methods and frameworks for creation of adaptive models are as follows:

- Rule-based – we look at these systems from some aspects: as a declarative interpretation of rules; as a hybrid representation based on logical deduction; as a users' stereotypes; as an overlay model of connecting and co-interacting with the model of the relevant applied area. Presenting the cognitions is connected with the accommodation of the system conventions, the attitude and the convictions of the users, and the stereotypes and the user groups that can be activated dynamically with the particular conditions, etc.

- Frame and Network-based – these models are associated with figuring the sciences as interrelations between separate facts of semantic net and frame structures. It can be used successfully on a small applied domain that can be easily identified and structured.

- Supposition-based – Such systems work with a multitude assumptions of the consumer that forms on the student's knowledge base and domain independent rules. The suppositions are facts on the user that the system takes with a certain level in security and cogency. The degree of cogency in the system is being raised if the user gives a good feedback and falls if he gives a bad one. The suppositions, established on the base of the direct communication with the user, are better defined that the system is adopted on the base of logical deductions. Formally, we can differentiate the system assumptions on three categories: what the student knows; what he doesn't know; and the student's aims, tasks, and plans. The first two can be realized by stereotype and overlay models as the knowledge of students are being adapted to relevant domain ontology. The third group is part of the Goal and Task Model of the e-Learning system. The most simple is the method of linearly parameterization. It is more complex but more reliable as the model uses formulas, predicates, ITL, policies, and grid models.

- Based on statistical rules and theoretical conclusions – This model permits the adapting of rules according to the state of the entrance data. The opportunities for setting-up the adaptation are based on the information from past learning sessions.

For the development of the adaptive model, we use separate elements from each of these methods we: use the stereotypes and the overlay model at the initial determination of common behaviours rules; define the concrete dependencies from the described school subject domain, by using of domain ontologies; make a system from assumptions for the learner, based on his stereotype, cognitions, and goals; store the information from the last learning sessions and processed it statistically; and deduced abstract conclusions for the user groups and the separate learners. The implementation of the model requires the consideration of the various adaptability aspects of horizontal and vertical principles. The first one is connected with the adaptation to some personal characteristics of the student. This model of realization in this aspect is discussed in [9]. There are two types of adaptation – adaptivity and adaptability. The first allows users to use different facilities for presentation and navigation in predetermined learning content. The second level includes mechanisms for adaptation to knowledge and preferences of students dynamically in the learning process. On this basis, we will distinguish the following three adaptive levels: Elementary Adaptive Level, Static Adaptive Level, and Dynamic Adaptive Level. The first two are connected with adaptivity, and the last one – with adaptability.

In the next section, we will look at these adaptive levels. We will focus our attention on the Static Adaptive Level and will comment on some ideas for the realization of the Dynamic Adaptive Level.

3. Adaptive levels and student-learning system interaction

Elementary adaptive level (EAL) – the adaptation in this level is connected by the use of static user information such as type of training, grade, class, name, access to learning material (by mobile or fixed device), etc. Here, we can use a stereotype approach. The authors of educational resources develop packages of lessons, tests, etc., in accordance with government educational requirements and standards for the typical student, school subject, the class and form of training. The created educational resources are common for all students in the described groups.

We can realize an adaptation on this level by the preparation of training materials, common for all students in the phase before the start of the learning process. These characteristics prove the relationship with the first interactive level – Standard Experience, because the physical structure and hierarchy of the learning content remains unchanged. However physical and cognitive interaction occurs for the users. The student receives the entire information independently if he knows it. At this level, users are an abstract group of people with common characteristics – background knowledge, preferences, cognitive performance, and more. This personalization is the lowest formal level. Although users have their accounts in the school e-Learning environment, they can work in it only on the predetermined way for all other users in the same stereotyped group.

Static adaptive level (SAL) – this level is based on the elementary level and is directly related with mechanisms to provide adequate learning materials for individual students according to their knowledge base, personal goals, and plans.

Before we present the adaptive mechanisms of this level, we will comment on the concept of persona as an aggregated user type. The persona is a description of a fictitious learner. This description is based on different methods, including the personal experience of the teachers, hypotheses, statistical methods, and heuristic analysis [10].

Adaptability of this level is realized through the collection preparation of educational materials and services, foreseeing the actions and behaviour of the persona. The realization is based on the log-information about past interactions between the student and LMS according to the set of rules defined by the teachers. It is necessary to define the background knowledge of this student. We can determine the knowledge in different ways – by initial testing, by results from completed to this moment training sessions, etc. Based on these values, the system joins this student to the persona, who is closest to these characteristics. The system compares the individual characteristics, plans, and objectives of the student with the typical didactic aims, defined in BES. As a result, this lesson that most closely matches with the basic knowledge, goals, plans, and personal characteristics of the student that is associated with this persona starts from the Lesson repository.

Moreover, special attention will be paid to the creation of courses by pedagogical specialists in the article. In accordance with pedagogical theory, this process is cyclical and begins by placing the main didactic aims, passes through specifying learning tasks, develops the profiles of aggregated user types (personas), the establishes learning scenarios with different personas, develops prototypes of the training process, shares this prototype among specialized pedagogical community of educators, experts and heuristic evaluation of this prototype testing in real learning environment, and corrects existing errors and inaccuracies. Each stage of this process requires a qualitative evaluation and heuristic analysis of the pedagogical community and the implementation of appropriate tools in a common environment – ex. Integrated Learning Design Environment (ILDE) [11] (Figure 2).

Figure 2. Creation of learning course in ILDE

Creation of the training course, according to the developed scenario is realized based on the selected standard for e-Learning. In developing the DeLC-system, we use the standard SCORM[2] [12]. The team developed a special SCORM-editor for the teachers and authors of the educational content – SELBO [13].

We will concentrate our attention on the two basic characteristics of the lesson – the content and the structure. The content of lessons is related with specific topics that are connected with some school subject domains. The e-lesson presents a semantic structure of the knowledge that is connected with some school subjects. The formalization can be realized through the creation of ontologies in which each concept from the respective area are associated with real information resources that represent them in the lesson. According to the main characteristics of the school subject domain, the authors of e-content in accordance with didactic aims define the structure of the lesson. The didactic aims are related with type of the lesson (for new knowledge, for exercises, summary, and testing). We use Bloom's taxonomy to formalize these

---

2 SCORM- Sharable Content Object Reference Model

aims with the cognitive levels – knowledge, comprehension, application, analysis, synthesis, and evaluation [14]. The teacher could structure the lesson in different ways depending on the predefined didactic aims. We came to the conclusion that there is a correspondence between the different types of e-lessons and the cognitive levels of Bloom's taxonomy. Therefore, we can formalize the different types of e-lessons according to didactic aims by creating standard scenarios for training and templates that describe them. The template is a combination of structure and learning scenarios.

To create electronic lessons by using algorithm requires a thorough knowledge of the standard SCORM, which creates objective problems for teachers who are not IT specialists. To partly solve this problem, we can use the SCORM Best Practices Guide for Content Developers (BPG) [15], which offers a number of basic templates and models that correspond to different educational scenarios.

In order to increase the formalization level of templates and models, we created a system for its parameterization. Thus, we received a number of different groups of templates that more fully meets the requirements and objectives of the learning process. We can use the following for the parameterization of templates:

- Number_of_SCOs – type Integer, to describe the number of SCOs[3] in the template. If the parameter value Has_test is "yes", the number of questions Num_Quest =Number_of_SCOs – 1;

- Has_test – type Boolean to determine whether there is a final test or not in the template. Defaults to "yes" and is realized with the last SCO;

- Num_Quest – number of questions in the final test

- The ordered pair (objective_n, min_value_n) connects each target variable (objective) and the minimum value for which LMS will mark it as successfully passed (n<Number_of_SCOs);

- The ordered pair (SCOn, template_num), for each n <Number_of_SCOs and template_num <= 10, which connects each SCO with instance of the main BPG-template;

Let's define two operatios:

- Set (SCO_Number_of_SCOs (Asset k); Objective_k) – for setting values of k-th target variable for the k-th issue of the last SCO, where k <Number_of_SCOs, and

- Read (SCO_k, Objective_k) – start-up of the information SCO_k if Objective_k has a value less than the predetermined.

In dialogue with the SCORM-based authoring tool for generating of electronic lessons, the teacher will determine the values of these parameters and the system will generate the structure of the desired template. If specific values of the parameters are not mentioned, the system will get the default values. After the parameterization, the teacher will receive the

---

3 SCO- Sharable Content Object

parameterized template with the SCORM rules that served as a guide to the sequence of educational activities in the educational scenario depending on the behaviour of the individual student.

For example, if we get parameter values: number_of_SCOs = 10; has_test = "yes"; (objective_n; 0.75) for each n <10; (SCO_n, template_2), for each n <10; Set (SCO10 (asset_n), objective_n) for each n <10; Read (SCO_n, objective_n) for each n <10, we get the following chart describing the scenario of the lesson (Figure 3):

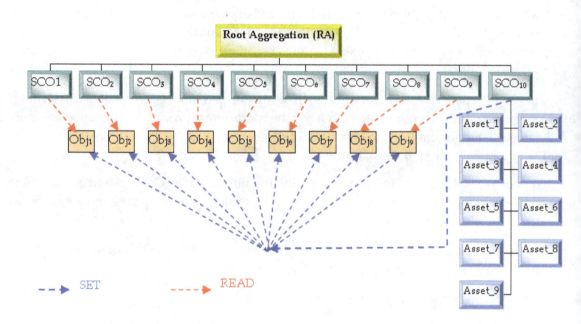

Figure 3. Parametrized Content Structure Diagram

Therefore, based on the Bloom taxonomy of didactic purposes, lesson types formalization of their structure and navigation rules can be created by the step by step algorithm for creating of e-lessons.

The teacher in some school subjects create e-lessons in a specialized development environment, which is in dynamic interaction with the respective ontology. This author's tool has to maintain information about the compulsory concepts in the relevant discipline according to Bulgarian Educational Standards. Concepts that are mandatory taught according to BES and those that are determined from the teacher for this lesson are marked with AND and those that contain additional information are marked with OR. The algorithm includes the following steps:

1. Through a dialogue with the system (e.g. personal assistant), the teacher defines the class, form of training, and didactic aims of establishing a lesson. The system filters relevant domain ontology and retrieves concepts – mandatory and complementary.

2. Depending on the subject area and selected didactic aims, the system offers the most appropriate templates that can be selected from.

3. In a step by step process, the teacher determines the values of parameters such as the number of data objects (SCOs), presence of preliminary and final test, minimum values of the target variables for their passing, number of attempts to solve the tests, etc. As a result, the system generates a parameterized template, which includes the structure of the lesson (SCORM CAM[4]) and the rules that will manage the learning process (SCORM Sequence & Navigation Model[5]).

4. The author connects the SCOs with nodes of the structural graph in the template of the lesson.

5. The author ccreated lesson (the system generates zip-package and imsmanifest.xml)

6. He upload created lesson in SCORM-environment of the education portal.

E-Learning resources (SCOs) are associated with concepts of relevant ontology. They are stored in some online SCOs Repository. In ontologies and related items, SCOs are presented into the development environment for creating electronic lessons [16]. The authors determine the structure of the e-lesson by using the parameterization of some basic templates. In this way, they create an instance of the template in which there are no free parameters. LMS manages educational processes and determines the training scenario in accordance with the structure of the lesson and learning scenario, which are related to the didactic aims, behaviour, and basic knowledge of the students. The e-lesson will be presented in the system as a specific instance of some basic template, which, by setting the values of parameters, is associated with specific learning resources.

One example is the Lesson "Summary on complex verb tenses» for 7th grade students for independent distance training". The didactic aim is to reach higher levels of Bloom's taxonomy – application, analysis, synthesis, and evaluation. The system offers BPG-templates №7, 8, and 10, and the teacher chooses Template 7. In this template, SCOs containing learning information are grouped in a separate Aggregation B. The student must answer questions from the preliminary test and if wrong (i.e. target variables that monitor test results are less than the minimum values), he has to become familiar with the educational content of the information SCOs. Then, he will make the final test in the last SCO. The template can be used in the creation of educational resources, which is necessary to verify and ensure a certain volume of back-ground knowledge. It is essential to fill the gaps and to allow the student to successfully pass the final test. LMS manages the values of the variables (objectives) and only if they are larger than the specified minimum, the training is considered to be successfully completed. The teacher gives the following values of the parameters through a dialogue in a step-by-step process: Number_of_SCOs=9; Has_pre_test="yes"; Num_Quest=9; Has_post_test="yes"; $(Obj\_n,1)$ – i.e., answered correctly for all questions from 1 to 9; $(Obj\_n; 0{,}75)$ – gave a very good answer to the questions for $\forall n \in [10, 18]$; (SCOn, pattern_2) for $\forall °n \in [3, 11]$; Set(SCO1 (Asset_k); Obj_k) for $\forall k \in [1, 9]$; Set (SCO2 (Asset_k); Obj_k) for $\forall k \in [10, 18]$; Read (SCO (k +2), Obj_k) for $\forall k \in [1, 9]$. The system generates a CAM- model and S & N rules. The teacher

---

4 CAM-SCORM Content Aggregation Model

5 S&N Model- SCORM Sequence and Navigation Model

writes the test questions and puts the SCOs in Aggregation B. These data objects (SCOs) include both basic information on various complex verb tenses as well as tasks and exercises for students who will have to pass successively through the levels «application» – «analysis» – «synthesis» – «evaluation». The teacher makes a SCORM-package of the lesson and uploads it in the SCORM-based school education portal (http://sou-brezovo.org). These characteristics prove the relationship with the second interactive level – Personal Experience – because the hierarchy of content changes and adapts to the user's behaviours and selections.

Dynamic adaptive level (DAL) – This level is related to the dynamic interaction between students and the system during the training process (in run-time). After selecting the most appropriate e-lesson from the Lesson DB, the LMS starts the learning process according to the training scenario. The learning scenario is realized by a sequence of actions that is previously defined by the author of the lesson. The system observes the intermediate results during the training and information from the already completed training sessions. Based on this information, the LMS adapts itself dynamically to the changing characteristics of the learning environment as it generates new "condition-action" rules and either continues the training process or stops it. If the parameters are not appropriate, the system has to choose and to start a new and more appropriate e-lesson.

We are convinced that in the process of dynamic interaction between the learners and the training system, it is essential to use intelligent agents who interact with the system and with each other to provide a flexible change of training scenarios depending on the behaviours and actions of the individual student. For the managing of the dynamic adaptation of LMS, we can use Interval temporal logic (ITL) and policies.

Morris Sloman in [17] defines the policies as a set of rules for activating different states and actions, depending on the behaviour of the consumers or the current state of the system. There are different techniques to formalize the policies – graphical modelling, using the object-oriented methods for defining of policies, etc. We will use the opportunities provided from ITL [18] as it builds on a classical logic tier and allows to describe dynamic processes in the course of their implementation. It is a flexible notation for handling events that varied in time intervals, allows series, and parallel compositing using a well-defined mathematical proof system. ITL includes four components – logic tier, temporal structures, conditions, and intervals. Classical logic manages variables, constants, functions, and predicates. If we want to describe the dynamic processes, it is necessary to add temporal structures as skip, chop, and chopstar. The states are specific transmission of values to the observed variables and the intervals are sequences of states.

We will describe the next three sets: S-set of students, O-set of available objects or resources, and A-actions that can be performed with these resources. Then, we can introduce the user authentication as one of the Boolean variables:

- $Autho^+(S, O, A)$ – Positive identification of the user S, who has right to use the resource O by performing action A. For example $Autho^+(Ivan, Lesson1, Read)$ or $Autho^+(Ivan, Test1, Write)$;

- Autho⁻(S, O, A) – Negative identification – the user S refusal to use the resource O by performing action A. For example Autho⁻ (Ivan, Lesson1, Write).

Upon the initial start-up of the system, these variables have a default value of "false". The mathematical model of **Autho** is a matrix with 3 columns – users, objects, actions, and n-number of lines for all users in the system. The access to resources will be allowed if they satisfied certain "condition-action" rules of the type: $F \to W$ i.e., F always followed by W in the final state of the observed subinterval. According to this definition, the Access Rules take the following form: $F \to autho^+(S, O, A)$ – rule for positive identification and $F \to Autho^-(S, O, A)$ – rule for negative identification. For example: If in the initial step the access was denied, but in the next moment, it is authorized in the duration of 10 time units then: $((Autho^-(S, O, A) \wedge skip) \vee (Autho^+(S, O, A) \wedge len <= 10) \to Autho^+(S, O, A))$. If two users M and N are grouped and one of them has access, then the second one also receives access: $In(M, N) \wedge Autho^+(M, O, A) \to Autho^+(N, O, A)$.

The Access Rules determine whether the particular user is entitled to access this learning resource or service. To realize the access itself, the management passes the Implementation Rules, which has the following more general form: $F \to Autho(S, O, A)$. There are two alternatives in access: Open Access and Restricted Access. Open Access has low security – i.e., if access is not prohibited, it is allowed: $\neg Autho^-(S, O, A) \to Autho(S, O, A)$. Restricted Access means the system checks whether access is allowed and it has meanwhile been prohibited i.e., $(Autho^+ (S, O, A) \wedge \neg Autho^-(S, O, A)) \to Autho(S, O, A)$.

Another way to access learning resources is the delegation of rights to the unauthorized user. For example, the teacher gives access rights to other teachers for reading a lesson: $Teacher(S, Lesson) \to Candeleg^+(S, \_, Lesson, Read)$. The rules for delegating access, which author A1 gives teacher T2 to make corrections in Lesson1 is: $(Autho(A1, Lesson1, Write) \wedge Candeleg(A1, T1, Lesson1, Write)) \to Autho(T1, Lesson1, Write)$.

The policy P is a collection of rules: $P \cong (w \wedge (\wedge ri) \wedge fin)$, where w is the initial state, w' is the final state, and $\wedge r_i$ is a conjunction of intermediate states. For example, the policy for Author of Lesson1 (Author), teacher, who use this Lesson1 (Teacher), and student (Student) is:

$$P1 \cong \left(\left(Author(S, Lesson1) \to Autho^+ (S, Lesson1, Read)\right)\right.$$
$$\left(Author(S, Lesson1) \to Autho^+ (S, Lesson1, Write)\right)$$
$$\left(Teacher(S, Lesson1) \to Autho^+ (S, Lesson1, Read)\right)$$
$$\left(Teacher(S, Lesson1) \to Autho^- (S, Lesson1, Write)\right)$$
$$\left(Student(S, Lesson1) \to Autho^+ (S, Lesson1, Read)\right)$$
$$\left(Autho^+ (S, Lesson1, A) Autho^- (S, Lesson1, A)\right) \to Autho(S, Lesson1, A)\right)$$

The first step towards the creation of our school e-Learning system is the standardization of key processes associated with the personalization of access to e-lessons.

The teachers create e-lessons in specialized SCORM-compliant and ontology-based development environment, then publish them in the education portal in a special Lesson-DB. Further to SCORM-metadata, we will use some additional specifications such as:

- **Info** – title of the lesson, school subject, author, etc. features that are supported by the SCORM-metadata;

- **Subdomain** – matrix with concepts that will be included in the lesson and the extent of their studying Subdomain(concept, m), where m=1,2,3 as: 1 – low level of studying (mandatory minimum, according to BES); 2 – good level и 3 – high level;

- **Num_Grade** (the grade, for which is intended the lesson) – an integer from 1 to 12;

- **Form_of_training** (form of training): 1 – regular training; 2 – self training;

- **Lesson_Status** (status of the lesson) – an integer between 1 and 4: 4-free for use by all users in this and other portals in DeLC-education network; 3-free for use only by students and teachers in the portal; 2-authorized use only for certain users; 1-unavailable for other users, except for the author; **Didactic_aims** (didactic aims, according to Bloom's taxonomy) – an integer between 1 and 5: 1 acquisition of new knowledge (level "knowledge" and "comprehension" in the Bloom's taxonomy); 2 actualization of old knowledge (level "comprehension", "application", and "analysis"); 3 exercise and improvement of knowledge (level "application", "analysis", and "synthesis"); 4-generalization (levels "analysis", "synthesis", and "evaluation"); and 5-exam (level "evaluation").

Therefore, any electronic lesson in the education portal is a vector with the above dimensions:

$$\text{Lesson}\Big(\text{Info}\big(\text{ID, title, domain, author,...}\big), \text{Subdomain}\big(\text{concept}, m\big),$$
$$\text{Num\_Grade, Form\_of\_training, Lesson\_status, Didactic\_aims}\Big)$$

For example, the lesson "Past imperfect tense of the verb", school subject "Bulgarian language", for 5th grade; author Sarafov, with concepts from matrix Subdomain, designed for regular students, free for use for all users in the education system, and is a lesson for new knowledge we get:

$$\text{Lesson1}\Big(\text{Info}\big(\text{ID, Past imperfect tense of the verb, Bulgarian language, Sarafov,...}\big),$$
$$\text{Subdomain} * 5, \ 2, \ 4, \ 1\Big),$$

where Subdomain* is present with Table 1.

Conceptions	Level of Studying
Verb	3
Person of the verb	2
Tense of the verb	2
Communication moment	3
Moment of action	3
Main orientation moment	2
Additional orientation moment	2

Table 1. Subdomain

When the student requires launching of a lesson around a chosen theme, the system checks the availability of the appropriate e-lesson from the Lesson DB. Lessons that meet the initial user requirements are usually more than one, so the system should provide an appropriate mechanism for selecting the most appropriate among them. After a dialogue with the student, the personal agent defines his personal aims, preferences, etc., and transmits this vector to the system for choices. After the comparison with the vectors of the uploaded e-lessons in the Lesson DB, the e-Lessons with the highest level of similarity are extracted. The result will be a number of e-lessons andthe system should choose the most appropriate. This selection can be realized by the use of some intelligent algorithm (ex. CBR-approach).

The preferences and personal goals of each student can also formalize the policy which defines the sequence of actions in this training scenario. After the identification of the student in the training environment, based on the profile and persona-stereotypical information and a dialogue with his personal agent, the system receives the necessary initial values of the observed variables. After determining the initial state, the policy management can be transferred to a special Policy-Engine, which is part of the infrastructure of the run-time environment of the educational e-Learning portal. Initially, based on the dialogue with the student, the Policy of Preferences registers in the Policy-Engine and then starts the Mechanism for Selecting of Lesson that makes a request to the Lesson DB. After the selection a particular lesson, this e-lesson is filed to SCORM-Learning Management System for implementation. The scenario, which will run activities in the learning process, are described and formalized in the SCORM Sequence & Navigation-model and the corresponding parameterized template by which is created this lesson. Policy-Engine can continually modify policies according to the information coming from the behaviour of the learner.

The learning scenario may include mandatory implementation actions (e.g. solving tests). If a student fails to successfully complete these actions, the learning process falls in a critical condition and the Policy-Engine has to choose more appropriate lessons. In this case, the learning process is temporarily interrupted and the LMS restarts the training process with the new lesson.

The Policy of Preferences is expressed by the rules of condition-action types. Conditions present a number of behaviors that trigger certain actions. The formal semantics of the model is based on ITL as the rules are the following:

when B [increase | decrease] preference in Lesson [low | medium | high], where B is behaviour and Lesson is the e-lesson.

The degree of preference can be expressed as an integer. The larger number represents a higher degree of preference. It is initially assumed that the student doesn't have any preferences and all values are 0. We define the meaning of low, medium, and high level of preferences as 1, 2, and 3. We will look at an example of training with two lessons on the same learning material. The first lesson is more difficult and presents the studying concepts in a higher level than the second one. The student initially has not decided what his preferences are. In the Policy-Engine, there are defined policies, which specify that the lessons that guarantee more than 70% results in the final test are preferable than those that only guarantee between 50% to 70% and the lessons that ensure less than 50% are not preferred. We can express the policy with the following rules:

Score (Lesson1, Lesson2):

When (1: test_result >= 70%) increase preference in Lesson to high

When (2: 50%<=test_result <70%) decrease preference in Lesson to medium

When (3:test_result<50) decrease preference in Lesson to low

The Policy-Engine determines the information needed for the implementation according to these rules. LMS through the SCORM RTE[6] and the mechanism of the target variables (objectives) determines the outcome of the student in solving the test. After each experience, the Policy-Engine checks the assumption as defined by the rules and determines whether they are appropriate. Let's assume that the student has an aim to study the learning material at a high level (3). The system starts Lesson1 and the results of the three consecutive attempts to resolve the final test are 55, 49%, and 60%. After the first attempt to solve the final test, the Policy-Engine activates the second rule because the result is between 50% and 70%. This determines the preference in 2. The next value is <50%. According to rule three, the Policy-Engine reduces the preference from 2 to 1. The last attempt to solve the test starts again with rule two and increases the preference from 1 to 2. This result is unsatisfactory for the personal aims of the student and as a result, the Policy-Engine defines the lesson as inappropriate. The learning process suspends the former lesson and continues with Lesson 2. The student's results from solving the final test for this lesson are 64%, 68%, and 72%. At the first attempt, the preferences rise to 2, the second is retained the same level, while the third attempt increases it to 3, which is quite satisfactory for the student's personal aims that the student has set.

The dynamic adaptive levels most directly correspond to the third type of interaction – Open Experience – because the communication is dynamic with continuous engagement between the system and student.

---

6 RTE- Run-Time Environment

4. Personalization and user modeling

User modelling is an important feature of any e-learning system, to personalize and tailor the e-Learning to individual characteristics, knowledge, didactic aims, and the preferences of the students [19], [20], [21]. On the basis of the previous section, we can describe the adaptability of the system for e-Learning to knowledge and the preferences of students in elementary, static, and dynamic levels [22].

The Elementary Adaptive Level is guaranteed by the profile information about the student before starting his training process in the system. Based only on this adaptive level, the e-learning system offers only learning resources that are common to all students of the same grade and form of training.

The Static Adaptive Level is based on the model for selecting the most appropriate lesson from the Lessons DB as the student is joined to a particular persona in the stereotypical hierarchy. By personas, students with similar characteristics are presented in the e-learning system together. The lessons are prebuilt by the parameterization of the basic BPG-templates and models from the authors of e-learning content in a special authoring environment. These lessons are placed in a special repository – Lesson DB – and are described in metadata as described above.

The Dynamic Adaptive Level is implemented through the Policies of Preferences and Policy-Engine, which dynamically monitors the behaviours of student and his preferences with the relevant lesson in the actual learning process and can replace the current lesson with another that is more appropriate for the individual student.

In the adaptation process in terms of the user modelling, we will look at: the information athering about the learner, processing the information and its update, and finding and presenting the appropriate training resources for the considered student. The model describes the notion of the e-learning system for user knowledge, for his preferences, and aims. This model must be continuously updated according to the dynamic changes in the process of accumulation of knowledge about the particular student (Figure 4). The algorithm includes the following steps:

- Step 1. Filling the static profile information. According to the grade and form of training, the student is associated to any persona in a stereotypical hierarchy. The initial parameters are filled in interactive mode or the system gets the default values from the general stereo-type model. Stereotyping and personas are used to transfer more general information about the group in the assumption of the individual user.

- Step 2. According to the persona, which is associated with the student, the system determines the common characteristics of the group and includes default values. Then, in the dialogue mode, the school subject, topic, and personal didactic aims of the student are determined. The rules are updated on the basis of collected information. The Policy-Engine launches the Searching Mechanism for the more appropriate lesson from the Lesson DB and submits it to the LMS for implementation.

- Step 3. The system manages individualized learning process. If there are any discrepancy found between personal aims, the knowledge of the student, and the rules, the Policy-Engine interrupts the current training scenario and restarts the Searching Mechanism for a new choice.

- Step 4. The system stores the new values of the parameters and change the rules by which Policy-Engine manages personal learning process of the individual student.

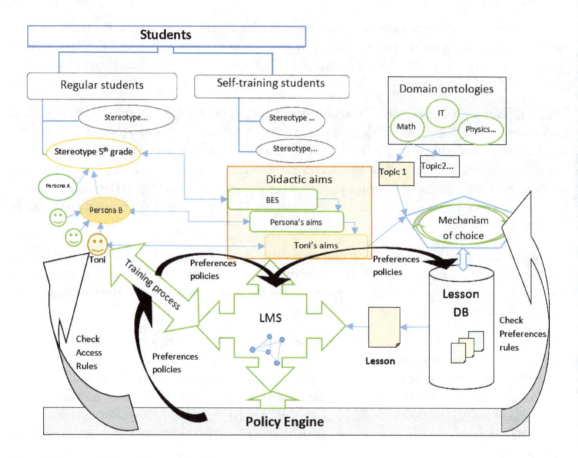

Figure 4. User modelling and personalization

The information in this user model can be considered as information specific to the school subject domain and information that is independent of it. The first type includes the data connected with the Dynamic Adaptive Level as an evaluation of the student; his background knowledge and records of his behavior (number of passed lessons, number of errors during solving test, number of inappropriate lessons, etc.). The information that is not dependent on the some subject domain is related to the personal goals of the learner, with his motivation, experience, preferences, interests, and personal data such as name, years, type of training, etc.

The presented algorithm provides a continuous actualization of information. Such one is independent from the specific school subject domain and one that is domain-dependent. The model is continuously updated to correctly present the student in the e-Learning environment.

We created several versions of SCORM-based e-Learning portal of the secondary school "Hristo Smirnenski"-Brezovo, which is based on the conceptual framework of the system DeLC and supports SCORM RTE [23]. The latest version of the environment ensures the personalization in the elementary and static levels. We developed the mechanism of parameterization of the basic BPG-templates and models, and created an authoring tool for the designing and packaging of SCORM-based e-lessons. Ontologies provide developers with predefined resources covering a specific school subject domain that can be used directly in the content. The establishment of educational environment is based on the adaptation of the corporate portal of the Delphi group. For the realization of the educational portal, we used the portal framework Liferay (http://liferay.com), which has implemented LMS of SCORM RTE [24]. There are many services implemented into the portal that supports the training process in different subjects and raises the level of interactivity in learning.

5. Conclusions and future work

The proposed user model allows to increase the level of personalization in the e-Learning system. This is essential for learners from all forms of training, but is particularly important for students using the distance form of training, pupils with special educational needs, and disabled children. The implementation at the elementary level of the model is provided by the Autho - rules, which depend on stereotyped groups and personas with their access rights to portal resources. Users could be students, teachers, parents, authors of learning content, and so on. If they are students, access must be allowed to educational materials for the appropriate grade, form of training, and so on. If they are teachers, according to their stereotypical information, the mechanism provides them an access to learning resources and services related to their school subjects. If they are authors of educational content, they are allowed access to the Lesson DB for editing and adding of e-Lessons. If they are parents, they are allowed an access to information about their children. Different scenarios for access formalize a sequence of different rules for each group of users managed from the Policy-Engine. The second level of user-modelling is realized through the model for selecting the most appropriate lesson from the repository of lessons – lesson DB and their meta-description by the lesson-vector. The Dynamic Adaptive Level is implemented through the set of Policies of Preferences. The Policy-Engine monitors the behaviour of students and their preference at the relevant lesson and can dynamically replace the current lesson with a more appropriate one.

Based on the MOOC Integrated Learning Environment (http://ilde.upf.edu/handson3), the authors of e-Learning resources successively pass through several steps – the definition of didactic aims, analysis of educational content, creation of personas, designing of learning scenario, creation of e-Lesson in specialized SCORM authoring environment, share a draft version of the created e-lesson for evaluation, and heuristic analysis from other pedagogical specialists. At each step, the authors directly share with their counterparts in the integrated environment. After the completion of the first cycle and depending on the evaluation, authors can then correct their lessons and again pass through the step-by-step cycle or publish the e-lesson in the Lesson DB of education portal. This process is cyclical and leads to the continuous improvement and refinement of the developed learning resources. It meets specified in figure 1 workflow. The published lessons are created in dialogue with educational specialists and tested directly in the real learning environment. This largely ensures the sustainability of the model and overcomes some of the problems in the development of e-Learning. The report is part of the work on the project IT 15- FMIIT-004 "Research in the field of innovative ICT business orientation and training" to fund "Scientific Researches" of Plovdiv University "Paisii Hilendarski".

Author details

Todorka Glushkova*

Address all correspondence to: todorka.glushkova@gmail.com

Plovdiv University "Paisii Hilendarski", Bulgaria

References

[1] Carliner, S., Patti Shank, editors, The e-Learning handbook: past promises, present challenges. 1st ed. USA: Pfeiffer; 2008. 560 p., ISBN: 978-0-7879-7831-0

[2] Allen, I. Elaine; Seaman, Jeff. Entering the Mainstream: The Quality and Extent of Online Education in the United States, 2003 and 2004. 1st ed. USA: Sloan Consortium (Sloan-C); 2004. 27 p., ISBN:0-9677741-8-7

[3] Abrami, R., Barrett, H., Directions for research and development on electronic portfolios. Canadian Journal of Learning and Technology. 2005; 31(3):1-15, ISSN 1499-6685

[4] Drucker, P., Need to Know: Integrating e-Learning with High Velocity Value Chains. 1st ed. USA: Delphi Group; 2000. 12 p., Delphi Group White Paper

[5] Stoyanov, S., I. Ganchev, I. Popchev, M. O'Droma, From CBT to e-Learning. Information Technologies and Control. 2005;3(4):2-10, ISSN 1312-2622.

[6] Stoyanovich, L.,Staab S., Studer R.,. e- Learning, based on the Semantic Web. In: WebNet2001-World Conference on the WWW and Internet; 23-27.10.2001; Orlando, Florida. USA:2001. p. 23-27, ISBN 1-880094-46-0.

[7] Shedroff, N., A unified field theory of Design. In: Jacobsen R., editor. Information Interaction Design. Cambridge: MIT Press; 1999. p. 267-292.

[8] Glushkova, T., Adaptive Model for E-Learning in Secondary School. In: Elvis Pontes, editor. E-Learning – Long-Distance and Lifelong Perspectives. 1st ed. Croatia: InTech; 2012. p. 3-22, ISBN 978-953-51-0250-2. DOI: 10.5772/29342

[9] Glushkova, T., Adaptive environment for e-Learning in secondary schools [PhD thesis]. Plovdiv University: Plovdiv University; 2011. 220 p. Available from: http://procedures.uni-plovdiv.bg/docs/procedure/163/1820394915693780406.pdf

[10] Lene, N., Personas. In: Rikke Friis, editor. The Encyclopedia of Human-Computer Interaction. 2nd ed. Denmark: The Interaction Design Foundation; 2014. https://www.interaction-design.org/encyclopedia/personas.html.

[11] Mor, Y., Mogilevsky, O., Learning Design Studio: Educational Practice as Design Inquiry of Learning. In: EC-TEL 20013; 17-21 September 2013; Paphos. Berlin: Springer; 2013. p. 233-245.

[12] Glushkova, T., Trendafilova, M.,Uzunova, N., Application of SCORM standard for e-Learning in secondary school. In: Informatics in the Scientific Knowlege- ISK'2006; 18-22 June 2006; Varna. Varna: VFU; 2006. p. 205-216, ISSN 1313-4345, ISBN – 10:954-715-303-X, ISBN-13:978-954-715-303-5.

[13] Stoyanov, S., D. Mitev, I. Minov, T. Glushkova. E-Learning Development Environment for Software Engineering Selbo 2. In: 19th Database and Expert Systems Application (DEXA 2008); 1-5 September 2008; Turin. Springer: 2008. p. 100-104, ISBN: 978-3-540-85653-5. DOI: 10.1109/DEXA.2008.89

[14] Bloom, B., Taxonomy of Educational Objectives Book 1: Cognitive Domain. 2nd ed. Addison Wesley Publishing Company; 1984 (first published June 1956). 204 p., ISBN13: 9780582280106

[15] Learning System Architecture Lab. SCORM Best Practices Guide for Content Developers. 1st ed. Pittsburgh, USA: Carnegie Mellon University; 2003. 80 p.

[16] Mitev, D., Popchev I. Intelligent agents and sevices in eLearning development environment Selbo 2. In: ISK'2008; 26-28 June 2008; Varna. Bulgaria: ISK; 2008. p. 275-284. DOI: ISBN-13:978-954-715-303-5

[17] Sloman, M.. Policy driven management for distributed systems. Journal of network and Systems Management. 1994; 2(3):333-360, ISSN 1064-75-70 (Print), 1573-7705(online).

[18] Moskowski, B. Reasoning about Digital Circuits [Dissertation]. Department of computer science: Stanford University Stanford, CA, USA; 1983. 148 p. Available from: http://dl.acm.org/citation.cfm?id=911281 DOI: AAI8329756

[19] Kobsa, A. User modelling and user-Adapted Interaction. Springer Netherlands. 2004; 14(5):469-475, ISSN: 0924-1868(paper) 1573-1391(online). DOI: 10.1007/s11257-005-2618-3

[20] Glushkova,T., User modelling of distributed e-Learning system for secondary school. In: DIDMATHTECH; 2006; Komarno. Slovakia: DIDMATHTECH; 2006. p. 117-123. ISBN: 978-80-89234-23-3

[21] Brusilovsky, P. Adaptive hypermedia. User Modelling and User Adapted Interaction, Ten Year Anniversary Issue. 2001; 11(1-2):87-110, ISSN: 0924-1868.

[22] Glushkova, T., Stoyanova, A., Interaction and adaptation to the specificity of the subject domains in the system for e-Learning and Distance training DeLC. In: Informatics in the Scientific Knowlege; 17-20 June 2008; Varna. Bulgaria: ISK; 2008. p. 295-307. ISSN: 1313-4345, ISBN: 13:978-954-715-303-526-28

[23] Glushkova, T, Stoyanov, S., Trendafilova, M, Cholakov, G., Adaptation of DeLC system for e_learning in Secondary school. In: CompSysTech'2005; 16-18 June 2005; Varna. Bulgaria: CompSysTech; 2005. p. IV.15.1-15.6. ISBN: 954-9641-38-4

[24] Glushkova, T., E-Learning environment for supporting of secodary school education. Cybernetics and Information Technologies. 2007; 7(3):89-106, ISSN: 1311-9702.

3

Barriers to E-Learning in SMEs — Are they Still There?

Andrée Roy

Additional information is available at the end of the chapter

Abstract

Facing pressure from an increasingly competitive business environment, small and medium-sized enterprises (SMEs) are called upon to implement e-Learning strategies to support their organizational training and developmental efforts. The purpose of this study is to identify the barriers and constraints SMEs experience when they want to use e-Learning and to determine, through a multiple case study, if the barriers to e-Learning actually experienced by SMEs in Atlantic Canada are the same as those that larger organizations are experiencing, and if they remain the same after all these years. Another purpose of this study is to present different approaches, such as the need to develop an e-Learning culture in Atlantic Canada and Canada in general, to create greater awareness and promotion of e-Learning, to determine an overall learning strategy to upgrade the technological skills of the employees and the SMEs, that can assist SMEs in surmounting the barriers they face when they want to use e-Learning.

Keywords: Barriers, constraints, e-Learning, SMEs, training,

1. Introduction

Small and medium-sized enterprises (SMEs) are considered a source of economic growth and are seen as a key sector for creating employment in many countries around the world. Consequently, training and learning are considered critical to SMEs' growth in many countries. To this end, references [1, 2] consider that in knowledge-based economies, a firm's investment in training and updating its employees' skills is a key element of its growth. However, SMEs do not provide sufficient training mainly because they cannot spare time for employees to attend external training programs and because internal training is too expensive. Therefore, SMEs should logically turn to e-Learning to provide training as the benefits associated with it are supposed to solve these problems. But the logic is not working. SMEs have not rushed to embrace e-Learning in order to train their employees. Why? What are the barriers and constraints they face?

In Canada, particularly Atlantic Canada, SMEs have played an important role in the economic development in various ways and their contribution towards a healthy economy has been recognized. They are defined as businesses having fewer than 500 employees and they represent the majority of businesses [3]. They are the fastest growing segment of the economy, and are considered the foundation of economic development [3–5]. Due to their great flexibility and adaptability, they represent the economy sector that creates the most employment [3, 6] and they remain critical to the economic prosperity of the region as in other parts of the world [see, for example, 7–9]. Yet, despite their great contribution to the region's economy, there are very few studies on them and even less on the training barriers they face, and this despite the fact that the most successful economies are those with the best trained individuals [1, 2, 10].

Capability development of small and medium firms remains critical to economic prosperity in Atlantic Canada as well as in other parts of the world [for example, see 3, 5, 7–9,11–13]. It is therefore important to know the barriers faced by SMEs regarding training, more specifically e-Learning, in order to be in a position to help them ensure their growth and their sustainability.

The purpose of this study is descriptive and prescriptive. After having identified the barriers and constraints SMEs experienced when they wanted to use e-Learning using a survey of the literature on the issue, the first objective is to determine through multiple case studies if the barriers to e-Learning actually experienced by SMEs in Atlantic Canada are still the same after all these years. If so, the second objective is to introduce possible solutions to assist SMEs in surmounting these barriers.

Thus, the remainder of this chapter is arranged as follows. Section 2 presents the method used for the study. Section 3 presents a literature census on the various barriers and constraints to the use of e-Learning by businesses. Section 4 determines through multiple case studies the barriers and constraints to e-Learning actually encountered by SMEs in Atlantic Canada and proposes different approaches to overcome those barriers. The conclusion and discussion will be included in section 5. The references are in section 6.

2. Method

Given the present state of knowledge on training in SMEs and on e-Learning, the method used for this study includes a census of the literature on training and e-Learning combined with a qualitative and exploratory research approach, i.e. multiple case studies. The literature census covers more specifically the barriers and constraints businesses faced when they wanted to use e-Learning. The case study method is well adapted in situations where theoretical propositions are few and field experience is still limited [14]. Multiple-site case studies allow one to understand the particular context and evolution of each firm in regard to e-Learning. Sixteen SMEs located in the Atlantic Region of Canada were studied in 2006, four in each of the provinces of New Brunswick, Nova Scotia, Prince Edward Island and Newfoundland. In 2012, 6 years later, four other SMEs located in New Brunswick and Prince Edward Island have been studied to verify if the businesses were still encountering the same problems in regard to e-Learning. These 20 businesses were selected because they were sufficiently successful (at least 10 years in business) and representative in terms of industry and size, for theoretical generalization purposes. These manufacturing SMEs stem from various sectors such as: construction, textile, oil and gas, pulp and paper and processed food sector. Following North American research [4, 15], a small enterprise (SE) is defined as having 20 to 99 employees, whereas a medium-sized enterprise (ME) has 100 to 499.

Data were collected through semi-structured tape-recorded interviews ranging approximately 2 hours each with the owner-manager or CEO and with the firm's HR manager or manager responsible for training. E-Learning users were also interviewed. The interviews consisted of a series of standardized open-ended questions related to e-Learning. The standardized open-ended interview, as explained by reference [16], is a structured approach in which participants are always asked identical questions designed to generate an open-ended response. This approach was utilized to solicit a variety of viewpoints based on individual experiences, but also to control researcher biases. All narrative interviews were transcribed, coded and analysed using open line-by-line coding to identify themes following reference [17] prescriptions with the assistance of the Atlas.ti application. For confidentiality reasons, fictitious names of individuals and firms participating in the study were used. For example, the first business interviewed is represented by the letter A, and a name starting with the letter A (Arthur, Andy) is given to the representatives of this business. The second business interviewed is represented by the letter B, and a name starting with a B (Bert, Bob) is used and so on. As presented in the research results section, these firms range in size from 60 to 490 employees and operate in industries whose technological intensity varies from low to high. All export except for one firm (M). The SMEs interviewed in 2006 were regrouped in four e-Learning profiles of increasing intensity based on the extent of their awareness and use of e-Learning (none, weak, average, strong). The four businesses interviewed in 2012 are grouped together, but not based on their e-Learning profiles of awareness and used of e-Learning. Three of these businesses were using e-Learning, and one was not.

3. Literature census

Some researchers such as references [18, 19] have identified the barriers to the traditional training taken up by SMEs. Some of the problems identified are lack of training time, delivery of tailored training programs, cost versus financial resources available for training, lack of knowledge on training opportunities available, returns on training offered and the fear of poaching by other businesses or losing the employees to another business. The lack of employees' desire for training and learning combined to a lack of awareness by SMEs of the necessity of having more skilled employees for business success have also been identified.

Barriers to e-Learning as a method of training for learners, both for businesses and educational institutions, have also been identified by various studies. For example, reference [20] mentions that the main barriers to the use of e-Learning in Canada are learners and technical infrastructure. Among other barriers mentioned by reference [20], we find the lack of knowledge towards e-Learning, the accessibility, the lack of commitment from senior management, the lack of quality courses, the development costs and the priorities of investment. According to reference [21], the bandwidth, the access to the Internet, the reluctance of the employees to use the technologies, the lack of investment on the part of companies in technology and the lack of university-level courses and non-academic courses relevant to the needs of businesses are also some barriers to e-Learning. In addition to the lack of relevant courses, the reluctance of employees towards training, the lack of expertise or technical capacity of the employees, reference [22] also mentions the lack of realism of businesses towards what e-Learning can and cannot do. Businesses' lack of realism towards what e-Learning can and cannot do is also mentioned by reference [23]. The barriers to e-Learning seem to be perceived differently by working adults and full-time students, with working adults viewing technology access and time for studying their principal constraints [5].

A more recent report, the State of e-Learning in Canada, done by reference [24] also mentions the learners and the technology as some of the main barriers. Other barriers mentioned in the 2009 report are the lack of support for the learners, the lack of knowledge towards e-Learning by the organization and, the financial problems, in which the e-Learning project are underfunded and, therefore, could not produce the anticipated gains. Other challenges and constraints mentioned in the 2009 State of e-Learning report are the reluctance to use chat rooms and discussion groups by the learners, the fact that many Canadians discontinue use of the Internet and the difficulty to harness the potential of the Internet to enhance learning opportunities. A similar study conducted in seven European countries by reference [25] also mentions that technology and attitudes of managers and employees seem to form the main drawbacks to e-Learning initiatives in SMEs. For reference [26], learners and the necessity for them to be self-motivated and self-disciplined are also a barrier to e-Learning. They also noted the lack of desire to assign a specific amount of time to learn during the work day and the lack of a good human resources development policy towards learning as some barriers to e-Learning.

Other researches done on Canadian SMEs also mentioned that the barriers encountered by SMEs in the use of e-Learning are the lack of access to the necessary technology, the lack of training and support both for SMEs and for the employees and the lack of knowledge on the e-courses and the content relevant to the needs of SMEs including false expectations of SMEs as to what e-Learning can and cannot do. The purchase costs of tailored courses and internal development costs are also barriers for SMEs. Finally, the level of interaction in the e-courses and the learners are also problematic according to references [27, 28].

According to reference [29], organizations reported more barriers to adopting e-Learning in 2011 than in 2010 but the top barriers remain the same: the lack of skills among employees, the lack of knowledge of technology, the lack of skills by training staff to implement e-Learning, the reluctance by line managers and unreliable ICT. The barriers facing companies when they want to use e-Learning are summarized in Table 1.

Barriers	Explanation of barriers
Accessibility	Difficulty for the learner and trainer to acquire or have access to the necessary technology (hardware, software, bandwidth) [5, 20–25, 27–44].
Training and support not available	Teachers and learners do not always understand how to use the technology required for the course (computers, software, Internet, TV, etc.) [5, 21, 27–30, 36, 38, 40–42, 44–47]. Support service not available or inadequate for teachers and learners [24, 26–29, 36, 40, 41, 44, 46, 47]. Lack of support from senior administration [5, 20, 21, 24–29, 36, 40, 41, 44]. Lack of involvement of different stakeholders and lack of strategic plan [25, 26, 36, 44, 48, 49].
Course and course content	Determine the purpose of the course: learning through technology or learning technology [26, 50]. Determine the course content and the order of the presentation of content [27, 28, 32, 44, 51–53]. Align the course's objectives with the course content and assessments [27, 28, 32, 34, 44, 46, 52]. Choose the method of training (an active method, which allows the learner to construct their learning, and have access to a teacher if necessary, is a better method than an affirmative one) [27, 28, 40, 45, 47, 52]. Determine the duration and cost [26–28, 34, 38, 46, 54]. Lack of university-level courses and non-academic relevant to businesses [20, 21, 27, 28, 41]. Lack of knowledge on e-Learning and e-courses and what e-Learning can and cannot do [22–24, 27, 28].
Interaction	Lack of human interaction (face to face) [27, 28, 31, 33, 35, 49, 55].
Learners	The profile of the learner may not always match the desired profile (including lack of skills of the learners) [21–25, 27–29, 37, 43, 52]. The following characteristics are desirable in order to ensure the success of the training: self-motivated [5, 20, 26–28, 31, 32, 45, 46, 51, 55, 56], able to work alone [27, 28, 45, 56], self-disciplined [5, 20, 26–28, 32, 44, 51, 55, 56], 'focused' [20, 27, 28, 32, 44, 51, 55].
Environment	The political, social and economic forces which may influence the choice of courses offered, the quality of courses and the place [23, 32, 41, 49].
Costs	Costs (infrastructure, development and/or purchase of course) required to support e-Learning [23, 27, 28, 31, 32, 38, 40, 44, 57–59].

Table 1. Barriers to the use of e-Learning

4. Research results

The majority of SMEs who participated in the 2006 case were well aware of e-Learning, but it remained to be defined for some. A detailed study of these SMEs stated knowledge about e-Learning and their use of it enables us to qualify their level of use. This analysis also allows us to categorizing SMEs into four distinct profiles of e-Learning users. There are SMEs that use e-Learning a great deal (strong use), those that use it quite a bit (average use), those that don't use it much (weak use) and those that don't use it at all (non-existent use) as indicated in Table 2.

The four SMEs who participated in the 2012 case study were all aware of e-Learning even the one who was not using it (profile V in Table 2). One of the SMEs in profile V was using e-Learning a great deal (strong use – SME name Q), one SME was using it quite a bit (average use – SME name R), one didn't use it much (weak use – SME name S) and the last SME didn't use it at all (non-existent use – SME name T).

Year	2006				2012
	Profile I _Strong_ (C, D, K, L)	Profile II _Average_ (B, E, M, O)	Profile III _Weak_ (A, F, I, J)	Profile IV _Non-existent_ (G, H, N, P)	Profile V _Mixed_ (Q, R, S, T)
Size					
Number of employees	300 to 485	60 to 280	150 to 350	75 to 400	150 to 490
E-Learning					
Utilization	Strong	Average	Weak	Non-existent	Mix

A 'strong' use means that the business regularly uses e-Learning to train its employees. An 'average' use means that the business has developed at least two courses in e-Learning format and that the production employees must take these courses. A 'weak' use means that only a few employees use it in the business and a 'non-existent' use means that the business does not use e-Learning to train its employees and that they do not use it to develop their knowledge. A 'mixed' use means that there is an SME for each of the above criteria.

Table 2. Profiles of e-Learning's utilization by SMEs.

SMEs encounter some barriers when they want to use e-Learning as a means of training. Even SMEs who rarely or never use e-Learning are aware that certain barriers may be encountered with e-Learning.

4.1. Perceived barriers of e-Learning by SMEs

The barrier which was most often mentioned in the 2006 case study (for more details on the 2006 case study, see references [27, 28, 60]), in fact which was mentioned by all SMEs interviewed, was the one connected with the bandwidth, which is part of the accessibility. The capacity to download e-Learning courses was not available because the required bandwidth was not always available in the workplace or in regions where employees reside. This problem was illustrated by the comments of Gérôme, who said at the time: « *The bandwidth is insufficient. It takes an eternity to download an e-mail, forget videos and other sophisticated things. It would be difficult to administer training of this style with the system such as it operates at present. By the time a course would be online, the employees would have left home* » (G:181–186).The bandwidth problem was never mentioned in the 2012 study. This may be due to the fact that several initiatives have been undertaken during the last years, both by the provincial government and the federal government, to improve access to the Internet across Canada and especially in remote areas.

In the 2006 study, some SMEs pointed out that they didn't have a training room equipped with the necessary equipment for this type of training, and some employees didn't have a computer at home. This barrier was not mentioned in the 2012 case study. However, one SME brings up the point that they only have computers in the 'office'.

Another barrier mentioned by the majority of SMEs, in both 2006 and 2012 cases, is the level of knowledge of employees towards computers. There are several employees whose level of knowledge is not sufficient, and some even have no interest in computers. The comments of Jules illustrate the problem; he says: « *There are some employees who are fascinated by computers and there are others who don't want to touch them... Is that the medium that is most suitable for these people to learn* » (J:652–654). Stan's comments give us another example of this persisting barrier; he says: « *Many of our employees have not finished their high school... they are not interested in computers... well, not learning on a computers* » (S:427–430). The lack of motivation and discipline to take a course online, and the lack of knowledge and capacity to support e-Learners by the organization were also mentioned in both studies. Theresa gives us an example of the lack of capacity to support e-Learners; she says: « *We don't have computers technicians here, we only have computers in the office...* » (T:223–224).

The lack of knowledge about the courses available is another barrier highlighted in both studies. It is not known what courses are offered, where they can be found, what their level of interaction is, what the possibilities of mentoring are, what the possibilities for evaluation are and what level of security is necessary in order to avoid problems and to ensure that it is the right person participating in the course. Hector gives us an example of the lack of knowledge about what is available; he says: « *There's no directory, or if there is one, I am not aware of it* » (H: 145–146). Quynh give us another example; she says: « *There was no college or university-level courses relevant to our business... we develop a partnership with a private college to fulfill our needs* » (Q:328–331).

The lack of human interaction in some courses was mentioned in the 2006 study and is still mentioned as a barrier in the 2012 study. Ron gives us an example of how the lack of interaction is a barrier that made it difficult to stay focused on the subject covered by the e-course. He says: « *You know, sometimes with some of these webinars, it gets so boring... The guy is speaking and speaking... I leave my computers on and I work on others things... I still hear what they are saying* » (R: 221–223). Denise gives us another example where interaction in e-Learning courses is impor-tant and the lack of it could be a barrier; she says: « *I prefer interaction in e-Learning. I prefer when there are discussions, and it is more my learning style to have conversations and discussions. I learn better when I can discuss and exchange ideas* » (D:803–805: 816–817: 869–870).

Another barrier stated by the SMEs in both studies is the profile of the learners and the SMEs. It appears that the profile of the learner and the profile of the SME do not always match the desired profile for e-Learning. Jules gives us an example of how the profiles of the SME and the employees could be barriers; he says: « *The 'learning by doing' method is frequently used to learn certain jobs. It is our preferred manner of training and we've used it since the beginning of the company in 1964... Some employees have chosen e-Learning, but it is usually on an exception basis, to develop their work knowledge and it was suggested by the employee and not the employer... They have to be self-disciplined and motivated to finish the course on-line and get their diploma* » (J:447–449: 989–919: 954–955). Quynh gives us another example how the profile of the employee could be a barrier; she says: « *The employees have to be dedicated, they have to be motivated and self-disciplined... it is not easy to find the time when you are working full time* » (Q:656–658). Denise gives us another example of barrier to e-Learning if the employee is not self-disciplined and self-motivated; she says: « *Since I have a three year-old daughter and that my work schedule is rather full, I can complete the work (course) at 3:00 AM...* » (D:82–83).

Finally, the cost of e-Learning was and is still an important barrier for SMEs. Denise, from the 2006 study, gives us an example; she says: « *The costs for a course like an MBA (on-line) are very high* » (D:687–693). Edna, also from the 2006 study, gives us another example of how the cost is a barrier; she says: « *The cost and time of development in-house are high* » (E:419–423). Lastly Quynh, from the 2012 study, is telling us how cost of e-Learning is affecting their business and is a barrier. She says: « *It costs us a lot of money to have courses developed and tailored for us... We could easily have done something else with that money* » (Q:917–918: 921–923).

The barriers cited by SMEs in the use of e-Learning, during the 2006 study and 2012 study, are illustrated in Table 3. These barriers, as shown in Table 4, can be grouped into broad categories, namely: lack of access to computers or the Internet (accessibility), the lack of training and support both for SMEs and for the employees (training and support), lack of knowledge on the courses and content relevant to the needs of SMEs including false expectations of SMEs as to what e-Learning can and cannot do (course and content), the level of interaction (interaction), the cost of purchases or development (costs) and the learner himself (learners). The barrier of the environment was not mentioned during the study conducted in 2006 nor during the study conducted in 2012. It is important to reiterate that the barrier associated to the bandwidth doesn't seem to be there anymore. The barriers faced by SMEs are similar to those found in the review of the literature.

According to reference [31], many SMEs may be more willing to engage in the use of the Internet and e-Learning if they can overcome the barriers that are preventing them from moving forward in this digital economy. Therefore, in order for e-Learning to be a doable and viable solution for all SMEs, we must eliminate or at least mitigate some of these barriers. Activities to promote e-Learning, at all levels of the firms, also have to be undertaken by different stakeholders. The various approaches presented below are a step in that direction.

- « *The necessary bandwidth is not available in all regions.* » Gérôme (G:264–267)
- « *The necessary bandwidth is not available everywhere.* » Ivan (I:886–896)
- « *Some employees do not have access to the Internet at home.* » Jules (J:1055–1064)
- « *We don't have* the *facilities for such courses. [...] They were conditioned to receive training in a certain way, with a teacher. It will be difficult to change this.* » Arthur (A:509–513: 613–617)
- « *Not all of our employees have a computer at home. We will have to organize a class with computers and give* the *employees some free time in order to get trained. There are costs associated with that.* » Jules (J:1086–1107)
- « *The employees don't have* computers access here. » Theresa (T:336)
- « *Employees do not have all the necessary knowledge.* » Ivan (I:822–830)
- « *As mentioned earlier, many of our employees don't have their 12th grade.* » Stan (S:477–477)
- « *First we would have to know what is available [...] The information is missing. There is no directory of what is available or, if there is one, I don't know* about it. » Hector (H:140–147)
- « *It is difficult to find courses relevant to what you need and it takes time.* » Bert (B:719–726)
- « *We had too many employees who were not studying but surfing on the Internet ... We had to restrict access to the Internet.* » Bert (B:531–543)
- « *There are people who need to be in class* in order *to learn. It depends on the type of learner you are. If you are able to learn alone and you do not need interaction, it is OK.* » Monique (M:637–647)
- « *It's scary when you do not know what it is.* » Gilbert (G:264–267)
- « *Some of our employees have done some courses over the Internet. [...] They are motivated ... they needed the courses for their job.* » Ron (G:826–829)
- « *The cost and time for development at the internal are high.* » Edna (E:419–423)
- « *The costs for a course like an MBA(on-line) are very high.* » Denise (D:687–693)
- « *It is expensive to develop courses in-house and it takes a lot of time. We need a champion to lead the case. [...] It took us a while to find the right platform.* » Bert (B:576:581–584:1044)
- « *It will be too expensive ... too expensive for what we need.* » Theresa (T:773–775)

Table 3. Illustrations of the barriers encountered by SMEs in the use of e-Learning

Barriers	SME (2006) Profile I Strong (300 to 485)				SME (2006) Profile II Average (60 to 280)				SME (2006) Profile III Weak (150 to 350)				SME (2006) Profile IV Non-existent (75 to 400)				SME (2012) Profile V Mixed (150 to 490)			
No. of employees	C	D	K	L	B	E	M	O	A	F	I	J	G	H	N	P	Q	R	S	T
Accessibility	x				x				x	x	x				x					
Training and support					x		x	x	x	x			x				x	x	x	x
Course and content					x	x						x	x	x	x	x	x	x	x	x
Interaction	x	x							x				x		x	x	x			
Learners	x		x	x	x				x		x						x	x	x	
Environment																				
Costs	x	x		x	x	x		x	x				x				x	x	x	x

Table 4. Barriers to the use of e-Learning according to SMEs

4.2. Approaches to overcome barriers to the use of e-Learning by SMEs

As mentioned earlier, the investment of a company in the training and update of the employees' skills is a key element of growth in the knowledge-based economies [1, 2]. Consequently, SMEs need to exploit e-Learning to address their training needs in order to ensure their growth and their sustainability [1, 2, 28, 61–63]. However, if we want business- es to use e-Learning, barriers need to be removed or at least reduced [24, 27, 28, 57, 59]. In addition, a culture more favourable to e-Learning must be developed [21, 24, 27, 28, 62, 64]. The culture change must also be transmitted and adopted by all stakeholders, i.e. by SMEs, governments and the various players in economic development and society in general [23, 24, 27, 28, 65]. Therefore, the approaches to incite SMEs to use e-Learning must include both actions to develop a culture more conducive to e-Learning and actions to remove or reduce barriers in using e-Learning [27, 28].

The development of a culture of learning and e-Learning passes, among other things, by valuing learning and having a better understanding of the e-Learning [2, 27, 28, 64, 66]. The comment issued by Denise illustrates indeed the need to develop a culture of learning and enhance learning. She says: « *We must develop a learning culture in society in general because without education or training, businesses cannot survive* » (D:985–999). For its part, the comment issued by Jules illustrates the need to learn more about e-Learning. He says: « *It is important that SMEs see practical examples of e-Learning, things that are already used by another company if you want them to invest or move in that direction. The best way to educate a group is to present the success of customers or other SMEs and to recommend them to verify this with them. […] It is also necessary to develop success stories* » (J:1546–1551: 1557–1565: 1582). Developing a culture of learning and e-Learning is also about building and sustaining an environment that inspires and supports employees to pursue learning [67]. The comment issued by Quynh illustrates the need for a business to create an environment that motivates and supports employees to pursue learning; she says: « *In our field, it is very important for us that our employees keep their skills up-to-date. This is why we develop a partnership with a private college in order to develop e-Learning courses to fulfill our needs. […] We also reimburse some university courses taken by our employee* » (Q:991–993:997–998).

Champions of learning and e-Learning are another way to develop a culture of learning and e-Learning [27, 28, 67]. Champions, at every level of the organization, can help towards the promotion and awareness of e-Learning. This promotion and awareness can be done by internal champions of e-Learning [27, 28, 67–70] as well as by external champions [1, 27, 28, 71, 72]. However, champions must have credibility and knowledge of e-Learning [27, 28]. The comment issued by Bert clearly illustrates the need for internal champions of e-Learning. He says: « *Developing courses in-house is expensive and it takes a lot of time. We need a champion to lead the case* » (B:576: 581–584). Ron's comment illustrates how internal champions can have an impact on the choice of taking or not an e-Learning course. He says: « *Word of mouth is important. Some of our employees have taken some e-Leaning courses because someone else has taken the course and given a good review. Some of our employees lead the show in regards of e-Learning* » (R:946–949). For its part, Edna illustrates the need for external champions of e-Learning. She says: « *I think it should be up to someone like an economic development agency to tell SMEs about what is available* » (E:613–615). Monique's comment also illustrates the need for external champions. She says:

« The information spreads quickly around here. If a person is satisfied with e-Learning, it won't take long for everyone to know. You can use agencies or groups to circulate the information. [...] I think we should encourage suppliers to give seminars to show what they have as courses. They could provide examples of people or businesses that use their courses. [...] They could show the different possibilities of e-Learning for various industries » (M:423–427: 848–851: 861–866).

As previously mentioned, in addition to actions in developing a culture more conducive to e-Learning, actions should be undertaken to remove or reduce barriers in using e-Learning if we want to encourage SMEs to use e-Learning. To this end, various actions including the improvement of the accessibility to e-Learning, the upgrading of SMEs' and employees' skills in technology and e-Learning and the offering of technical support must be undertaken.

Accessibility has been one of the major barriers to e-Learning in the 2006 study. The lack of bandwidth in some regions was reducing the ability of companies and employees to download training courses in e-Learning format. Ivan's comment goes in this direction. He says: *« The Internet is the Internet. There are places where it is not fast [...] We need more bandwidth »* (I:886–898). Gérôme also mentions the need for more bandwidth; he says: *« The speed of the line (bandwidth) has to be greater, we should have a better network »* (G:268–270). For its part, Jules says: *« Some employees may not have access to the Internet at home »* (J:1055–1064).

Initiatives have been undertaken in the last years to overcome the accessibility barrier and in the 2012 case study, none of the SMEs mentioned this barrier, which tends to support references [26, 29] findings. According to reference [26], technological improvement and the design of high-capacity networks for sharing data have allowed for solving most of the limitations of the traditional learning methodology both by facilitating access to information and by adapting programs to individual needs. According to reference [29], the increase in bandwidth is now achieved.

One of the factors which also discourage businesses to use e-Learning is the lack of support available [27, 28]. The lack of support was a barrier to the use of e-Learning in the 2006 study and is still a barrier. Thus, in order to ensure that SMEs and learners do not drop out or refuse to use e-Learning, they must be given the necessary support to use e-Learning [2, 23, 24, 27, 28, 57, 59, 64, 73, 74]. To this effect Ivan said: *« It will take some support. There are some people who do not know how to download and install the necessary software »* (I:886–901). He adds: *« Universities or another organization should make resources available by e-mail or telephone to provide a consulting service for SMEs. They could also leave a phone number that people could call, say between 4:00 pm and 6:00 pm, if they have questions. The questions would be answered by students. This would be part of their training, and this would be an improvement for the business community. This would be a way to get people interested »* (I:1086–1098). For its part, Denise says: *« It is necessary to speak the language of SMEs and employees »* (D:1020). Theresa gives us another example of the need of some support in order to use e-Learning; she says: *« We will need some external support. As I have said earlier, we don't have computers on the floor and we don't have computers technicians here »* (T:442–443).

In firms where the availability of resources is limited, e-Learning based on cloud computing could be an interesting alternative since it creates virtualized resources (hardware and software) that can be made available to users [75–81]. Users connect their devices (computers, tablets, smart phones, etc.) to the server where applications have been installed and use them to train themselves [75, 79, 80]. There is no burden of maintenance. Software and hardware updates are done by the providers [81]. Users can also receive external computing support from the cloud supplier [77, 78]; which is an important aspect for smaller firms [77]. Nevertheless, top management commitment and support is still a requirement for cloud e-Learning [77].

The lack of knowledge towards e-Learning and the technology is among the factors that discourage SMEs and employees from using e-Learning [2, 24, 25, 27–29, 74]. The comment of Hector is an example; he says: « *First, it is necessary that SMEs are equipped with people who can prepare the material for e-Learning. The IT equipment and the applications have to work. [...] People who do the promotion have to know what they are talking about. It will take trained people to promote e-Learning to other businesses* » (H:386–398: 410–412). Thus, in order to ensure that learners do not drop out or refuse to use e-Learning, we must ensure that employees have the equipment, the software, the skills and the necessary knowledge needed to use e-Learning [24, 31, 64, 69, 74]. Reference [58] suggests offering training seminars in IT skills to people working in SMEs in order to help small firms integrate information and communication technologies in their business activities and improve their competitiveness. Ivan gives us an example of the necessity to train employees; he says: « *Employees do not have all the necessary knowledge. We might have to train them before they can use computers and e-Learning* » (I:822–830). It is also necessary to provide basic courses to those who do not know how to use computers. Jules's comment goes in this direction; he says: « *Some of our employees do not have the knowledge and skills necessary [...]* » (J:654–658). Stan's comment also expresses the need for better-trained employees. He says: « *Some of our employees don't have what's needed... we will have to offer them some training* » (S:611–612). For her parts, Theresa expresses her firm's incapacity to support e-Learning; she says: « *We don't have computers technicians here...* » (T:223).

Cloud-based e-Learning could be an alternative to the lack of knowledge on technology since the SMEs and the employees don't have to be knowledgeable on the necessary technologies because the technology itself is being offered by the provider [77–80]. Moreover, since the e-Learning applications run on provider's infrastructure, the need to keep high-end computers and highly qualified technicians is eliminated with cloud-based e-Learning [81].

The lack of information about what is available on the Internet is one of the barriers identified in the use of e-Learning [27] by both authors and SMEs themselves despite references [73, 82] showing a large number of courses available on the Internet. To overcome this barrier, some researchers [for example, see 82–84] suggested using tools to explore the availability of e-Learning, and thus better understand what is available on the Internet. For their part, references [27, 28, 69] suggest creating and distributing tools to help companies use e-Learning. Reference [58] also suggests the development of information counters in order to provide information and empirical evidence to SMEs. The comment of Gérôme illustrates well the need of a toolbox; he says: « *The most interesting way would be to bring me a catalogue and to tell me what is available as training [...]* » (Gérôme G:595–597). Edna also expresses the need for a toolbox for SMEs or access to different resources. She says: « *I think if the economic development agencies have libraries of courses pertinent to SMEs to train their employees, SMEs would see e-Learning as a very effective way to provide training. I think that it is necessary to develop inventories of existing courses or to give access to portals such as 'Soft Skill' where there is a library that contains hundreds of useful courses to SMEs to train their employees* » (Edna E:615–625: 627–643). Ron's comment also expresses the need for help finding what is available in terms of e-Learning. He says: « *If someone could tell us what is available as training [...]. Which courses are good ones [...]. It would be very helpful* » (R:974: 977: 980).

Costs are also a barrier to e-Learning. In-house development or external tailored development of e-Learning courses and/or buying general e-courses can cost a lot of money [27, 28, 31, 32, 38, 40, 44, 58, 59, 64]. Ron is giving us an example how in-house development can cost a lot of money to a small business; he says: « *It takes a lot of time to develop courses in-house and it is expensive* » (R:815–816). The comment of Quynh is an example of how buying external courses could be expensive; she says: « *An on-line MBA costs a lot of money, especially one with a good university such as...* » (Q:717–719). To overcome this barrier, reference [2] suggests ensuring that the costs of education and training be shared. Reference [2] also suggests that governments can design financial incentives and tax policies that encourage individuals and employers to invest in education and training. For reference [64], some changes in the supports available to e-Learning funding are required for Canada to 'leapfrog' to a stronger adoption of e-Learning. Facilitating SMEs' access to funding will also help improve SME's access to training interventions, according to reference [58].

Since cloud e-Learning's task is to ensure that users, such as SMEs, can simply use the computing resources (infrastructure, software, platform) and e-Learning resources (courses) on demand and pay money according to their usage [75–77, 79, 81], cloud computing is a cost alternative for providing training in SMEs [75, 78–80]. By lowering operation costs through cloud computing, a firm can redirect the saved money towards the development of in-house content or purchase content developed by other organizations [80].

5. Conclusion and discussion

In recent years, e-Learning has grown into a widely accepted learning model by larger organizations and to some extent by SMEs. The technological advances along with a reduction of their costs allow SMEs to reconsider the e-Learning model in order to train their employees.

In Atlantic Canada, a growing number of SMEs are aware of e-Learning, and use it to train their employees. During this study, three quarters of the SMEs participating used e-Learning to various degrees to train their employees. Nevertheless, they encounter numerous barriers when they want to use e-Learning.

The barriers that need to be addressed and are preventing SMEs in using e-Learning are the same as those which larger organizations are facing. The lack of training and support for both SMEs and employees is a major barrier. There is no support service regarding technology and e-Learning in some firms and the technical infrastructure is inadequate in others. The learners' lack of skills is another problem. There is a large number of employees whose level of knowledge is inadequate for e-Learning and who don't have any interest in computers, even less in e-Learning. The lack of knowledge on e-courses and content relevant to the needs of SMEs including false expectations of SMEs as to what e-Learning can and cannot do is another barrier. The level of interaction of e-courses is also a challenge for SMEs. E-courses where there is some level of interaction are judged more interesting and appropriate for effective learning. The cost of purchases of e-courses or the cost of in-house development is an important barrier. Finally, the culture towards learning and e-Learning is also an obstacle. The accessibility which was a barrier in the 2006 study doesn't seem to be a barrier anymore for SMEs, nor for the employees/learners at home.

Therefore, in order for e-Learning to be a viable and feasible solution for all SMEs and for the full potential of e-Learning to be achieved by SMEs, conditions favourable to e-Learning must be created and maintained. Efforts are required to eliminate or at least alleviate some of the barriers SMEs run into while using e-Learning. Activities to promote e-Learning have to be undertaken at all levels of the firms as well as different stakeholders if we want SMEs to fully engage in the use e-Learning. The various actions presented below to alleviate and to eliminate some of these barriers are a start in that direction.

Indeed, a number of actions could facilitate the adoption of e-Learning by SMEs and address the barriers they face in its adoption. The first set of actions should focus on the need to develop an e-Learning culture within the SMEs: an e-Learning culture where managers and employees are truthfully committed and motivated to lifelong learning using e-Learning because they believe it is essential to their individual development and their firm's growth. This requires greater awareness and promotion of learning and e-Learning's value through the dissemination of knowledge among SMEs as to the nature, possibilities and advantages of e-Learning for workplace training. It also requires a better awareness and promotion of the supply and appropriateness of e-Learning services and products available.

A second set of actions should focus on eliminating or at least alleviating the barriers to the efficient and effective use of e-Learning by SMEs. Inadequate infrastructure, technological problems and lack of support services are major barriers to e-Leaning and can eliminate the motivation to learn through e-Learning. Inadequate or lack of necessary skills of the employees to learn through e-Learning is also a barrier faced by SMEs. This implies that employees must possess the computer knowledge and skills required to use e-Learning effectively, and that they should be provided with computers and e-Learning software at work that are user-friendly and appropriate to the task at hand if we want to eliminate these barriers. This also implies better management and technical support of employees in regard to e-Learning, support which was found lacking in a number of SMEs. Cloud-based e-Learning could be a solution since it can alleviate some of these barriers. Finding relevant courses to the need of SMEs is also a barrier. This implies a need for a better dissemination of information on existing e-courses and other possibilities. Finally, the cost of in-house development of e-courses and of purchases of external tailored e-courses is another major barrier to the use of e-Leaning. Cloud-based e-Learning could be a solution here and at the same time lower the burden of cost.

Considering the limitations of our research, it should be noted that our sample includes 16 SMEs in the first case studies and 4 SMEs in the last case studies. This constrains the possible generalization of results; thus further research is needed in order to confirm our conclusion. Nevertheless, this research sheds light on the barriers faced by SMEs when they want to use e-Learning to fulfil their training needs and introduces some ideas on how to address these barriers.

For e-Learning's full potential to be achieved, favourable conditions to learning must be created and maintained in Atlantic Canada and Canada in general. Stakeholders such as governments, economic development agencies, SMEs, employees, learning institutions and society in general have an important role to play in developing a culture more conducive to learning and e-Learning. Stakeholders also have a role to play in facilitating access to e-Learning in order to ensure the growth and sustainability of SMEs.

Author details

Andrée Roy*

Address all correspondence to: andree.roy@umoncton.ca

Université de Moncton, Moncton, Canada

References

[1] OECD. (2004) *OECD Employment Outlook*. Paris: OECD Publishing.

[2] OECD. (2012) *Better Skills, Better Jobs, Better Lives: A Strategic Approach to Skills Policies*. Paris: OECD Publishing.

[3] APECA. (2005) *État de la petite entreprise et de l'entrepreneurship dans la région de l'Atlantique 2005*. Moncton: Direction générale des politiqueset des programmes.

[4] Mittelstaedt, J.D., Harben, G.N. and Ward, W.A. (2003) 'How small is too small? Firm size as a barrier to exporting from the United States', *Journal of Small Business Management*, Vol 41, No. 1, pp 68–84.

[5] Roffe, I. (2007) 'Competitive strategy and influences on e-learning in entrepreneur-led SMEs', *Journal of European Industrial Training*, Vol 31, No. 6, pp 416–434.

[6] Brady, A. (1995) 'Small is as small does', *Journal of Business Strategy*, Vol 16, No. 2, pp 44–52.

[7] Varum, C.A. and Rocha, V.C. (2013) 'Employment and SMEs during crises', *Small Bus Econ*, Vol 40, pp 9–25.

[8] Yoshida, Y. (2012) SMEs' important role in creating jobs in the post-crisis. In *Skills Development Pathways in ASIA* (pp 133–135). Paris: OECD Publishing.

[9] Kongolo, M. (2010) 'Job creation versus job shedding and the role of SMEs in economic development', *African Journal of Business Management*, Vol 4, No. 11, pp 2288–2295.

[10] Smith, A. and Hayton, G. (1999) 'What drives enterprise training? Evidence from Australia', *The International Journal of Human Resource Management*, Vol 10, No. 2, pp 251–272.

[11] Bowale, K.E. and Ilesanmi, A.O. (2014) 'Determinants of factors influencing capacity of small and medium enterprises (SMEs) in employment creation in Lagos State, Nigeria', *International Journal of Financial Research*, Vol 5, No. 2, pp 133–141.

[12] Jayawarna, D., MacPherson, A. and Wilson, A. (2007) 'Training commitment and performance in manufacturing SMEs; Incidence, intensity and approaches', *Journal of Small Business and Enterprise Development*, Vol 14, No. 2, pp 698–720.

[13] Matlay, H. (1999) 'Vocational education and training in Britain: A small business perspective', *Education & Training*, Vol 41, No. 1, pp 6–13.

[14] Yin, R.K. (1994) *Case Study Research: Design and Methods*, 2nd Edition. Thousand Oaks, CA: Sage Publications.

[15] Wolff, J.A. and Pett, T.L. (2000) 'Internationalization of small firms: An examination of export competitive patterns, firm size, and export performance', *Journal of Small Business Management*, Vol 38, No. 2, pp 34–47.

[16] Gall, M.D., Gall, J.P. and Borg, W.R. (2003) *Educational Research: An Introduction*, 7th Edition. Boston, MA: A & B Publications.

[17] Miles, M.B. and Huberman, A.M. (1994) *Qualitative Data Analysis: An Expanded Sourcebook*, 2nd Edition. Thousand Oaks, CA: Sage Publications.

[18] Joyce, P., McNulty, T. and Woods, A. (1995) 'Workforce training: Are small firms different?', *Journal of European Industrial Training*, Vol 19, No. 5, pp 19–25.

[19] Westhead, P. and Storey, D. (1996) 'Management training and small firm performance: Why is the link so weak?', *International Small Business Journal*, Vol 14, No. 4, pp 13–24.

[20] Bolan, S. (2001) 'Canada behind in e-learning', *Computing Canada*, Vol 27, No. 9, p 4.

[21] Schweizer, H. (2004) 'E-learning in business', *Journal of Management Education*, Vol 28, No. 6, pp 674–692.

[22] Economist Intelligence Unit. (2004) *Europe Company: Making the Most of e-Learning*. New York, NY: EIU ViewsWire.

[23] Medarova, V., VladimírBures, V. and Otcenaskova, T. (2012) 'A review of obstacles to successful e-Learning deployment in SMEs', *Journal of Innovation Management in Small & Medium Enterprises*, Vol 2012, No. 2012, pp 1–9.

[24] Canadian Council on Learning. (2009) *State of e-Learning in Canada 2009*. Ottawa: Canadian Council on Learning available at: www.ccl-cca.ca

[25] Admiraal, W. and Lockhorst, D. (2009) 'E-Learning in small and medium-sized enterprises across Europe: Attitudes towards technology', *Learning and Training. International Small Business Journal*, Vol 27, No. 6, pp 743–767.

[26] Calvo, N. and Rungo, P. (2010) 'Analysis of emerging barriers for e-Learning models: An empirical study', *European Research Studies*, Vol 13, No. 4, pp 33–43.

[27] Roy, A. (2010) 'SMEs: How to make a successful transition from conventional training towards e-Learning', *International Journal of Advanced Corporate Learning*, Vol 3, No. 2, pp 21–27.

[28] Roy, A. (2013) E-Learning: Tool to ensure growth and sustainability of SMEs. In *Collectif, Case Studies in e-Learning Research: For Researchers, Teachers and Students* (pp 122–140). Reading, UK: Academic Conferences and Publishing International Limited.

[29] Little, B. (2012) 'The rise and rise of do-it-yourself e-learning', *Training & Management Development Methods*, Vol 26, No. 3, pp 613–618.

[30] Banes, D. (2005) 'Accessible e-learning', *E.learning Age*, November 25, p 28.

[31] Collins, C., Buhalis, D. and Peters, M. (2003) 'Enhancing SMTEs' business performance through the Internet and e-learning platforms', *Education + Training*, Vol 45, No. 8/9, pp 483–494.

[32] Dunn, R.L. (2003) 'Getting into e-learning for workplace training', *Plant Engineering*, Vol 56, No. 9, pp 63–71.

[33] Melymuka, K. (2002) 'Executive education on a shoestring', *Computerworld*, Vol 36, No. 11, pp 24–25.

[34] Noble, D. F. (2002) *Digital Diploma Mills: The Automation of Higher Education*. Toronto: Between the Lines.

[35] Nonprofit World. (2002) 'Reach out and train someone: The many faces of distance learning', *Nonprofit World*, Vol 20, No. 2, pp 24–29.

[36] Rayfield, R. and Imel, L. (2002) 'Making interactive video distance learning work', *Principal Leadership*, Vol 2, No. 4, pp 56–61.

[37] Retová, J. and Pólya, A. (2012) 'The accessibility of e-learning systems for disabled', *Studia Commercialia Bratislavensia*, Vol 5, No. 17, pp 124–130.

[38] Sambrook, S. (2003) 'E-learning in small organizations', *Education & Training*, Vol 45, No. 8/9, pp 506–516.

[39] Sanderson, P.E. (2002) 'E-learning strategies for delivering knowledge in the digital age', *Internet and Higher Education*, Vol 5, No. 2, pp 185–188.

[40] Sharma, K., Pandit, P. and Pandit, P. (2011) 'Critical success factors in crafting strategic architecture for e-learning at HP University', *International Journal of Educational Management*, Vol 25, No. 5, pp 423–452.

[41] Swensson, L., Ellstrom, P.-E. and Aberg, C. (2004) 'Integrating formal and informal learning at work', *Journal of Workplace Learning*, Vol 16, No. 7/8, pp 479–491.

[42] Tiene, D. (2002) 'Digital multimedia & distance education: Can they effectively be combined?', *T.H.E. Journal*, Vol 29, No. 9, pp 18–25.

[43] Thomas, D. (2007) 'Accessibility and e-learning', *E.learning Age*, June 2007, pp 12–14.

[44] Uhomoibhi, J.O. (2006) 'Implementing e-learning in Northern Ireland: Prospects and challenges', *Campus-Wide Information Systems*, Vol 23, No. 1, pp 4–14.

[45] Moore, K.B. (2002) 'Professional development through distance learning', *Scholastic Early Childhood Today*, Vol 16, No. 6, pp 6–7.

[46] Perez, S. and Foshay, R. (2002) 'Adding up the distance: Can developmental studies work in a distance learning environment?', *T.H.E. Journal*, Vol 29, No. 8, pp 19–24.

[47] Serwatka, J.A. (2002). 'Improving student performance in distance learning courses', *T.H.E. Journal*, Vol 29, No. 9, pp 46–51.

[48] Servage, L. (2005) 'Strategizing for workplace e-Learning: Some critical considerations', *Journal of Workplace Learning*, Vol 17, No. 5/6, pp 304–317.

[49] Spaulding, S. (2002) 'Distance education, broadcast media, virtual reality, and cyberspace: Is the future passing us by?', *Comparative Education Review*, Vol 3, No. 46, pp 119–130.

[50] Fulton, L. (1998) 'Learning in a digital age: Insights into the issues', *T.H.E. Journal*, Vol 25, No. 7, pp 7–10.

[51] Cutshall, S. (2002) 'Going the distance: When online learning works', *Techniques*, Vol 77, No. 5, pp 22–23.

[52] O'Dell, T. (2009) *Generational Difference in Satisfaction with e-Learning in a Corporate-Learning Environment* [thesis]. ProQuest Dissertation and Theses.

[53] Phillips, V. (1998) 'Virtual classrooms, real education', *Nation's Business*, Vol 86, No. 5, pp 41–45.

[54] Stevenson, N. (2000) *Distance Learning Online for Dummies*. New York, NY: Hungry Minds Inc.

[55] Jha, S.K., Shahabadkar, P.K. and Singhal, S.K. (2012) 'Developing architecture of an e-learning system – A case study', *Journal of Information and Operations Management*, Vol 3, No. 1, pp 129–132.

[56] Brandao, C. (2002) 'Teaching online: Harnessing technology's power at Florida Virtual school', *T.H.E. Journal*, Vol 29, No. 10, pp 37–42.

[57] Industrie Canada (2001) *L'évolution de l'apprentissage en ligne dans les collèges et les universités*. [online], http://www.rescol.ca/mlg/sites/acol-ccael

[58] Panagiotakopoulos, A. (2011) 'Barriers to employee training and learning in small and medium-sized enterprises (SMEs)', *Development and Learning in Organizations*, Vol 25, No. 3, pp 15–18.

[59] Web-Based Education Commission. (2000) *The Power of the Internet for Learning: Moving from Promise to Practice*. Washington, DC: Government Printing Office.

[60] Roy, A. (2009) 'The training process of SMEs: What motivates SMEs to use e-Learning', *International Journal of Advanced Corporate Learning*, Vol 2, No. 3, pp 66–73.

[61] Berris, J. (2006) 'A job like mine', *E.learning Age*, October 26, p 26.

[62] Edwards, M.G. (2009) 'An integrative metatheory for organisational learning and sustainability in turbulent times', *The Learning Organization*, Vol 16, No. 3, pp 189–207.

[63] Filipczak, B. (1994) 'The training manager in the '90s', *Training*, Vol 31, No. 6, pp 31–35.

[64] Contact North. (2012) *Online Learning in Canada: At a Tipping Point – A Cross-Country Check-Up 2012*. Ontario: Ontario's Distance Education & Training Network available at: http://contactnorth.ca/sites/default/files/pdf/trends-and-directions/onlinelearningincanadareport_june_2012_-_final_0.pdf

[65] Middleton, C. (2003) 'The rate of learning must be greater than the rate of change', *Industrial and Commercial Training*, Vol 35, No. 6/7, pp 306–308.

[66] Taran, C. (2006) 'Enabling SMEs to deliver synchronous online training – Practical guidelines', *Campus-Wide Information Systems*, Vol 23, No. 3, pp 182–195.

[67] BC Public Service Agency (2012) *Developing the Best: A Corporate Learning Strategy for the BC Public Service*. [online], http://www2.gov.bc.ca/local/myhr/documents/learning_education/corporate_learning_strategy.pdf

[68] Clawson, T. (2004) 'Teach the boss', *Human Resources*, Vol 12, pp 38–40.

[69] Tanquist, S. (2001) 'Marathon e-learning', *T + D*, Vol 55, No. 8, pp 22–24.

[70] Terry, L. (2000) 'Get Smart Online', *Upside*, Vol 12, No. 5, pp 162–164.

[71] Manufacturiers et exportateurs du Québec. (2003) *La formation par les TIC ou e-learning: le pourquoi et le comment: guide d'aide à la décision en contexte manufacturier*. Montréal: Manufacturiersetexportateurs du Québec.

[72] TechnoCompétences. (2002) *E-learning: guide pratique de l'apprentissage virtuel en enterprise*. Montréal: TechnoCompétences.

[73] Roffe, I. (2004) 'E-learning for SMEs: Competition and dimensions of perceived value', *Journal of European Industrial Training*, Vol 28, No. 5, pp 440–455.

[74] Zielinski, D. (2000) 'Can you keep learners online?', *Training*, Vol 37, No. 3, pp 64–75.

[75] Masud, A.H. and Huang, X. (2012) 'An e-Learning system architecture based on cloud computing', *World Academy of Science, Engineering and Technology*, Vol 6, No. 2, pp 736–740.

[76] Marston, S., Li, Z., Bandyopadhyay, S., Zhang, J. and Ghalsasi, A. (2011) 'Cloud computing – The business perspective', *Decision Support Systems*, Vol 51, No. 1, pp 176–189.

[77] Alshamaila, Y., Papagiannidis, S. and Li, F. (2013) 'Cloud computing adoption by SMEs in the north east of England: A multi-perspective framework', *Journal of Enterprise Information Management*, Vol 26, No. 3, pp 250–275.

[78] Dong, B., Zheng, Q., Yang, J., Li, H. and Qiao, M. (2009) An e-Learning ecosystem based on cloud computing infrastructure. In: *Ninth IEEE International Conference on Advanced Learning Technologies (ICALT '09)*, 15–17 July 2009, Riga (pp 125–127). Latvia: IEEE.

[79] Bora, U.J. and Ahmed, M. (2013) 'E-Learning using cloud computing International', *Journal of Science and Modern Engineering*, Vol 1, No. 2, pp 9–13.

[80] Karim, F. and Goodwin, R. (2013) 'Using cloud computing in e-learning systems', *International Journal of Advanced Research in Computer Science & Technology*, Vol 1, No. 1, pp 65–69.

[81] Mitakos, T., Almaliotis, I., Diakakis, I. and Demerouth, A. (2014) 'An insight on e-learning and cloud computing systems', *Informatica Economica*, Vol 18, No. 4, pp 14–25.

[82] Harris, P. (2005) 'Small businesses bask in training's spotlight', *T + D*, Vol 59, No. 2, pp 46–52.

[83] Charp, S. (2002) 'Assisting educators on the use of technology', *T.H.E. Journal*, Vol 29, No. 11, pp 10–11.

[84] Pantaziz, C. (2002) 'Maximizing e-learning to train the 21st century workforce', *Public Personnel Management*, Vol 31, No. 1, pp 21–26.

4

Using Phonically Based E-books to Develop Reading Fluency

Charles Potter

Additional information is available at the end of the chapter

Abstract

The purpose of this chapter is to describe the 'Tales of Jud the Rat' reading fluency programme and its logic, and to present preliminary results from its use as a form of e-learning. The first section of the chapter provides an overview of the development of the 'The Tales Jud the Rat' series. Literature relevant to the neurolinguistic basis of the materials is then reviewed. Results from initial case study and the first cohort of children who have worked on this programme with their parents are presented in the third section, while the final section of the chapter provides an evaluation of the current status of the programme and indicates its potential uses.

At this stage in the development of the programme, there is plenty of material available, and the ebooks and supporting methodology are currently being used by the parents, therapists and teachers of over seventy children with reading difficulty across our country. Some of the children live over a thousand kilometres from my rooms. Others are in schools or clinics. The results have been promising both with primary school children as well as with adolescents in high school. Parents, therapists, teachers and children have also provided positive evaluations of the effects improved reading fluency has had on reading ability more generally, as well as on school work.

Keywords: Reading difficulties, dyslexia, reading fluency, rate of work, structured phonics, analytical phonics, seven vowel system, large print, ebooks, visual tracking, 3 × 3 oral impress method, distance education

1. Introduction

'Learning to read requires mastering the system by which print encodes the language.' [1]

I am an educational psychologist who specialises in work with children with learning and reading difficulties. As part of this work, I have been developing a reading fluency programme based on a series of ebooks.

The text of the ebooks has been written based on neurolinguistic theory[1], and the ebooks are designed to be used with a form of oral impress procedure based on paired reading. This is simple to implement. It differs from the type of paired reading procedures documented in the literature, as it involves additional repetition to develop phonic associations and automaticity in reading.

The ebooks are set in large print with wide spaces between words to provide maximal visual cues and also to prevent crowding, which has emerged in recent literature as a factor affecting reading in dyslexic children. The oral impress procedure also builds in visual tracking to maintain visual attention. Repetition on both the phonological and the visual level is thus provided both in the text of the ebooks as well as in the procedures used to work with the children. Visual attention is maintained through the use of a pointer working from the top of the line, and not from the bottom, for the reason that the top of the line provides greater visual cues than the bottom of the line.

As the materials are in electronic form, they provide a form of e-learning which can be used in contact, as well as at distance. The ebooks are designed to be used by parents and can also be used by therapists, teachers and schools to develop fluent reading. Assessment and evaluation are built into the programme's structure, linked to an awards system for children using the materials.

This chapter is written in three parts. The first part of the chapter presents a literature review. The second part describes the development of the characters and setting of a set of reading materials called 'The Doctor Skunk Stories', which were developed for a child who lived some 6,000 miles away from my rooms. This part of the chapter is based on a longitudinal case study. The third part of the chapter then describes the subsequent development of the materials into an assessment-based reading programme and presents results of the first cohort of children who have worked on this programme with their parents.

At this stage in the development of the programme, there is plenty of material available, and the ebooks and supporting methodology are currently being used by the parents, therapists and teachers of over seventy children with reading difficulty across our country. Some of the children live over a thousand kilometres from my rooms. Others are in schools or clinics. The results have been promising with younger children as well as adolescents. Parents, therapists, teachers and children have also provided positive evaluations of the benefits improved reading fluency has had on reading ability more generally, as well as on school work.

---

1 The approach to automaticity in reading adopted in this chapter is based on the work of the Russian neuropsychologist A.R. Luria, and the term "neurolinguistic" follows Luria's work on the physiological basis of language-based functions (Luria, A.R. (1976). Basic Problems of Neurolinguistics. The Hague: Mouton B.V.) as well as the approach suggested by Arbib and Caplan of the Center for Systems Neuroscience at the University of Massachusetts, Amherst (Arbib, M.A. and Caplan, D . (1979). Neurolinguistics must be computational. Behavioral and Brain Sciences, 2, 3, pages 449- 460) in which neurolinguistics draws insights from modern neuroanatomy, neurochemistry and neurophysiology.

2. Literature on automaticity in reading

2.1. Orientation

The literature on reading is complex on a theoretical level, and it is impossible in a short literature review to do justice to this. I have thus written the first section of the literature review which deals with automaticity in reading from a functional and applied perspective, and would refer readers interested in psycholinguistic theories of reading to a good source, such as Adams [2] or Perfetti [3, 4, 5].

The definitions of the terms I am going to provide at the beginning of this chapter are functional ones for the reason that the first stage in development of 'The Tales of Jud the Rat' materials was based on applied work conducted over a number of years with one child. As these initial materials were used by a parent and a peer tutor implementer working in Europe, 6,000 miles away from my rooms in Johannesburg, the initial literature I am going to review is based on research on reading fluency programmes implemented through parent and peer-tutored paired reading. This is followed by review of the neurolinguistic literature which has provided the theoretical basis for the development of the 'The Tales of Jud the Rat' materials in their current form.

2.2. Definition of terms

Reading decoding involves a child or adult's ability to read words both individually and in sequence. This involves the ability to use sound–letter associations to sound out individual words by analysing their parts and then to link these parts together to form words. The process of analysis and synthesis of individual words then needs to be done sequentially, with sufficient fluency to comprehend both the individual words and strings of words being read.

Fluent reading involves the ability to decode individual words and join the parts together quickly and accurately, so that the words can be understood both individually and in sequence. Cognitive processes of perception, language, sequencing and working memory are involved in fluent reading, and for this reason, assessment of reading also involves side-by-side assessment of perceptual, language, working memory and sequential abilities.

Reading can be defined as a complex cognitive process of making meaning from text, which depends on adequately developed perception, language, working memory and sequential abilities. As reading comprehension is affected by reading fluency, reading fluency can be defined as:

'The ability to read phrases and sentences smoothly and quickly, while understanding them as expressions of complete ideas.' [6]

Smooth, quick reading is based on the notion of automaticity [7], which underpins the abilities to read with speed and accuracy as well as expression. Automaticity is developed in reading when there has been sufficient practice to enable a complex functional act to become fluent enough to form the basis for higher mental processing. As Logsdon [8] suggests:

'Reading fluency refers to the ability to read with adequate accuracy, speed, expression, and automaticity. Reading fluency is very important to one's overall ability to understand, or comprehend, what is read.'

2.3. Automaticity in reading

On a theoretical level, automaticity in reading is based on the suggestions made by Luria [9] concerning the development of automaticity in the hierarchical processing of information by the working brain. LaBerge and Samuels [10] were the first researchers to focus on automaticity as a function of how reading fluency develops. They proposed a model of information processing in reading, in which visual information is transformed through a series of processing stages involving visual, phonological and episodic memory systems until it is finally comprehended in the semantic system.

LaBerge and Samuels further proposed that the processing occurring at each processing stage was learned while the degree of learning could be assessed with respect to two criteria: *accuracy* and *automaticity*. At the accuracy level of performance, attention was assumed to be necessary for processing; at the automatic level, it was not.

Again following Luria [11], who had suggested the value of repeated modelling and practice in developing automaticity in writing, Samuels suggested that automaticity in reading could be trained through procedures involving repeated reading, As Samuels commented,

'It is important to point out that repeated reading is not a method for teaching all reading skills. Rather, it is intended as a supplement in a developmental reading program. While the method is particularly suitable for students with special learning problems, it is useful for normal children as well.' [12]

Support for LaBerge and Samuels' work was provided independently by Carol Chomsky [13] at Harvard University. Chomsky concluded that the repeated reading procedure she had used with students had been facilitating for both slow and halting readers, 'increasing fluency rapidly and with apparent ease'. Other researchers such as Carbo [14], Morgan and Lyon [15] and Ashby-Davis [16] provided additional support through studies using different repeated reading methods to model and develop automaticity through repetition.

The goal of each of these different studies was the development of reading fluency, which Allington [17] pointed out was a characteristic of poor readers, but was seldom treated. The notion of fluency has then recurred in subsequent literature. Adams [18], for example, has suggested that the most salient characteristic of skillful reading is the speed with which text is reproduced into spoken language.

Fluency is thus associated with oral reading. Fuchs et al. [19] have defined oral reading fluency as the oral translation of text with speed and accuracy. On the basis of review of theoretical arguments and several studies substantiating this phenomenon, Fuchs et al. concluded that oral reading fluency is an indicator of overall reading competence.

The U.S. Congress [20] has defined the essential components of reading instruction as involving explicit and systematic instruction in:

a. phonemic awareness;

b. phonics;

c. vocabulary development;

d. reading fluency, including oral reading skills; and

e. reading comprehension strategies.

(SEC. 1208. DEFINITIONS).

There would thus be justification for incorporating the assessment of reading fluency as one aspect of psychometric measurement of reading, with implications for both research and practice based on assessment of reading ability (e.g. [21]).

2.4. Developing reading fluency through paired reading methods

The literature suggests that reading fluency can be developed by paired reading methods, which have been described differently by different researchers. Carol Chomsky [22] called the technique 'repeated reading'. Carbo [23] used tape-recorded books with struggling readers to good effect and called her method 'talking books'. Morgan and Lyon [24] called their technique 'paired reading', while Ashby-Davis [25] called her method 'assisted reading'. Other terms used by researchers include 'neurological impress' [26, 27, 28] and 'reading by immersion' [29].

The use of these different terms would suggest that paired reading is an umbrella term, in which there are a number of variations in method. For this reason, I have used the term '3 × 3 oral impress method' to describe the procedure for paired oral reading I have developed, as the method I use differs from the strategies for developing reading fluency used in the studies reviewed in the rest of this section.

The earliest study indicating the value of paired reading in a classroom setting was conducted by Heckelman [30, 31], who reported that 24 students involved in using what he called 'the neurological impress method' made exceptional gains in reading ability. The mean gain in reading comprehension was 1.9 grade levels after using the method daily for 15 min (a total of seven and a quarter hours) over a 6-week period. Heckelman hypothesised that this method was 'one of the most direct and fundamental systems of reading' involving a 'combination of reflexive neurological systems'.

Hollingsworth [32] also reported positive results from the use of an impress method in teaching reading and defined impress or neurological impress techniques as the use of unison reading methods in which teacher and student read aloud simultaneously. No attention would be called to the pictures accompanying the story, nor would the teacher attempt to teach sounds of words or word recognition skills.

Morgan and Lyon [33] involved parents in the process of providing tuition for children with reading difficulties and called the technique 'paired reading'. In Morgan and Lyon's study, the paired reading tuition procedure was described as a simple and flexible remedial technique for general application, incorporating simultaneous reading and verbally reinforced individual reading, and utilising textual material suited to the child's interests and chronological age rather than his reading age.

In Morgan and Lyon's study, the parents of four reading-retarded children were trained in how to provide paired reading tuition at home for a quarter of an hour daily. Over 12 to 13 weeks of tuition, the group's reading ages improved markedly. Marked advances in reading comprehension were also noted.

The researcher who has done most to promote and popularise paired reading methods, however, has been Topping [34–37], who has been Professor of Educational Psychology and Director of the Centre for Paired Learning at the University of Dundee. Topping's Centre has focused in particular on the development and evaluation of the effectiveness of methods for non-professionals (such as parents or peer tutors) in providing support in the acquisition of basic skills in reading, spelling, writing, science, maths and information technology. As part of this work, Topping has published widely on paired reading as well as peer tutoring and other forms of cooperative learning.

Topping [38] focused on the value of paired reading in the context of a large-scale dissemination project, and reported on the instructional procedures and outcomes from ten different peer tutoring projects. Pre-and post-test data were reported for all these ten evaluative studies. Four of the studies also provided baseline data and two studies provided comparison group data. Two studies then provided follow-up data for the short and long term respectively.

The evidence reviewed under these different conditions suggested that peer tutored paired reading accelerated children's reading progress in all these settings. All children were reported to have made progress, with peer tutors gaining more than tutees. On the basis of these positive results, Topping [39] also suggested that peer tutoring and paired reading were two potentially powerful techniques which could be combined, and that structured pair work between children of different ability had great potential for effective cooperative learning. Good organisation by the teacher was the key.

2.5. Parent involvement in paired reading

Based on the work of a number of paired reading programmes, Topping [40] suggested that paired reading methods provided an ideal way for teachers to involve parents in the process of developing reading competence. He also wrote a handbook [41] indicating ways in which parents could use paired work with their children to develop basic skills in reading, spelling and writing.

In addition, Topping reported the results of a number of studies indicating the effects of paired reading on reading ability based on reading age gains relative to increase in chronological age [42–44]. Based on analysis of results of 18 studies which focused on the effects of paired reading, Topping concluded that variables such as the duration of the intervention period and the acceleration of learning did not affect the results. In addition, based on analysis of the results of projects which included follow-up data and as there were no reports to the contrary in any of the other studies, Topping concluded that gains in reading ability appeared to be sustained.

Other researchers have also indicated the value of parental involvement in children's reading. Morgan and Lyon [45] described paired reading tuition procedure as a simple and flexible remedial technique which incorporated simultaneous reading and verbally reinforced individual reading. Parents could be trained to use the method. Hewison and Tizard [46] reported that the factor which emerged as most strongly related to reading achievement was whether or not the mother regularly heard the child read. IQ differences did not account for the superior reading performance of the coached children. Maternal language behaviour also had little effect on the association between coaching and reading performance. The important variable was the amount of parental coaching received by the children, which had a highly significant positive association with reading test scores.

In addition, there has been evidence of the value of paired reading programmes involving parents cross-culturally. Vanwagenen, Williams and Mclaughlin [47] reported positive effects of assisted reading on reading rate, accuracy and comprehension on three 12-year-old Spanish-speaking children learning English, while in South Africa, Overett and Donald [48] trained 29 parents from low socio-economic backgrounds to use a paired reading technique. Overett and Donald then compared their results with those of a control group composed of 32 parents. The results indicated a statistically significant increase for the experimental group, with statistically significant improvements in reading accuracy and comprehension, as well as reading attitude and involvement. A broader ecosystemic analysis was also conducted, which suggested that positive relationships between children and significant others in the family were nurtured and other children in the family were benefiting. Interactions between family and school, and school and the local community library were also enhanced.

Positive results have also been reported in other cultural contexts. In Hong Kong, Lam et al. [49] involved parents in paired reading with pre-schoolers, working with 195 preschoolers (mean age = 4.7 years) and their parents. The sample was drawn from families with a wide range of family income, and the preschoolers were then randomly assigned to experimental and control groups.

Training was provided to the parents in the experimental group, who received 12 sessions of school-based training on paired reading over a period of 7 weeks. These parents were then asked to do paired reading with their children at least four times a week in each of these 7 weeks.

At the end of the 7-week intervention, Lam et al. reported that the children in the experimental group had better performance in word recognition and reading fluency than their counterparts in the control group. The children who had been exposed to paired reading were also reported as more competent and motivated in reading by their parents.

In addition, parental changes in relationships and self-efficacy were found to mediate the impact of the intervention on some of the child's outcomes. Lam et al. reported that the parents in the experimental group had higher self-efficacy in helping their children to be better readers and learners, and that these parents also had better relationships with their children. However, family income did not moderate the effectiveness of the programme, with families with high and low income deriving similar benefits from the programme.

2.6. Are parents and peer tutors effective in assisting their children to learn to read?

Overall, the literature reviewed in this section would suggest that both practice and modelling of the reading process by a competent reader are important in paired reading. Repetition is also a crucial factor, especially in working with children with reading or reading fluency difficulties. Parents as well as peer tutors can be used to provide support to struggling readers for the reason that it is the contact, support and modelling of the reading process which are important factors as opposed to variations in implementation of paired reading procedure. Organisation and clear direction are also important factors in implementing a successful paired reading programme.

In their review of the literature on paired reading, Cadieux and Boudreault [50] concluded that paired reading is an effective means of improving reading performance and that nothing indicates that reading gains made through paired reading are not sustained over time. Those studies which have examined processes demonstrate variable levels of compliance with the paired reading technique. However, this factor does not appear to be closely linked with reading gains.

There is also a wider literature supporting parental involvement in assisting their children to read. Hannon, Jackson and Weinberger [51] reported considerable similarities between the parents' and teachers' strategies in terms of the relative frequencies with which they made different kinds of responses while hearing their children read. The most frequent responses for each group were providing words or giving directions about reading, with a greater proportion of parents' responses being made after reading mistakes or miscues, while teachers were likely to make responses both after reading mistakes or miscues, as well as at other times.

Hannon, Jackson and Weinberger reported that both parents and teachers used phonic techniques in responding to reading mistakes or miscues. For parents, this usually meant 'sounding out' words, while for teachers this meant a wider range of responses. Both parents and teachers focused on children's understanding, but for the parents this was generally in response to reading mistakes or miscues, while for teachers this was generally to establish that what the children had read had been comprehended. Hannon, Jackson and Weinberger reported differences in the pattern of positive feedback, praise and criticism between parents and teachers but suggested that these could be due to differences in the social context of reading in the parent and school settings.

Overall, Hannon, Jackson and Weinberger concluded that no justification exists for considering that parents are incompetent in working with their children in developing reading ability. They also concluded that there was scope for reviewing the roles of both parents and teachers in developing reading competence in early childhood education, and this could be facilitated by further research.

Ellis [52] utilised a pre-test/post-test experimental design to investigate the effects of a 12-week parent and child reading intervention on the reading ability and self-perceptions of reading ability in second- and third-grade students. Twenty parents, randomly assigned to the experimental group, participated in the weekly programme sessions. The sessions emphasised simple techniques that parents could use at home to help their child in reading, such as relaxed reading, paired reading and praise and encouragement.

Ellis reported significantly greater improvements in reading as measured by the number of errors made on graded passages for the experimental group. No significantly greater improvements were made by the experimental group in terms of the number of errors made on graded word lists or graded comprehension questions, or in self-perceptions of reading ability. Overall, the findings supported the notion of parental involvement in reading to improve reading ability.

2.7. Type and difficulty level of materials used in paired reading

The literature is not as clear on the type of reading materials to use in paired reading programmes, and also reflects different opinions on difficulty level of materials in paired reading. Carol Chomsky [53] reported that struggling readers decoded slowly and with difficulty and that, despite their hard-won decoding skills, they were also passive to reading. Chomsky recommended that what was needed was material which would engage attention and also make large amounts of textual material available.

Other researchers have used taped books in paired reading (e.g. [54]), or instructional level materials (e.g. [55]). Based on Wasik's review of volunteer tutoring programmes in reading [56], Cadieux and Boudreault gave a standard material package of instructional level material to all participants in their study of paired reading, which was based on available materials reflecting the type and progression of instruction in reading and word attack skills received in school. The package included flash cards containing phonograms (letters, consonant–vowel syllables and consonant–vowel–consonant syllables) which were used for letter reading and syllable recognition activities, as well as first-grade books containing illustrations which were used to practice reading using text. The children received two or three books at each tutoring session, chosen to suit the level of the reading abilities of the child and parent.

In contrast, Deegan [57] has suggested that the student and teacher should select a text that is near frustration level reading and around 200 words in length. Deegan has also suggested that textual characteristics influence the effectiveness of paired reading and that rhythmic and repetitive texts can increase student participation.

Given difference of opinion relating to difficulty level, Morgan, Wilcox and Eldredge's [58] study is of particular interest. These researchers investigated the effect of difficulty levels on second-grade delayed readers using dyad reading, with the aim of establishing how far above a poor reader's instructional level dyad reading should be conducted. The aim was to establish which level of difficulty was associated with the greatest improvement in reading level, word recognition, comprehension and rate. In their study, 51 poor readers were randomly assigned to three experimental groups: (a) dyad reading using materials at their instructional reading level, (b) dyad reading using materials which were two grades above their reading level and (c) dyad reading using materials which were four grades above their reading level. The research was conducted over 95 sessions, with all groups involved in paired reading for 15 min daily during their classroom reading time.

At the end of the school year, Morgan, Wilcox and Eldredge compared reading gain scores of the three groups. They also compared the post-test scores for word recognition, comprehension and reading rate for each group. No significant differences were found between classrooms. The results indicated that all three groups had made gains in reading skills regardless of the difficulty level of the materials used. The second and third groups which read material significantly above their reading level made greater gains than those reading at their instructional level.

Morgan, Wilcox and Eldredge reported that those students who were assisted in reading material two years above their level made the greatest gains. From informal observations, it appeared that poor readers in the third group (i.e. poor readers reading difficult material) seemed to be less motivated to read books four years above their reading level. Morgan, Wilcox and Eldredge commented that these books had significantly less pictures and more words and the children did not seem ready to make the transition from picture books to chapter books. At this level of difficulty, some students appeared to be turned off and paid less attention.

Overall, while all the children improved with dyad reading regardless of the difficulty levels of materials, the results suggested that the difficulty level of materials used for dyad reading may make a difference in student progress. The researchers did not indicate the exact point at which frustration defeated the purpose of paired reading, but suggested that additional research was needed to establish this. Nevertheless, Morgan, Wilcox and Eldredge concluded that children did not have to be taught with instruction-level materials. Poor readers appeared to improve significantly more when they read with a partner at higher levels that exposed them to more unknown words and complex language structures. The results also indicated that to progress more rapidly, students need to be exposed to more difficult material.

Stahl and Heubach [59] reported the results of a 2-year project in which they re-organised the basal reading instruction provided in 14 classes so as to stress fluent reading and automatic word recognition. The reorganised reading programme consisted of three parts: a basal reading lesson which included repeated reading and partner reading, a choice reading period during the day and a home reading programme. The reorganised reading programme was then implemented over a period of 2 years.

Stahl and Heubach reported that the children in all 14 classes made significantly greater than expected growth in reading achievement. All but two children who entered second grade were reading at grade level or higher by the end of the year, while growth in fluency and accuracy appeared to be consistent, reflecting over the whole year. Students' and teachers' attitudes towards the programme were also positive.

In evaluating the contribution of the different components in their programme, Stahl and Heubach reported that self-selected reading partners appeared to work best. Children chose partners primarily out of friendship, and tended to choose books that were at or slightly below their instructional level. However, children in the study also benefited from more difficult materials, provided that scaffolding and support were provided.

2.8. Implications

The literature on paired reading reviewed in this section reflects some differences in preferred methodology, as well as some difference between recommendations concerning the type of materials felt to be most appropriate for use in the process. Overall, however, there would appear to be consensus concerning the value of paired reading, with all of the studies indicating the potential of including parents as well as peer tutors as partners in the process of teaching children to read fluently.

In many of the studies reviewed in this section, paired reading showed positive results on reading fluency over a relatively short period of time. In addition to effects at the reading fluency level, transfer effects of paired reading into reading comprehension were also noted. This would suggest benefits from paired reading methods not only at the level of automaticity (i.e. on speed and accuracy of reading) but also on the higher-level cognitive processes involved in comprehension.

There are also areas of lack of clarity in the literature. Difficulty level of materials would be an important variable to consider in developing paired reading programmes. Certain authorities suggest the value of fun reading materials, others the value of instructional level reading materials and others the value of reading material chosen to be at or near frustration level. There is thus a lack of consensus in this area.

What is clear from the literature, however, is that quality of scaffolding and support in paired reading is important, especially where difficult materials are chosen for use in paired reading programmes. How reading errors are corrected would appear to be less important, as the literature suggests that a wide variety of strategies have been used for doing so, particularly by teachers. It would, however, be important that the procedures used in paired reading are clear enough to be consistently used by parents, tutors and teachers, and that recommended procedures for correcting the errors made by children are also defined.

Overall, it would also be important to stress that while paired reading methods have potential value for developing reading fluency, other methods have also produced positive results. A study by Homan, Klesius and Hite [60], for example, compared repeated reading strategies with non-repetitive strategies on students' fluency and comprehension. In their study, they focused on the transfer effects of the previously mentioned procedures on both comprehension and fluency with sixth-grade students. Homan, Klesius and Hite's results indicated equivalent benefits for repetitive and non-repetitive methods, with significant comprehension improvement over a 7-week period.

Similarly, working in a developing country context, Shah-Wundenberg, Wyse and Chaplain [61] investigated parental support for children's reading of English in an inner-city school in India. The children in the study had oral proficiency in the regional language but were beginning to acquire conventional forms of literacy in English. A quasi-experimental design involving a sample of 241 children was used to evaluate the effectiveness of two approaches to parents supporting reading: paired reading and hearing reading. Interviews and observations with a smaller sub-sample of parents and children were also used to explore the implications of the data more deeply.

In Shah-Wundenberg, Wyse and Chaplain's study, paired reading and hearing reading were found to be equally effective in developing children's beginning English reading skills, reading accuracy and comprehension, relative to controls. The data also indicated that parents had engaged in a variety of mediation behaviours to enhance their children's English reading development. In addition, parents reported that participating in their children's reading in both conditions had been both enriching and empowering, suggesting that parental involvement can benefit children's English reading development.

The development of the reading fluency programme described in the rest of this chapter should thus be viewed as one of a number of potential approaches to enhancing the development of reading ability. Its potential advantages to parents, therapists, teachers and schools lie in the fact that it is based on a theory of structured phonics which has been developed with children who have had reading and spelling difficulties, that the material is delivered via the internet and email, and that the programme can be used at distance. 'The Tales of Jud the Rat' thus provides a form of e-learning which has the potential to enable paired reading methods to be used in a variety of contexts to develop fluent reading. There would also be potential for combining this programme with other instructional approaches [62].

3. Literature relevant to the Phonological Side of 'The Tales of Jud the Rat' reading fluency programme

3.1. Phonological and language correlates of reading ability

A wide variety of different studies have indicated an association between phonological and language development and reading ability. Based on meta-analysis of 61 samples of data, Scarborough [63, 64] reported that the highest average correlations and effect sizes were between measures requiring the processing of print (e.g. letter-sound knowledge) and reading ability, followed by measures of oral language proficiency (e.g. phonological awareness). There were a number of average predictive correlations above 0.50 and still more above 0.40, but of the oral language predictors, only phonological awareness was found to have a causal relationship with learning to read [65, 66].

Overall, the evidence from predictive research within the phonologically based paradigm was both convergent and compelling [67, 68, 69]. In addition, a number of neurolinguistic studies (e.g. [70, 71, 72]) indicated that dyslexic readers process written stimuli atypically, suggesting abnormal functioning of the left hemisphere reading system.

These neurolinguistic studies were of particular interest in suggesting particular areas of the brain associated with reading difficulties. Schulte-Körne and her colleagues [73] used mismatch negativity (MMN) to investigate the relationship between dyslexia and central auditory processing in 19 children with spelling disability and 15 controls at grades 5 and 6 level. While there were no group differences for tone stimuli, a significantly attenuated MMN was found in the dyslexic group for the speech stimuli, suggesting that dyslexics have a specific speech processing deficit at the sensory level which could be used to identify children at risk at an early age.

Shaywitz et al. [74] reported that learning to read requires phonological awareness, which can be defined as an awareness that spoken words can be decomposed into the phonologic constituents that the alphabetic characters represent. Phonological awareness is characteristically lacking in dyslexic readers, for the reason that dyslexic readers have difficulty in mapping alphabetic characters onto the phonologic constituents of the spoken word.

Shaywitz and her colleagues used functional magnetic resonance imaging (MRI) to compare brain activation patterns in dyslexic and non-impaired subjects as they performed tasks that made progressively greater demands on phonologic analysis. Brain activation patterns were found to differ significantly between the groups with dyslexic readers showing relative underactivation in posterior regions (Wernicke's area, the angular gyrus and striate cortex) and relative overactivation in an anterior region (inferior frontal gyrus). Shaywitz et al. thus concluded that the impairment in dyslexia is phonologic in nature and that brain activation patterns may provide a neural signature for this impairment.

Similar conclusions were reached by Brunswick et al. [75], who reported that dyslexic readers process written stimuli atypically, based on abnormal functioning of the left hemisphere reading system, and that the deficits are localised in the neural system underlying lexical retrieval. Klingberg et al. [76] used MRI analysis to examine the structure of white matter in dyslexic and normal adult readers and found differences between normal readers and individuals with poor reading ability. These differences occurred bilaterally in the temporo-parietal white matter underlying perisylvian cortical areas. An overlapping region in the left temporo-parietal white matter also yielded significant correlation between white matter microstructure and reading ability across all 17 subjects. This correlation was apparent both in the poor reading group and in the control group, indicating a structural neural correlate of reading skill in both normal and poor readers and also indicating that white matter underlying left temporo-parietal cortex plays a critical role in reading ability.

Burton [77] reported that there were functional sub-regions within the inferior frontal gyrus that correspond to specific components of phonological processing (e.g. orthographic to phonological conversion in reading, and segmentation in speech). Temple et al. [78] suggested that difficulties in reading are associated with both phonological and orthographic processing deficits, and that dyslexia may be characterised in childhood by disruptions in the neural bases of both phonological and orthographic processes important for reading.

In addition, the neurolinguistic literature indicated that a number of areas of the cortex were involved in fluent reading, as well as in processing different types of reading material. Bentin et al. [79] conducted research based on the analysis of event-related potentials (ERPs) elicited by visually presented lists of words. Based on this evidence, Bentin et al. concluded that different levels of processing are involved for visual, phonological/phonetic, phonological/lexical and semantic material in both hemispheres of the brain, and that a cascade-type process involving different but interconnected neural modules may be involved in the processing of print material, each responsible for a different level of processing of word-related information.

Similar conclusions were reached by Brown et al. [80] on the basis of examination of the MR images of 16 men with dyslexia and 14 control subjects, and comparison of these using a voxel-based analysis. Brown et al. reported evidence of decreases in gray matter in dyslexic subjects, not only in the left temporal lobe and bilaterally in the temporo–parieto–occipital juncture but also in the frontal lobe, caudate, thalamus and cerebellum. Brown et al. thus concluded that widely distributed morphologic differences affecting several brain regions may contribute to the deficits associated with dyslexia.

The above research thus suggested associations between impaired neurological processing and reading disability in dyslexic children. Equally important, however, were the indications from the neurolinguistic literature that reading difficulties were not immutable and that improvements in reading ability also had physiological correlates. Specifically, the development of reading ability would be accompanied by improvement in connectivity between the variety of cortical and sub-cortical centres involved in the reading process. These studies are reviewed in the following section.

3.2. The development of reading ability has correlates on a neurological level

A number of studies suggest that there are associations between the development of reading ability and improvement in neurological processing of print material. Patterns of central processing might initially not be well developed in dyslexic children, but would be responsive to instruction.

Simos et al. [81] studied magnetic source imaging scans during a pseudoword reading task with a sample of eight children aged from 7- to 17-years-old, both before and after 80 hours of intensive remedial instruction. All children were initially diagnosed with dyslexia, having severe difficulties in both word recognition and phonological processing. After remedial training, the dyslexia-specific brain activation profiles became normal, suggesting that change in central processing of print had occurred following intensive remedial training.

Shaywitz et al. [82] reported that provision of a phonologically mediated reading intervention over a period of a year improved both reading fluency and the development of the fast-paced occipito-temporal systems serving skilled reading. After the year-long intervention, children taught with the experimental intervention had made significant gains in reading fluency and demonstrated increased activation in left hemisphere regions, including the inferior frontal gyrus and the middle temporal gyrus, These improvements appeared to be stable; as 1 year after the experimental intervention had ended, these children were activating bilateral inferior frontal gyri and left superior temporal and occipito-temporal regions. This indicated the phonologic reading intervention had facilitated the development of those fast-paced neural systems that underlie skilled reading.

Similar conclusions concerning change in neurological processing in children were reached by Maurer et al. [83], who investigated the development of coarse neural tuning for print by studying children longitudinally before and after learning to read, and compared these patterns to those exhibited by adults who were skilled readers. Maurer et al. reported that coarse neural tuning for print peaked when children learned to read. Coarse N1 tuning, which had been absent in non-reading kindergarten children, emerged less than 2 years later after the children had mastered basic reading skills in second grade. The coarse N1 tuning had become larger for words than symbol strings in every child. Coarse N1 tuning was also stronger for faster readers. On this evidence, Maurer et al. concluded that fast brain processes specialise rapidly for print when children learn to read, and play an important functional role in the fluency of early reading.

3.3. Neural connectivity is associated with fluent reading

Shankweiler et al. [84] also concluded that cortical integration of speech and print in sentence processing varies with reader skill. These researchers used functional magnetic resonance imaging (fMRI) to investigate the association between literacy skills in young adults and the distribution of cerebral activity during comprehension of sentences in spoken and printed form. The results from different analyses all pointed to the conclusion that neural integration of sentence processing across speech and print varies positively with the reader's skill. Further, Shankweiler et al. identified the inferior frontal region as the principal site of speech–print integration and a major focus of reading comprehension differences.

Additional studies used advances in fMRI to identify a relationship between white matter structure (as an indicator of myelination) and reading ability (e.g. [85, 86]). This area of the neurolinguistic literature was based on the premise that myelination was not only an index of the maturity of the insulation of individual fibres in the brain but was also an index of efficiency in neurological transmission [87, 88].

Hasan et al. [89] used diffusion tensor imaging to study the structure and distribution of white matter within the corpus callosum areas connecting the two hemispheres of the brain in children with dyslexia and those of typically developing readers of comparable age and gender. Hasan et al. reported that the posterior corpus callosum area was enlarged in children with dyslexia relative to the same area as measured in typically developing children. In addition, there were microstructural differences (e.g. the mean diffusivity of the posterior middle sector of the corpus callosum), which correlated significantly with measures of word reading and reading comprehension. Reading group differences between dyslexic and typically developing children were also found when using fractional anisotropy, mean diffusivity and radial diffusivity to measure the microstructural characteristics of the posterior corpus callosum.

Vandermosten et al. [90] also used diffusion tensor imaging tractography to examine the integrity of the three-dimensional white matter tracts connecting the left temporo-parietal region and the left inferior frontal gyrus, for which atypical functional activation and lower fractional anisotropy values have been reported in dyslexic readers. Their study revealed structural anomalies in the left arcuate fasciculus in adults with dyslexia. In addition, Vandermosten et al. were able to demonstrate a correlational double dissociation, which suggested that the dual route reading model has neuroanatomical correlates. In the sample studied, the left arcuate fasciculus seemed to sustain the dorsal phonological route underlying grapheme–phoneme decoding in reading, while the left inferior fronto-occipital fasciculus seemed to sustain the ventral orthographic route underlying reading by direct word access.

3.4. Repetition of phoneme-grapheme relationships is likely to build neural connectivity

Later in this chapter, there is reference to the longitudinal work I conducted in the 1990s with a dyslexic child called Q. There were indications from the neurologist's reports that Q's dyslexia was linked to a disorder of neural network connections, as well as a function associated with possible cortical immaturity (Dr Graeme Maxwell, personal communication). The research evidence reviewed in the previous sections was not available at this time, and it was only at the end of the 1990s that neurolinguistic evidence began to emerge that many dyslexic children process reading material at a central level in ways different to normally developing readers [91, 92, 93].

Subsequent evidence suggested that the neural connections formed through the reading process involved a number of cortical areas [94], while also indicating a developmental trajectory by which exposure to written language engages areas originally shaped by speech on the path toward successful literacy acquisition [95, 96]. Equally important was the evidence from studies reviewed in the previous section (e.g. [97, 98, 99]), which suggested that connectivity in the brain could be enhanced through involvement in the process of learning to read, and that phonologically and phonemically based instruction could be particularly helpful in this process.

What my own clinical observations and the literature implied was that in Q's development as well as in the development of other dyslexic children, neural connections would not initially be strongly developed. Changes in connectivity as well as in white matter structure would also be likely to accompany phonologically based reading acquisition.

On a programmatic level, this implied that repeated reading of phonically based material would be likely to develop connections between the variety of cortical areas involved in fluent reading. Conversely, where repeated reading of phonically based material leads to observable changes in reading fluency, this would probably also point to increased functionality in the neural connections which underpin central processing of printed material.

In short, there was a two-way association involved. This suggested that in children with reading difficulties, increased time on task in reading tasks involving repetition of phoneme–grapheme relationships would be likely to build greater reading ability, as well as greater neural connectivity. This has informed the development of the 'Jud the Rat' reading materials described later in this chapter.

3.5. Limitations in correlational research

While the research reviewed in this section implies two-way associations between phonological- and language-based factors, reading ability, instruction in reading and brain connectivity, it is important to note that there are a number of limitations in correlational research.

As Scarborough [100] has suggested, two-way associations in the literature on reading may not be linear ones, for the reason that the development of reading is a multi-faceted process. In addition, Scarborough has suggested that there are many inconsistencies within the evidence on the relationship between phonological and language factors and reading disabilities, which may indicate that there is a second causal chain (e.g. a persisting underlying condition which may account for all the two-way associations observed).

Studies by Galaburda [101], Poldrack [102] and Stein [103] have also suggested the high likelihood that some other mechanism (e.g. of magnocellular, auto-immune system or genetic origin) may account for the anatomical differences between the brain structures of dyslexics and normal readers. Underlying attentional or working memory factors (what Ahissar et al. [104, 105], have called an

anchoring-deficit) may also account for the evidence that only 5–10% of children who are fluent readers in the early grades at school stumble later, while between 65% and 75% of children designated as reading disabled early continue to read poorly throughout their school careers (and beyond), despite evidence that these readers have learned to read [106]. Anchoring deficit factors could also account for periods of 'illusory recovery', in which symptoms of reading disability appear to be remediated, but then reappear at later stages in schooling, suggesting that language skills may develop in a non-linear fashion [107].

In short, while the evidence of the associations between phonological and language factors and reading disability would appear to be compelling, other underlying factors besides a core phonological deficit may contribute to reading disability [108, 109, 110]. A number of other theories (e.g. those relating to how print material is processed visually) are thus reviewed in the following section. These theories have provided the rationale behind the use of large print in the 'Jud the Rat' materials, as well as the use of visual attentional cueing in the process of implementing the materials.

4. Literature relevant to the visual and visual-attentional sides of 'The Tales of Jud the Rat' reading fluency programme

4.1. Rapid visual and auditory processing as predictors of reading difficulty

A number of studies have indicated that developmental dyslexics do poorly in tests requiring rapid visual and auditory processing. Witton et al. [111] reported that neuronal mechanisms that were specialised for detecting stimulus timing and change were dysfunctional in many dyslexic individuals. The dissociation observed in the performance of dyslexic individuals on different auditory tasks also suggested a sub-modality division in the auditory system similar to that already described in the visual system.

Both Farmer and Klein [112] and Stein and Walsh [113] reported that dyslexia was associated with difficulties with moving visual stimuli. Hari and Renvall [114] also reported that dyslexic subjects often suffered from impaired processing of rapid stimulus sequences and suggest that sluggish attentional shifting can account for the impaired processing of rapid stimulus sequences in dyslexia. Amitay et al. [115] concluded that disabled readers suffered from both visual and auditory impairments, showing impaired performance in both visual and auditory tasks requiring fine frequency discriminations.

Talcott et al. [116] reported that both visual motion sensitivity and auditory sensitivity to frequency differences were robust predictors of children's literacy skills and their orthographic and phonological skills. Cohen-Mimran and Sapir [117] reported auditory temporal processing deficits in children with reading disabilities, and that children with reading difficulties had difficulty in discriminating between pure tones with short, but not long, interstimulus intervals, whereas controls performed well with both short and long interstimulus intervals.

Rapid auditory processing deficits have also been found to be consistent predictors of later reading achievement [118]. Lervåg and Hulme [119] reported that rapid automatised naming (RAN) measured with non-alphabetic stimuli before reading instruction had begun was a predictor of later growth in reading fluency, and continued to exert an influence on the development of reading fluency over the next 2 years after reading instruction had begun. Equally important were indications that there was no evidence of reciprocal influence of reading fluency on the growth of RAN skill. This would suggest that RAN is a function which taps the integrity of the left-hemisphere object-recognition and naming circuits which form critical components of the child's developing visual word-recognition system.

4.2. The influence of instruction on rapid processing ability

The literature, however, also indicates that rapid processing dysfunctions are responsive to training. Temple et al. [120] reported disruption of the neural response to rapid acoustic stimuli in dyslexia, with normal readers showing left prefrontal activity in response to rapidly changing, relative to slowly changing, non-linguistic acoustic stimuli. Dyslexic readers, in contrast, showed no differential left frontal response. Temple et al. also reported that dyslexic readers who participated in a remediation program showed increased activity in left prefrontal cortex after training.

Temple et al.'s results would suggest that the left prefrontal regions are normally sensitive to rapid relative to slow acoustic stimulation, but are insensitive in the case of dyslexic readers. Equally important are the indications that the left prefrontal cortex would appear to be plastic enough in adulthood to develop such differential sensitivity after intensive training.

Gaab et al. [121] reported that children with dyslexia had a fundamental deficit in processing rapid acoustic stimuli, but that this was responsive to training. While typical-reading children showed activation for rapid compared to slow transitions in left prefrontal cortex, children with developmental dyslexia did not show differential response in these regions to rapid and slow transitions in acoustic stimuli. After 8 weeks of remediation which provided training in rapid auditory processing, phonological processing and language skills, Gaab et al. reported that the children with developmental dyslexia showed significant improvements in both language and reading skills. They also showed activation for rapid relative to slow transitions in the left prefrontal cortex after training. Gaab et al. thus concluded that neural correlates of rapid auditory processing were disrupted in children with developmental dyslexia, but could be ameliorated with training.

These findings suggested that many children with reading difficulties have difficulties with rapid visual processing, difficulties with rapid auditory processing, as well as impairments of perceptual processing of rapidly changing acoustic stimuli. These findings also suggest that reading disabilities are often accompanied by impaired perceptual skills as well as specific perceptual deficits and perceptual difficulties which have neurological correlates. As with other areas of functioning, the relationship between behaviour and underlying neural connectivity would appear to be a two -way association, in which improved perceptual processing leads to improved neural connectivity, and vice versa.

4.3. The magnocellular theory of dyslexia

Overall, the research reviewed in the previous section would suggest that many children with dyslexia or poor reading ability have difficulties in processing rapidly changing signals, both auditorally as well as visually [122]. Visual processing difficulties, as well as auditory processing difficulties, have neurological correlates, suggesting the possibility of a general underlying attentional or processing difficulty affecting the development of reading ability.

The magnocellular theory of dyslexia [123, 124] suggests that underlying difficulties in auditory and visual processing can be traced to difficulties in the magnocellular component of the visual system. As Stein and Walsh comment:

'Developmental dyslexics often complain that small letters appear to blur and move around when they are trying to read. Anatomical, electrophysiological, psychophysical and brain-imaging studies have all contributed to elucidating the functional organization of these and other visual confusions. They emerge not from damage to a single visual relay but from abnormalities of the magnocellular component of the visual system, which is specialized for processing fast temporal information. The m-stream culminates in the posterior parietal cortex, which plays an important role in guiding visual attention. The evidence is consistent with an increasingly sophisticated account of dyslexia that does not single out either phonological, or visual or motor deficits. Rather, temporal processing in all three systems seems to be impaired. Dyslexics may be unable to process fast incoming sensory information adequately in any domain.' [125]

Stein and Walsh's conclusions have been supported by a number of studies. Salmelin et al. [126] used magnetoencephalography to identify impaired word processing in the occipito-temporal areas of dyslexics, while Livingstone et al. [127] reported that dyslexic subjects exhibited diminished visually evoked potentials to rapid, low contrast stimuli, but normal responses to slow or high contrast stimuli. Livingstone et al. suggested that the abnormalities in the dyslexic subjects' responses to evoked potentials were associated with a defect in the magnocellular pathway at the level of visual area 1 or earlier.

Livingstone et al. also compared the lateral geniculate nuclei from five dyslexic brains to five control brains, reporting abnormalities in the magnocellular, but not the parvocellular, layers in the dyslexic brains studied. As previous studies using auditory and somatosensory tests had shown that dyslexics perform poorly on tasks requiring rapid discriminations, Livingstone et al. hypothesised that many cortical systems can be divided into a fast and a slow subdivision; and further that that dyslexia is associated with difficulties in rapid processing within these fast subdivisions.

Similarly, Vidyasagar and Pammer [128] reported that impaired visual search in dyslexia relates to the role of the magnocellular pathway in attention, leading Vidyasagar [129] to suggest that attentional gating in primary visual cortex provides a physiological basis for dyslexia. Sireteanu et al. [130] also investigated the performance of children with developmental dyslexia on a number of visual tasks requiring selective visual attention and found that dyslexic children did not show the overestimation of the left visual field (pseudoneglect) characteristic of normal adult vision. Dyslexic children also showed shorter reaction times and a dramatically increased number of errors on these tasks, suggesting that children with developmental dyslexia have selective deficits in visual attention.

Misra et al. [131], for example, have identified a number of neurological correlates of rapid processing deficits, reporting that the majority of children and adults with reading disabilities also exhibit pronounced difficulties on naming-speed measures such as tests of rapid automatised naming, which required speeded naming of serially presented stimuli. In their study, functional magnetic resonance imaging was used to evaluate the neural substrates that were associated with performance on rapid naming tasks. Activation was found in neural areas associated with eye movement control and attention as well as in a network of cortical structures implicated in reading tasks, including the inferior frontal cortex, temporo-parietal areas and the ventral visual stream. Whereas the inferior frontal areas of the network were similarly activated for both letters and objects, activation in the posterior areas varied by task. These results suggested that rapid naming tasks recruited a network of neural structures which were also involved in more complex reading tasks, and suggested that rapid naming of letters pinpointed key components of this reading network.

4.4. Prevalence of magnocellular deficits: Evidence from multiple case studies

Vidyasagar and Pammer [132] have proposed that dyslexia is a deficit in visuo-spatial attention, not in phonological processing. However, the evidence from multiple case studies of disabled readers suggests that dyslexics may suffer from visual and auditory impairments but only a few suffer from a specific magnocellular deficit.

Amitay et al. [133], for example, reported that only six out of the thirty reading disabled subjects in their study had impaired magnocellular function, and that the performance of the other twenty four reading disabled subjects on magnocellular tasks did not differ from that of controls. Amitay et al. also reported that many of the reading disabled children showed impaired performance in both visual and auditory non-magnocellular tasks which required fine frequency discriminations. Overall, Amitay et al. concluded that some reading disabled subjects have generally impaired perceptual skills, while many reading disabled subjects have more specific perceptual deficits. The 'magnocellular' level of description, however, did not capture the nature of the perceptual difficulties in any of the reading disabled individuals in the sample, as the six subjects with impaired magnocellular function were also consistently impaired on a broad range of other perceptual tasks.

Similarly, Ramus et al. [134] analysed sixteen dyslexic subjects and reported that all sixteen dyslexics suffered from a phonological deficit. Ten of the subjects could be characterised as suffering from an auditory deficit, four from a motor deficit and two from a visual magnocellular deficit. The results thus indicated that a phonological deficit can appear in the absence of any other sensory or motor disorder. A phonological deficit is also sufficient to cause a literacy impairment, as demonstrated by five of the dyslexics. Auditory disorders, when present, aggravated a phonological deficit, contributing to the literacy impairment.

These data thus indicated that auditory deficits could not be characterised simply as rapid auditory processing problems, as would be predicted by the magnocellular theory. Nor were they restricted to speech. Contrary to the cerebellar theory, Ramus et al. also found little support for the notion that motor impairments had a cerebellar origin or reflected an automaticity deficit. Overall, Ramus et al. concluded that the phonological theory of dyslexia could account for all sixteen of the subjects in their sample. There were also additional sensory and motor disorders in certain individuals.

Ziegler et al. [135] reported that children with dyslexia had significant deficits for letter and digit strings, but not for symbol strings. Visual-attentional theories of dyslexia could not explain these findings, as visual attentional theories postulated identical deficits for letters, digits and symbols in dyslexics. Ziegler et al. also reported that dyslexics showed normal W-shaped serial position functions for letter and digit strings. This finding suggested that their deficit could not be attributed to an abnormally small attentional window. In addition, the data indicated that the size of the deficit was identical for letters and digits, suggesting that poor letter perception in dyslexic children was not just a consequence of lack of reading.

What could account for Ziegler et al.'s data was that the process of mapping symbols onto phonological codes was impaired, as this was the case for both letters and digits. In contrast, symbols that did not map onto phonological codes were not impaired. This dissociation suggested that impaired symbol-sound mapping rather than impaired visual-attentional processing was the key to understanding dyslexia.

4.5. Both visual and visual attentional factors need to be taken into account in teaching reading

Despite convergent evidence that dyslexia is a language disability which has its foundations in difficulties in phonological and phonemic processing, both Schulte-Körne and Bruder's [136] review and Stein's more recent [137] review of current literature suggest that rapid processing, attentional and magnocellular factors are important influences on reading ability which should not be overlooked. Research from both Australia [138] and from Italy [139] also indicate that it is important to take account of visual attentional factors in remediating language-based learning difficulties.

In addition, visual features stemming from layout of reading material have been found to influence reading as well as comprehension outcomes [140]. Spinelli et al. [141] have suggested that dyslexic readers are affected by crowding of multiple characters and large numbers of words onto printed pages. Visual features of text such as print size [142], visual span [143], spacing of letters [144], spacing between letters [145, 146], as well as font size and spacing between words relative to print size and visual acuity limits [147] are also important to consider when publishing materials for poor readers.

The above research has implications for the development of reading materials for dyslexic children. As I had found in working with Q, research post 2000 indicated that dyslexic children would be likely to respond best to reading material which took account of factors such as length of words [148, 149], amount of text in paragraphs [150] and amount of text on pages [151].

How I have taken account of phonological and phonemic factors, as well as crowding, visual and visual-attentional factors, in writing the 'Tales of Jud the Rat' series as well as in developing the procedures used in the implementation of the materials is covered in the rest of this chapter.

5. The first stage of development of the 'Tales of Jud the Rat' programme: Extended case study

5.1. The need for graded reading materials of gradually increasing difficulty

Janet Lerner [152, 153, 154] has suggested that the methods used for children with learning difficulties can be used with all children. The reason for this is that all children respond to good teaching. Shaywitz et al. [155] also emphasise continuities across normal and dyslexic readers, interpreting dyslexia as occurring at the lower end of a normal distribution of reading abilities. While a diagnosis of dyslexia often has a high degree of stability over time, there are also a large number of children who are diagnosed as dyslexic in early grades who no longer meet dyslexic criteria in later grades at school. Thus the distinction between developmental dyslexics and other poor readers may be of limited usefulness.

Similarly, Elliott and Grigorenko [156] argue that the evidence suggests that both dyslexics and other poor readers benefit from structured phonological treatment. This implies that if a method is workable for a child who has severe reading difficulties, it is also likely to work for a child who has less severe learning difficulties, or for a child who has no difficulties at all.

This has been the principle guiding the development of the materials used in the reading fluency programme. These have been developed in two stages, working with children involved my practice in Johannesburg.

The first stage in the development of the reading fluency programme was based on the need for graded reading materials of gradually increasing difficulty for a child who was severely dyslexic (Child Q). These needed to be implemented at a distance of 6,000 miles from my rooms.

5.2. Implementation side-by-side with a method for teaching structured phonics which was both visual and verbal

Child Q worked with me over a number of years. She and her parents were South African but lived in Europe. The referral came internationally, and I was then consulted by the child's mother, who indicated that her child (called Q for the purpose of case study) had severe learning problems. These were intractable.

Q had been assessed as having developmental learning problems in Britain from age 5. This had been followed by a number of language and remedial interventions, which had been effective in developing skills, but not effective in increasing reading ability. When Q first came to see me at the age of 8, she did not know all her letters. It was also evident that she had both language and reading difficulties. Despite major phonological and expressive language difficulties, Q was of high intelligence, and had well-developed visual imagery and visualisation abilities.

As available instruction was not working effectively, Q's mother spent 2 h in Q's school daily, working individually with her child on a programme sent to her first by fax, and then by email. The initial programme I provided focused on phonically based instruction using synthetic phonics material. In addition, as the five vowel system previously used with Q had not been effective and as Q's strengths lay in visualisation, I utilised a system for teaching structured phonics to develop both word attack and spelling ability. This was both visual and verbal, based on a seven vowel system and colour coding.

Initially, developmental reading materials were provided by the teachers at Q's primary school, while the material provided by myself was designed to support the word analysis, spelling and sequential writing sides of Q's instructional programme. I also sent Q's mother material to teach number concept and arithmetic, with which Q had major difficulties.

Over the first year Q's progress was steady, but as her programme entered its second year, it became clear that there was insufficient graded reading material available in the school to support the gradual increase in the level of reading instruction which Q needed. Additional reading schemes were bought by the school; but as the second year progressed, we simply ran out of reading books which were available at the school and at her level. There was no alternative other than to develop reading material specifically designed to support the gradual increase in the level of phonic skills Q needed, as well as the amount of reinforcement of phonic skills required in her reading programme.

5.3. The Doctor Skunk stories

As Q was a South African child living abroad, the first two reading books I wrote were stories written about South African wild animals. However, I struck an immediate problem on a phonic level. South African wild animals have names like 'giraffe', 'elephant', 'eland', 'gemsbok', 'lion', 'leopard' and 'cheetah'. How would I be able to reconcile these indigenous names with Q's phonological and phonic needs?

To determine Q's phonic needs, I was using both standardised tests as well as a self-developed clinical test called the phonic inventories [157, 158, 159, 160], which classroom-based research [161, 162, 163, 164, 165, 166, 167, 168, 169] had identified as both valid and reliable, as well as predictive of learning difficulties at both junior and high school levels [170, 171, 172, 173]. Used clinically, the information yielded by the instrument was diagnostic and indicated that Q needed phonic materials targetting word endings such as 'ss', 'ff', 'll', 'ck', 'ng', 'tch' and 'dge', as well as vowel digraphs such as 'ai', 'ee', 'ea', 'oa', 'ay' and 'ou'.

In the first two reading books I wrote, it was impossible to reconcile the names of South African animals with these phonic needs. The word 'lion', for example, was spelled in a completely opposite way to the diphthong 'oi', which was one of the vowel digraphs which Q had not yet established. 'Cheetah' included the 'ee' vowel digraph, and also included a schwa sound made by an 'a' followed by a silent 'h' at the end of the word. 'Buck' had a short vowel and a 'ck' ending. Tiger also met long vowel phonic criteria, but unfortunately tigers are not found on the South African veld.

I thus abandoned the aim of indigenising Q's reading material. As Q lived near a park, I focused instead on creating a more universal reading world of a small village set next to a park. In the village lived a number of phonically regular short vowel animals such as 'rat', 'cat', 'dog' and 'skunk'. The books were set in large print to increase the visual cues from the letters and words, and the paragraphs were kept short to enable Q to focus on the words she was reading by avoiding clutter. As the stories progressed, the short vowel animals interacted with long vowel animals such as 'mole', 'bird' and 'owl' and more complex polysyllabic but phonically regular animals such as 'rabbit', 'weasel', 'hamster', 'hedgehog' and 'badger'.

The main characters in the stories became the phonically regular short vowel 'Jud the Rat' and 'Jill the Dog', who first interacted with other short vowel characters such as 'Tom the Cat' and 'Doctor Skunk', and later with long vowel characters such as 'Max the Mole' and 'Mrs Weasel', and then with polysyllabic characters such as 'Len Hamster', 'Mr and Mrs Rabbit' and 'Bill the Hedgehog'. As the stories progressed, the characters met others who lived at a distance from the village such as 'Mrs Horse', 'Captain Ferret' and 'Colonel Tortoise'.

At basic levels in the stories there was a 'shop' and each character had a 'house' in the village. There was also a 'farm' close by where there were 'cows' which provided 'milk' and 'hens' which provided 'eggs', while further away from the village and at higher levels in the stories there were more phonically complex 'mountains', 'a valley', 'a country club' and even 'Benjamin Horse's Stud Farm'.

At basic levels in the stories, the animals entertained themselves by having 'fun' and at intermediate levels by having 'tea and cake' and 'a picnic', while at higher levels the animals met with 'brothers' and 'sisters' and 'in-laws' and 'cousins'. One of the 'uncles' drove a 'shiny red motorbike with a bright green sidecar', while other animals rode 'from up the valley' on the 'bus from town' driven by 'Sid the Badger'.

At higher levels in the stories there was 'a party' in 'Farmer Jim's barn' with music provided by 'Harry Hopper and the Doodlebugs', who accompanied 'Cheryl Crow' and 'The Mice Girls'. Harry Hopper's band played polysyllabic 'guitars' and 'saxophones' and 'trumpets' through 'amplifiers'. More traditional music was also provided at the party on phonically counter-intuitive 'violins' by 'The Veteran Insects String Band', until Doctor Skunk came along and performed as the phonically intuitive 'Screaming Lord Skunk' and then wrecked the proceedings.

It will be gathered from the above that the Doctor Skunk stories were based on structured phonic principles which gradually increased in level, and were designed to teach as well as to entertain. For in the absence of other appropriately graded reading materials, it was important to keep Q interested, with material which appealed to her well-developed visual imagery and her delightful sense of humour, while at the same time addressing the basic progression in phonic complexity which Q needed to learn to read fluently.

5.4. What were the effects of this type of reading instruction?

In her longitudinal case study of the effects of instruction on Q's phonic, reading and spelling development, Sfetsios (2002) [174] described the development of the reading materials used in Q's programme as follows:

'Simultaneously with the introduction of rule-based instruction through the spelling, dictation and written side of the programme, an attempt was made to sequence the skills introduced in the reading side of the programme, in order for the written and reading sides of the programme to reinforce one another.

It was evident that Q needed a gradual progression when reading, and found changes in language register confusing (Professor Potter, personal communication, 2002). What had been established through the written side of the programme was that constant reinforcement was necessary before Q was able to use a particular phonic rule in reading, or orthographic rule as this applied in writing and spelling. Difficulties were pronounced where this involved a combination of vowels or chunking of letters. The Phonic Inventories (see Appendix A) indicated that she had particular difficulty with the consonant clusters commonly used in word endings, and the decision was made to target these and focus on the rules involving combinations of consonants used at the ends of words after short vowels. This was the focus before any attempt was made to target the long vowel sounds represented in vowel digraphs and diphthongs.

The reading materials available in Q's school essentially moved too quickly to provide the basis for learning and overlearning necessary to reinforce the alphabetic rules introduced in the written side of the programme, and the type of consistent use of a gradually expanding core vocabulary necessary for Q to progress (Professor Potter, personal communication, 2002). The indication on the reading side was thus for a reading programme which reinforced the skills introduced in the written side of the programme, and which did not increase in complexity too quickly. Here we found that conventional reading schemes were not sufficient, either singly or in combination as a part of a broader reading scheme. The font size used in the books was also problematic, in that Q responded better to larger as opposed to smaller font sizes.

Against this background, the decision was taken to develop one story and a core set of characters and extend them in the beginning, creating a context and world of meaning with which Q could become familiar, and then extending these parameters to new and wider contexts. The story would need to work from the familiar, and introduce a graded and gradually extending vocabulary. Q was very interested in animals. She also lived in an area adjacent to parkland in Holland. These two aspects were therefore selected as contextual features of the story created. The Doctor Skunk stories (see Appendix R, pp.1xxxiv–1xxxvii) revolved around a group of animals who lived in a parkland, each animal representing human qualities to which Q could relate and enjoy. The story had a strong comical angle and ensured that Q maintained interest in the antics of the growing number of characters over the 6-year remedial period.

In practice, the Doctor Skunk stories provided the vehicle both for the development of reading as well as a springboard for the development of Q's imagery and imagination, and for her own descriptive and creative writing (see Appendix R, pp. xciii–xcv). It should be borne in mind that owing to her developmental difficulties, Q had lost out on many situations involving social interaction through play and involvement with other children as a contributing and functional partner in learning activities at school. The key to Q's learning to read was the fact that she was able to discover humour and enjoyment in the reading act, and to maintain her interest in reading while experiencing success in working with text, both in reading and writing (Professor Potter, personal communication, 2002).

Four years later at the time Q went to high school, she was still interested in the characters in the Doctor Skunk stories and their antics, and had covered 23 books involving several thousands of pages of text in large print. The gradually increasing difficulty of the orthography used in the text had taken her from the level of short vowels and three letter words to the ability to decode the work she was required to handle at school (see Appendix R, p.1xxxvii). By the time it was possible to reduce the font size on the printed page after 4 years of this type of work, she had also developed the skills required to read more widely, and for enjoyment.' [175]

The gains in reading, spelling and dictation made by Q over a four and a half year period are presented in Table 1 below

	July 1997 M's age: 10 years 2 months	February 1998 M's age: 10 years 9 months	June 1998 M's age: 11years 1 month	June 2000 M's age: 12 years 11 months	April 2001 M's age: 13 years 11 months	August 2001 M's age: 14 years 3 months	December 2001 M's age: 14 years 7 months
	Age	Age	Age	Age	Age	Age	Age
Oral Reading							
Rate	7.9	7.7	7.9	8.9	7.10	8.2	8.0
Comprehension	7.11	8.7	9.5	9.8	9.1	9.11	9.11
Silent Reading							
Rate	7.0	7.5	7.4	8.0	7.3	7.9	8.0
Comprehension	8.6	9.7	9.12	10.3	9.2	10.2	9.5
Listening	9.2	9.2	9.2	10.2	9.2	10.2	9.2
Flash Words	7.10	8.0	8.2	9.6	9.2	9.7	9.11
Word Analysis	8.0	8.3	8.2	9.11	9.5	9.11	9.11
Spelling (Durrell)	7.3	8.0	8.0	9.6	8.2	8.8	8.2
Handwriting	7.4	8.3	8.3	8.9	9.2	9.0	8.5
Spelling							
Schonell Form A	7.2	7.6	8.4	8.7	8.5	9.4	8.6
Schonell Graded Dictation							
Test A	-	-	7.6	8.1	-	-	-

Test B			'No score	8.0	8.0	9.6	8.0
Test C	-	-	-	7.6	8.5	10.0	7.0
Test D	-	-	-	-	-	-	6.1
Daniels and Diack							
Graded Reading Test	7.2	-	-	-	-	-	-
Standard Spelling Test	7.3	-	-	-	-	-	-
Visual Memory	7.9	7.0	8.5	8.8	8.8	8.8	8.8
Hearing Sounds in Words	8.6	7.11	9.0	-	-	-	-
Auditory Phonic Spelling	-	-	8.8	10.8	10.2	10.2	7.3

'There is no score as it was found that Q was not ready for this level of dictation

Table 1. Q's Progress as Measured by Durrell Analysis of Reading Difficulty Age Scores

From Table 1, it will be clear that Q made gains, despite weaknesses in the phonological, phonemic and language areas, and difficulties with rate of reading. Her strengths lay in visual imagery and visualisation, which were utilised in her reading programme, as well as in the methods used to teach her spelling and sequentialisation. However, despite a programme which focused on phonological and phonemic development combined with tailor-made reading, writing and spelling programmes, Q did not develop to be a fluent reader. Both rate of reading and rate of work continued to be particular problems. She was nevertheless able to cope mainstream schooling up to the end of junior high school, requiring scaffolding and support to do so. She then completed her final years of schooling in a remedial school.

Summarising Q's progress, Sfetsios commented,

'Gains made with Q in reading, spelling and dictation have been hard won. Success has been a result of much dedication and support of her mother and father, remedial therapists and tutors, however, above all, it is a credit to Q's motivation and persistence. Her continuing willingness to undertake a programme that has been built step-by-step and skill-by-skill has resulted in her moving from only being able to recognise 16 letters of the alphabet to success-fully attending a mainstream British High School.' [176]

6. The second stage of development of 'The Tales of Jud the Rat' reading fluency programme

6.1. A set of graded phonic ebook materials for paired reading

It is very infrequently that I encounter children in my practice who have as intractable reading and spelling difficulties as those of Q. Early in 2013, however, I encountered another child (A) who was not making progress in reading, despite therapy directed at phonological and phonemic development, combined with a programme of reading, writing and spelling support. It was evident that there were major difficulties in A's reading fluency, despite progress in the development of phonological and phonic skills, as well as word analysis and sentence reading abilities.

As with Q, the report from A's neurologist (Dr Graeme Maxwell, personal communication) [177] indicated that there were attentional difficulties combined with attentional lapses, stemming from cortical immaturity and a slow myelinisation process. On a functional level, it was evident that A was not making progress in reading despite the fact that his school was sending out a variety of graded reading books which were then read orally at home and in his remedial support sessions in the afternoons.

At this stage (mid 2013), I took the decision to relook at the Doctor Skunk stories, and to develop additional material in a format in which they could be used to support A's need to become a more fluent reader. This required writing more graded material based on phonic associations which were introduced and then repeated. This set of ebooks ('The Tales of Jud the Rat') would then be sent to A's parents by email and implemented via a form of paired reading aimed at using repeated reading to develop automaticity and reading fluency.

I first tried out the material with A in my sessions with him. Once it was evident after 6 months of instruction that this type of programme was producing effects, the material was then made available for wider use; at the beginning of 2014, I suggested to the parents of seven other children in the practice who were not fluent readers that they should also use the programme. In this way, an initial cohort of children started working with the reading fluency materials.

This consisted of three children (A, B and C) of junior primary school level, three (D, E and F) were at upper primary school level and two children (G and H) who were at junior high school level. Each of these children had been diagnosed as being of average to upper intelligence with scatter in the IQ profile, and as having learning and reading difficulties. Each of these children was also being seen by the same neurologist, who had diagnosed attentional deficits and cortical immaturity linked to slow rate of myelination.

The ebook-based reading fluency programme followed by this initial cohort of children is described in the next section. This will be followed by discussion of the neurolinguistic research which has provided the theoretical basis of the programme materials and the oral impress method and visual tracking methods used in programme implementation. The assessment and evaluation process will then be described, followed by presentation of results. Implications will then be discussed at the end of the chapter.

6.2. An ebook series of gradually increasing level of difficulty

It was only near the end of the first stage in the development of the 'Doctor Skunk' stories that the books I had written began to be delivered as attachments to emails. During the second stage of development of the programme, email delivery was used with all children. One reason for this was that a large amount of additional graded material had been written over the second half of 2013, based on recent (post 2000) neurolinguistic literature. In addition as, there were now eight children of different ages and reading levels in the 2014 cohort, ebook delivery of the second series materials ('The Tales of Jud the Rat') became an integral feature of the reading fluency programme.

An additional reason for ebook delivery is that many children's parents travel considerable distance to the rooms in Johannesburg where I run my practice. One family travels 500 kilometers weekly. A number of other parents in the practice live over a hundred kilometers away from my rooms, travelling long distances to see me. The reason that they do so is that there is a high level of demand for instruction as well as materials for children with reading difficulties, particularly from areas outside Johannesburg. This is probably a feature linked with deteriorating schools in the public sector in South Africa, as well as a dearth of appropriate scaffolding and support in the schools close to where many parents live.

All parents in my practice, however, have email, and for this reason, 'The Tales of Jud the Rat' reading fluency programme has been developed in a form in which it can be delivered by email and then downloaded and used by parents at home. As the reading fluency materials have been designed to complement the sessional work I do, parents are provided with tutorial support by email, as well as questions and answers by cellphone. As new books in the series are also sent out by me, I am able to monitor the rate at which the children are covering the material, and through this establish the amount of paired reading done using the programme at home.

My own sessions thus work side-by-side with the implementation of the reading fluency programme by parents. In this way, I can focus in my sessions on developing basic skills in phonological and phonic development, as well as the sequentialisation and working memory skills which underpin writing, spelling and learning at school. I am also able to do work to develop the abilities to use these basic skills in reading comprehension and school-related work.

The aim has been to provide a large body reading fluency materials which are appropriately graded, which are readily available and inexpensive, and which can be used daily at home. As the materials have been written to meet the needs of parents of children in my practice who have rate of work problems linked to reading fluency difficulties, through the materials parents have thus become partners in the learning process.

6.3. Use of phonic strategies in writing the materials

My experience in working with Q had informed the decision that the 'Doctor Skunk' stories should be written on phonemically based principles. Developments in the neurolinguistic literature post 2000 then ensured that this principle should be carried forward into "The Tales of Jud the Rat" series. Specifically, I ensured that all words used in the ebooks would be able to be decoded using phonically based strategies. In addition, words used would then be repeated.

This would be done so that 'The Tales of Jud the Rat' materials would be suitable to be used by teachers and therapists working in a phonologically based paradigm. They would also be suitable for use by parents to develop automaticity in sound–letter associations through repeated reading. In addition, being phonically based, the materials could also be used for the purposes of teaching phonic analysis and spelling rules.

In short, my experience in working with Q suggested that repetition of phonic associations was necessary in developing fluent reading, and that there were side-by-side improvements in connectivity on a neural level (Dr Graeme Maxwell, Q's neurologist, personal communication) [178]. As this reciprocal link was also indicated in the neurolinguistic literature post 2000, there was clear support for the use of phonic strategies in writing 'The Tales of Jud the Rat' materials.

6.4. Use of repetition of phonic associations to build decoding ability

As with the 'Doctor Skunk' stories used with Q, the 'Tales of Jud the Rat' materials were designed to enable repetitions which were phonically based, and exposure to phonic rules which proceeded up in level very gradually. As there was a need for plenty of repetition, there was also a need for plenty of material.

The 'Doctor Skunk' stories had been implemented side-by-side with instruction in phonics, using a combination of the synthetic phonic principles embodied in the Orton/Gillingham [179] approach and the analytical phonics principles suggested by Sister Mary Caroline [180]. As the field had now moved on, 'The Tales of Jud the Rat' materials were designed to provide the degree of repetition necessary to reinforce remedial teaching done within both the Orton/Gillingham paradigm as well as teaching done within more modern phonologically based paradigms (e.g. [181]).

Underpinning both sets of materials was an assumption that repetition of phonic associations would lead to probable benefits at a neurological level. The 'Doctor Skunk' stories were based on the Wernicke-Geschwind hypothesis [182], the assumption being that a combination of amount of time on task and amount of repetition would enable associations to form within the occipito-temporal areas of the left hemisphere of the brain.

Given the more precise indications concerning neural connectivity which had emerged from neurolinguistic research post 2000, 'The Tales of Jud the Rat' materials assumed that neural connectivity would be improved by repetitive exposure to phonically graded material set in large print, specifically between the left occipital and parietal lobes in which large print would be processed, the temporal/occipital lobes in which sound–letter associations would be processed and also those areas of the left temporal and frontal lobes in which higher levels of language processing take place. Writing and spelling based on these associations would then be encoded in medial areas of the left side of the brain in both right-handed people as well as in the majority of left-handed people.

In short, stronger associations at a central level would be likely to lead to positive results, as a number of studies reviewed in this chapter had indicated that this would be likely to be the case.

6.5. Use of material set in large print: Visual features of the ebooks

The literature post 2000 also indicated that there are visual features in text which may influence the way in which dyslexic children learn to read [183, 184]. 'The Tales of Jud the Rat' materials were thus also designed to take into account visual attentional as well as visual features of text.

A feature of ebooks and electronic print is that they can be set in different fonts and print sizes. The ebooks in 'The Tales of Jud the Rat' series were set in large print and made use of short sentences and paragraphs as well as large amounts of white space on the page. This was done so that the material could avoid crowding, as this was to likely to affect dyslexics on a visual level (e.g. [185, 186]).

Print size was one important variable. O'Brien, Mansfield and Legg [187] had reported constant reading rates across large print sizes in dyslexics, but that a sharp decline in reading rates occurs once print is presented below a critical print size, indicating that dyslexic readers would require larger critical print sizes to attain maximum reading speeds. O'Brien, Mansfield and Legg's results indicated that reading rate-by-print size curves followed the same two-limbed shape for dyslexic and non-dyslexic readers. The reading curves of dyslexic children, however, showed higher critical print sizes and shallower reading rate-by-print size slopes below the critical print size. Non-dyslexic reading curves also showed a decrease of critical print size with age. Statistical analysis indicated that a developmental lag model of dyslexic reading had not accounted for the results, since the regression of critical print size on maximum reading rate differed between the two groups.

Research reported by Brennan, Worrall and McKenna [188] indicated that a number of other aspects of the design and formatting of materials used in written communication (e.g. use of simplified vocabulary and syntax, large print and increased white space) can influence comprehension. Brennan, Worrall and McKenna worked with aphasic adults, and reported that adding pictures, particularly Clip Art pictures, may not significantly improve the reading comprehension of people with aphasia, but that simplified vocabulary and syntax, large print and increased white space were significant features to consider when using all written communication with people with aphasia.

Martelli et al. [189] suggested the value of using white space when presenting materials for dyslexic children learning to read, for the reason that crowding may influence reading speed. Levi [190] also pointed out that crowding was an important influence on visual discrimination and object recognition which has a relationship with dyslexia. Based on review of the literature, Levi suggested that there were two stages involved in the development of object recognition which can be localised to the cortex. The first stage involves the detection of simple features, while the second stage is required for the integration or interpretation of the features of an object. In addition, there is evidence that top–down effects (i.e. effects of interpretation and comprehension) mediate the bottom–up effects of crowding, while the role of attention in this process remains unclear.

Overall, Levi suggested that there is a strong effect of learning in shrinking the spatial extent of crowding, indicating that instruction ameliorates the influence of crowding on reading ability. Legge and Bigelow's review [191] also indicated that both size and shape of printed symbols determine the legibility of text, and for this reason, the PDFs of the ebooks in 'The

Tales of Jud the Rat' series were set in large print, using Arial, which is a simple uncluttered font.

6.6. Use of visual tracking to maintain visual attention in the implementation process

Stein's review [192] indicates that visual attentional factors are likely to influence reading ability. In addition, Sireteanu et al. [193] have suggested that children with developmental dyslexia show selective visual deficits in attention, with dyslexic children showing shorter reaction times as well as dramatically increased numbers of errors.

For this reason, the procedures used for implementing 'The Tales of Jud the Rat' materials have been designed to provide a combination of phonically based material and large print, as well as visual tracking. The assumption is that this combination would assist developing phonological and visual associations while also maintaining visual attention, and that this combination, in turn, would be helpful in building connectivity on a magnocellular level.

Visual tracking is thus built into the implementation process of 'The Tales of Jud the Rat' materials, with a pointer being used from the top of the line focus attention on words read, as well as attention on those visual features in words which provide maximum cues in the decoding process. Visual and visual attentional decoding processes are then combined with phonic repetition throughout the core series of ebooks. The reason for this is that research evidence suggests that rapid automatised naming (RAN) is a correlate of early reading skills and that RAN continues to exert an influence on the development of reading fluency over the next 2 years after reading instruction has started [194].

Given needs for longitudinal intervention where reading problems are major or intractable (such as in Q's case), the series of 'The Tales of Jud the Rat' ebooks has been designed to provide enough graded reading material for the programme to be used for at least 2 years and for up to 4 years with any child, should this be necessary. This means that the combination of use of large print, visual tracking and phonic repetition can be continued for an extended period, until an age appropriate level of reading fluency has been developed.

How this is done is described in the following sections.

7. Provision of material of gradually increasing complexity: The core and extension readers

7.1. The core large-print reading series

Carol Chomsky [195] has suggested that struggling readers decode slowly and with difficulty and that, despite their hard-won decoding skills, they are also passive to reading. Chomsky also suggests that what is needed is material which will engage attention, and also make large amounts of textual material available.

The core series of large print readers is designed to provide a large amount of material which can be used to develop reading fluency. There are currently 19 ebooks which are graded in terms of level. The titles of the ebooks in the core reading fluency programme can be found on my website at http://www.charlespotter.org, while the programme as a whole is designed as follows:

Core Series: Title of book	Extension	Award
1. JUD THE RAT AND TOM THE CAT		
2. TOM THE CAT TRIES TO TRICK JUD THE RAT, BUT GETS VERY WET AND COLD		
3. TOM THE CAT TRIES TO BE CLEVER, BUT LANDS UP SICK IN BED	Supplementary Series One: The Stories of Sid the Badger – Basic Level Readers	Supplementary Series One: The Stories of Sid the Badger – Basic Level Readers
4. JILL THE DOG		
5. TOM THE CAT MAKES A MISTAKE, BUT LANDS UP BEING SUCCESSFUL		
6. HOW JUD THE RAT REALISES HE HAS BEEN TRICKED, AND TRIES TO SAVE FACE	Supplementary Series Two: The Stories of Bill the Hedgehog – Intermediate Level Readers	Certificate: Reading Fluency Level Two + Book Prize
7. JUD THE RAT'S HOUSE		
8. THE SMELLY END OF THE STREET		
9. TOM THE CAT CATCHES JUD THE RAT, BUT JUD STILL GETS AWAY	Supplementary Series Three: The Chronicles Doctor Skunk: Part One – Higher Level Readers	Certificate: Reading Fluency Level Three + Book Prize
10. JILL THE DOG'S SHOP		
11. TOM THE CAT'S SECRET		
12. JILL THE DOG SOLVES PART OF THE PUZZLE		
13. SID THE BADGER FINDS THE ANSWER		
14. TOM THE CAT'S TRAP	Supplementary Series Four: The Chronicles of Doctor Skunk Part Two – Higher Level Readers	Certificate: Reading Fluency Level Four + Book Prize
15. JUD THE RAT AND MAX THE MOLE		
16. DOCTOR SKUNK'S VISIT		
17. HOW DOCTOR SKUNK GOT BACK TO THE STREET AND THEN WENT HOME		
18. JUD THE RAT SPOILS TOM THE CAT'S BIKE RIDE		
19. TOM THE CAT GETS HIS OWN BACK	Supplementary Series Five: Stories of the Valley and Legends of the Deep Woods -- Extension Readers	Certificate: Reading Fluency Level Five + Book Prize

Table 2. Dr Charles Potter's reading fluency programme: design

Each of the elements in the programme is ebook-based, supported by email tutorials. The ebooks are also designed to be delivered by email. This provides the flexibility for the core programme of large print readers to be implemented both as a support programme for parents working with me on a sessional basis, or at distance.

7.2. Reducing font size and extending vocabulary: The extension readers

The evidence from the literature is convergent in indicating that reading difficulties are language based [196], though a combination of auditory and visual as well as attentional factors may also influence reading abilities [197], There is also evidence that increased reading fluency influences reading comprehension [198] and that conversely, top–down effects involved in language and reading comprehension mediate the influence of auditory, visual and attentional and fluency factors on reading ability [199].

For this reason, it will be evident from Table 2 above that reading fluency is conceptualised as a variable having stages. These stages can be determined both from reading behaviour as well as performance on reading tests measuring reading accuracy and reading rate.

As certain children may require substantial work before an age-appropriate level of reading fluency is developed, there are five supplementary series in the programme. Each of these supplementary series consists of between five and seven ebooks. At lower levels in the programme, there are extension stories based on rhythm and rhyme, as well as stories based on sequenced storytelling. At higher levels, there are extension stories drawn from the original 'Doctor Skunk' series written for Q, as well as extension stories designed to link with tales of imagination and legends. There are also procedures for use of the materials for building skills in analytical phonics, spelling and sequential spelling, as well as an awards programme for children completing a certain number of books and reaching particular levels of reading fluency. Despite having a large number of ebooks available, the aim is that the materials in the programme should be used only as long as is necessary to develop an age appropriate level of reading fluency. What this means is that decisions concerning the need for continued use of large print and repetition are evidence-driven and taken both quantitatively as well as qualitatively. In addition, as the evidence from the paired reading literature is not convergent concerning optimal levels of difficulty of reading material, the books in the core series are written based on predominantly short words which can be decoded using phonic rules. Books in the extension material also include more complex vocabulary.

Specifically, once there is evidence that reading fluency is developing from one stage to the next and evidence that age-appropriate top-down effects are operating (i.e. improvements in reading fluency as well as comprehension are taking place), children working through the 'The Tales of Jud the Rat' series are directed to supplementary and extension materials. In these ebooks both print size and repetition of words are reduced, At the same time, the amount of repetition in the paired reading procedures used for implementation of the reading fluency programme is also reduced.

7.3. Reading fluency as one element in a broader intervention

It will be apparent from the above that the 'Tales of Jud the Rat' programme can be used for purposes of clinical teaching as well as in other situations in which observation is used to determine needs for intervention. The assumption is that one size may not fit all, and that as Scarborough [200] suggests, the variables involved in reading acquisition may not be linear. In addition, multiple case studies suggest variation in the aetiology of adult dyslexics [201] as well as children [202].

What this means is that not all children need the same thing, and that not all dyslexic children are likely to respond to the same treatment. The reading fluency programme is thus conceptualised as one element in a broader intervention. Its value lies in its potential for providing sufficient time on task for automaticity in reading to be developed. At the same time, the results obtained also reflect the skill of the teacher or therapist in using the tools and the programmes available to him or her, and 'The Tales of Jud the Rat' series is only one of a number of possible tools and programmes.

What this also means is that for optimum results, paired reading using 'The Tales of Jud the Rat' programme should be combined with other programmes involving phonic teaching [203] as well as exposure to other texts in which vocabulary is broader and difficulty levels are higher [204]. As reading and spelling are linked processes, how this is done (i.e. how the programme is structured and how other additional instructional programmes are organised and implemented) is essentially based on assessment, evaluation and clinical judgement as interpretive processes, as described in the following sections.

7.4. Assessment and evaluation as informing clinical judgement

The ebooks in the reading fluency programme are not a panacea. They can best be described as an exercise programme designed to provide a structured and sequenced means for developing reading fluency as one element in a broader instructional programme. If the reading fluency programme is implemented by parents for 20 min a number of times a week, its potential value lies in enabling time on task in reading to be substantially increased, using graded materials which have been developed on a conceptual basis linked to recent developments in neurolinguistic research.

As it is important to establish the need for as well as the effects of the 'Tales of Jud the Rat' programme as well as the need for other interventions targeting the development of phonic analysis, reading comprehension, spelling and sequential writing ability, there are systems for assessment and evaluation linked to the materials. These are based on a process of action research [205], in which assessment is used to establish needs for intervention, followed by a process of planning and implementation in which evaluation is integral.

Placement in the programme is initially made on the basis of reading level. Based on the process of evaluation, awards are also made both for effort as well as improvement. These awards are linked to extension activities, in the form of ebooks which are at a higher level, as well as end books for broader reading.

Children are placed in the programme based on a system of assessment and evaluation involving quantitative indicators from four core reading, spelling and sequential spelling tests. Reading fluency and reading comprehension are also assessed via other reading tests, and supported by additional testing of phonemic knowledge and reading comprehension abilities. During implementation, these data are then linked to qualitative indicators of reading fluency based on parental reports. This is done by informal interviews as well as questionnaires.

The evaluation is thus multi-method [206, 207], based on both quantitative and qualitative evidence linked to other available data on school and classroom performance as well as reading habits. Once placement has been made at a particular level in the reading materials, the first ebook is sent out by email. This is supported by a written tutorial, and if possible a trial session in how to support the paired reading procedure with visual tracking, and how to pace repeated reading.

Once parents have tried out the materials, a formative evaluation questionnaire is completed. Only at this stage is the child brought into the programme. As the sequence of the core reading series is published on the author's website, the child's progress through the core reading materials can be tracked both by parents and their teachers or therapists. Summative evaluation is then completed after a number of books have been worked through, as the basis for achieving awards, as well as entry into the intermediate- and higher-level series.

This decision is based on clinical judgement and can be made at any level in the programme, but generally occurs once the child has reached reading fluency level three. Parents are involved in this process, as well as in the system of awards and the summative evaluation process conducted at the end of each calendar year, which involves post-testing.

8. Results

Though 'The Tales of Jud the Rat' reading programme has been developed on a clear theoretical rationale, in the final analysis any reading programme is merely a tool which is as good as the user. I have learned a great deal from working with parents as well as other therapists and teachers as part of the formative and summative evaluation process. This has shaped not only the sequence of the programme but also the awards system and the use of supporting and extension reading materials which now form an integral part of the structure of the programme.

Overall, the results have been very promising. Based on use of the materials for a period of 6 months as part of a broader-based remedial intervention, the results of the first cohort of children are presented in Table 3 below.

It will be evident from the above that all children in the initial cohort placed on the programme have made good progress, as indicated by gains in reading age after 6 months programme usage. Evaluative comments made by both parents and children have also been very positive. These can be summarised in Table 4 as follows.

Perhaps, the most important qualitative indicator, however, is that all parents who were using the materials at the end of 2014 have asked to continue using them this year (2015). Equally important is the evidence that many of the children using the programme have reported improvements in rate of work at school. Based on these positive indicators, an increasing number of children are currently working with the materials, some working with their parents as part of their weekly contact with me, and some working with their parents or with teachers or other therapists at distance from my rooms.

Children in Reading Fluency Programme	Grade Level at School	Schonell One Word Reading Test	Holborn Sentence Reading Test	Schonell Single Word Spelling Test	Schonell Dictation Tests
Child A *Pretest*	*start Grade 2*	*6 years 9 months*	*6 years 9 months*	*6 years 6 months*	-
Child A Post-test	end Grade 2	7 years 7 months	8 years 3 months	7 years 5 months	< 6 years 0 months
Child B *Pretest*	*start Grade 3*	*7 years 7 months*	*8 years 6 months*	*7 years 8 months*	*6 years 0 months*
Child B Post-test	end Grade 3	8 years 8 months	9 years 2 months	8 years 7 months	9 years 0 months
Child C *Pretest*	*start Grade 3*	*7 years 0 months*	*7 years 7 months*	*7 years 5 months*	*< 6 years 0 months*
Child C Post-test	end Grade 3	8 years 11 months	8 years 6 months	9 years 0 months	7 years 6 months
Child D *Pretest*	*start Grade 5*	*7 years 7 months*	*8 years 6 months*	*7 years 4 months*	*7 years 5 months*
Child D Post-test	end Grade 5	9 years 0 months	9 years 2 months	9 years 1 month	8 years 6 months
Child E *Pretest*	*start Grade 5*	*7 years 7 months*	*8 years 0 months*	*8 years 1 month*	*< 6 years 0 months*
Child E Post-test	end Grade 5	9 years 2 months	8 years 11 months	8 years 7 months	8 years 8 months
Child F *Pretest*	*start Grade 7*	*8 years 2 months*	*8 years 6 months*	*6 years 8 months*	*6 years 9 months*
Child F Post-test	end Grade 7	10 years 7 months	9 years 10 months	8 years 8 months	7 years 9 months
Child G *Pretest*	*start Grade 8*	*8 years 11 months*	*9 years 2 months*	*8 years 6 months*	*8 years 9 months*
Child G Post-test	end Grade 8	11 years 3 months	9 years 10 months	9 years 6 months	8 years 9 months
Child H *Pretest*	*start Grade 8*	*10 years 6 months*	*9 years 2 months*	*9 years 11 months*	*10 years 7 months*
Child H Post-test	end Grade 8	"/> 12 years 6 months	13 years 5 months	10 years 11 months	12 years 0 months

Table 3. Progress of 2014 Cohort as Measured by Reading, Spelling and Dictation Age Scores

Children in Reading Fluency Programme	Improvement in Reading Accuracy	Improvement in Reading Rate	Improvement in Reading Hesitancy and Confidence	Improvement in Ability to Read New Material	Improvement in Reading Comprehension
Child A	*	*	*	*	*
Child B	*	*	*	*	*
Child C	*	*	*	*	*
Child D	*	*	*	*	*
Child E	*	*	*	*	*
Child F	*	*	*	*	*
Child G	*	*	*	*	*
Child H	*	*	*	*	*

Table 4. Summary of Qualitative Evaluations by Parents: 2014 Cohort

Overall, the experience has been a very positive one. While the results we have are preliminary, the evidence so far would also suggest that parents can use the programme with their children and that schools, teachers and therapists can also use the materials to support the work they are doing. The evidence also suggests that those children who proceed through the programme at the rate of one ebook a month make substantial progress.

9. Summary and evaluation

This chapter has presented eight major assets of 'The Tales of Jud the Rat' series.

a. The material has been developed based on clinical teaching as well as neurolinguistic theory.

b. The material is graded, based on structured phonic principles.

c. The material is set in large print to increase visual cues as well as reduce crowding.

d. There is plenty of material available, and there is enough for the core reading materials to be used for as long as is necessary to develop reading fluency, even with readers who require a 2-year intervention (or more) as their reading problems are severe or intractible,

e. The material is available in electronic ebook form. This implies that all material can be sent out by email and used at a distance. All core tests and evaluation procedures can also be applied at a distance.

f. There are established procedures for implementation, which include visual tracking.

g. Once downloaded, 'The Tales of Jud the Rat' material is implemented using repeated paired reading to develop automaticity in reading.

h.   The implementation and evaluation procedures are simple, and can be used by parents and peer tutors, as well as by teachers and therapists.

While the research evidence reviewed in this chapter would suggest that automaticity forms the foundation for both increases in reading rate and accuracy as well being associated with improvement in reading comprehension, there are a number of disadvantages of the programme.

• The material targets reading fluency and does not overtly target reading comprehension.

• While the literature suggests that the development of automaticity is an essential skill and the evidence from parent use of 'The Tales of Jud the Rat' material suggests that the children who have used the programme have improved in a number of different aspects associated with fluent reading, the results we have so far are not definitive.

• The 'Tales of Jud the Rat' programme has so far only been used under clinical settings, and my own clinical experience suggests that the results of any one programme will only be as good as the other aspects of instruction which accompany it. Put another way, any educational programme is merely a tool. It will produce best effects where the programme implementer is skilled, and in situations where the programme is used in conjunction with other instructional programmes which also target improvement.

Despite these potential weaknesses, we have had good results with 'The Tales of Jud the Rat' series, and there are probably a number of reasons why this is so. The first reason is that the material is phonically based and proceeds up in level very gradually. There is plenty of repetition. The programme is also compatible with other instructional programmes. If one believes in Gillingham and Stillman's approach, for example (and many therapists still do), what this means is that 'The Tales of Jud the Rat' material can be used to reinforce remedial teaching done within the Orton/Gillingham paradigm [208], teaching done using an analytical phonics approach (e.g.[209]), as well as teaching done within more modern phonologically based paradigms (e.g. [210]).

Given the potential for increase in time on task in reading using material which involves frequent repetition of phonic associations, there are also probable benefits at a neurological level. In addition, visual tracking is built into programme implementation and this is also likely to lead to probable benefits at a neurological level. In short, increased time on task would be likely to develop automaticity in reading, implying stronger associations at a central level. As the literature suggests that the directionality in these associations is two-way, automaticity at a central level would be likely to lead to positive results in reading more generally, and the studies reviewed in this chapter indicate that this is indeed likely to be the case.

Based on the literature, there are also a number of other probable reasons for positive results. One is that 'The Tales of Jud the Rat' materials are repetitive, and take into account visual attention as well as visual features of text [211, 212]. The ebooks are set in large print and make use of short sentences and paragraphs as well as large amounts of white space on the page. What this means is that the material is likely to avoid crowding, which has been emerging in the literature as a feature affecting dyslexics on a visual level (e.g. [213, 214]). In addition, there are theoretical reasons why a combination of phonically based material and large print would be helpful on a magnocellular level, especially in a situation in which both repetition of phonic associations and visual tracking are built into programme implementation.

However, it is important to state that there is no empirical evidence that this is actually so, and these theoretical bases of a programme remain possibilities until there is empirical evidence available to support assertions like these, or prove otherwise. Though the results presented in this chapter are positive, they are small-scale and preliminary. In addition, there are many weaknesses in data from pre-test, post-test and pre-experimental designs, especially when these designs are used clinically. Specifically, difficulties in weak research designs are likely to be compounded where therapy or instruction is undertaken with the aim of improving test scores and where a variety of teaching strategies are used to do so.

As they are based on clinical evidence and case study, the results presented in this chapter are positive but difficult to disaggregate, and larger-scale comparative research would be necessary to do so. Nevertheless, the clinical evidence presented is recurrent and indicates that there is likely to be benefit from using the materials even in the absence of both longitudinal and/or comparative studies. The value of both partner reading and peer tutored reading as well as parental involvement in assisting children with their reading is already clear from the literature (e.g. [215, 216, 217, 218, 219]). This is essentially what 'The Tales of Jud the Rat' programme provides, and the evaluative issue may thus not be whether this particular method is better than any other, but whether it is able to provide an appropriately structured and low-cost way for parents or peer tutors to achieve improvements in reading fluency.

The results we have obtained would support the indications in the literature of the value of increasing the amount that children read, as well as providing exposure to accessible texts. As Fisher and Berliner [220] have suggested, the amount that students read in classrooms is critically related to their reading achievement. In addition, Hiebert and Fisher [221] have suggested that children of lower primary school age performing in the bottom quartile require the following experiences with text:

Accessible Text

Provision of text which is accessible through being decodable, which includes both high-imagery and high-frequency words, which limits the number of unique words per text, and which repeats key words.

Increased Text

Provision of increased opportunities for reading involving exposure to text during classroom instruction, with the aims of increasing both word recognition and fluent reading skills.

Repeated Text

Provision of opportunities for repeated reading of text, with the aims of increasing exposure to new words and developing reading fluency.

The evidence from my practice would suggest the value of providing greatly increased time on task in reading accessible, graded texts using a methodology combining repetition with visual tracking. Both parents and children in my practice report steady improvement in reading fluency, and evaluate the 'Tales of Jud the Rat' reading fluency materials positively Positive qualitative evaluations have been accompanied by the changes in test scores presented in Tables 3 and 4 in this chapter.

The evidence from my practice would also support Hiebert and Martin's [222] comment that repetition has been the forgotten variable in reading instruction. Both parents and therapists have commented positively on the phonic structure of the programme as well as the use of repetition within the texts as well as in the methodology used in implementing the programme. It is also of interest that, despite the large amount of repetition which is a feature of the programme, the stories have been rated as entertaining by both children and their parents.

There have also been wider benefits. One parent reports that her child receives the books. His older sister then reads them. The family's domestic help then reads them, and her children then also use them to learn to read. The ebooks are also currently being used as the basis for reading fluency programmes being implemented with ten higher- and twenty lower-income families in Mpumalanga province. I await the results of these pilot programmes with interest.

In summary, I have found in my own work that 'The Tales of Jud the Rat' material provides a way of enabling parents to provide graded daily reinforcement of reading, by using ebooks which target reading fluency and automaticity in decoding at home. The majority of the children I work with have reading difficulties, and in this context 'The Tales of Jud the Rat' programme has been very helpful.

In implementing the programme, clear guidelines are given to parents in how to engage productively in improving the reading fluency of their children, and this enables me to ensure that time on task in reading is increased at home. The involvement of parents then leaves me with more time to focus in therapy on programmes which improve other aspects of reading and writing ability. These include programmes for developing synthetic and analytical phonic skills and word attack, as well as tasks involving oral and written language skills designed to build oral and written language comprehension skills. I am also able to spend more time in assessment and counselling of children and parents, as well as in working on programmes for developing skills in silent reading, as well as word analysis, single word spelling and sequential writing and spelling.

What can be claimed is that a great deal of material in 'The Tales of Jud the Rat' programme is already available but I am still developing parts of it, and also revising aspects of the material where formative evaluation has shown that this is necessary. It can also be claimed that the programme has provided clear benefits based on observable differences as well as changes in test scores. Based on positive evaluations, the materials are being added to, but are already in a form in which they can be used by others.

The number of families using the programme has increased rapidly, and the material may also have wider relevance for use in the classroom. Low-cost material of this type is often difficult to obtain especially in developing world contexts, or where parents, teachers and therapists live at distance from major towns or from educational bookshops. Positive results with the 'Tales of Jud the Rat' series so far suggest that the material provides a low-cost path to reading improvement which can be used in direct contact or at distance by parents, peer tutors, teachers, therapists and schools.

Author details

Charles Potter*

Address all correspondence to: pottercs@gmail.com

Private Practice, Johannesburg, South Africa

References

[1] Rieben L, Perfetti CA (Eds.) Learning to Read: Basic Research and Its Implications. New York: Routledge, 2013, p. vii.

[2] Adams MJ. Beginning to Read: Thinking and Learning About Print. Cambridge, MA: MIT Press, 1990.

[3] Perfetti CA. Psycholinguistics and reading ability. In: Gernsbacher MA. (Ed.) Handbook of Psycholinguistics. San Diego, CA: Academic Press, 1994, pp. 849–894.

[4] Perfetti CA. The universal grammar of reading. Sci Stud Reading 2003;7(1):pp.3–24.

[5] Perfetti CA. Representations and awareness in the acquisition of reading competence. In: Rieben L, Perfetti CA. (Eds.) Learning to Read: Basic Research and Its Implications. New York: Routledge, 2013, pp. 33–44.

[6] Logsdon A. What is reading fluency? http://learningdisabilities.about.com/od/glossar1/g/rdgfluency.htm, 2012a.

[7] Luria AR. The Working Brain: An Introduction to Neuropsychology. Harmondsworth, UK: Penguin Education, 1973.

[8] Logsdon A. What is reading fluency? Learn about reading fluency. http://learningdisabilities.about.com/od/readingstrategies/a/What-Is-Reading-Fluency.htm, 2012b.

[9] Luria AR. The Working Brain: An Introduction to Neuropsychology. Harmondsworth, UK: Penguin Education, 1973.

[10] Laberge D, Samuels JS. Toward a theory of automatic information processing in reading. Cogn Psychol 1974;6(2):293–323.

[11] Luria AR. The Working Brain: An Introduction to Neuropsychology. Harmondsworth, UK: Penguin Education, 1973.

[12] Samuels SJ. The method of repeated readings. The Reading Teacher 1979;32(4):403–8.

[13] Chomsky C. After decoding: what? Language Arts 1976;53(3):288--96.

[14] Carbo M. Teaching reading with talking books. The Reading Teacher 1978;32(3):267–73.

[15] Morgan R, Lyon E. Paired reading — a preliminary report on a technique for parental tuition of reading retarded children. J Child Psychol Psychiatr 1979;20(2):151–60.

[16] Ashby-Davis C. A review of three techniques for use with remedial readers. The Reading Teacher 1981;34(5):534–8.

[17] Allington RL. Fluency: the neglected reading goal. The Reading Teacher 1983;36(6): 556–61.

[18] Adams MJ. Beginning to read: Thinking and learning about print. Cambridge, MA: MIT Press, 1990.

[19] Fuchs LS, Fuchs D, Hosp MK, Jenkins JR. Oral reading fluency as an indicator of reading competence: a theoretical, empirical, and historical analysis. Sci Stud Reading 2001;5(3):239–56.

[20] U.S. Congress. No Child Left Behind Act: Reauthorization of the Elementary and Secondary Education Act (PL 107–110). www.ed.gov/offices/oese/esea/. 2001.

[21] Norton ES, Wolf M. Rapid automatized naming (RAN) and reading fluency: implications for understanding and treatment of reading disabilities. Annu Rev Psychol 2012;63:427–52.

[22] Chomsky C. After decoding: what? Language Arts 1976;53(3):288–96.

[23] Carbo M. Teaching reading with talking books. The Reading Teacher 1978;32(3):267–73.

[24] Morgan R, Lyon E. Paired reading — a preliminary report on a technique for parental tuition of reading retarded children. J Child Psychol Psychiatr 1979;20(2):151–60.

[25] Ashby-Davis C. A review of three techniques for use with remedial readers. The Reading Teacher 1981;34(5):534–8.

[26] Heckelman RG. A neurological impress method of reading instruction. RG Heckelman – 1962 – Merced County Schools Office, Merced CA.

[27] Heckelman RG. A neurological-impress method of remedial-reading instruction. Acad Therap 1969;4(4):277–82.

[28] Heckelman RG. N.I.M. revisited. Acad Therap 1986;21(4):411–20.

[29] Hoskisson K, Krohm B. Reading by immersion: assisted reading. Elementary English 1974;51(6):832–6.

[30] Heckelman RG. A neurological impress method of reading instruction. RG Heckelman – 1962 – Merced County Schools Office, Merced CA.

[31] Heckelman RG. A neurological-impress method of remedial-reading instruction. Academic Therapy 1969;4(4):277–82.

[32] Hollingsworth PM. An experiment with the impress method of teaching reading. The Reading Teacher 1970;24(2):112–4.

[33] Morgan R, Lyon E. Paired reading — a preliminary report on a technique for parental tuition of reading retarded children. J Child Psychol Psychiatr 1979;20(2):151–60.

[34] Topping K. Paired reading: a powerful technique for parent use. The Reading Teacher 1987a;40(7):608–14.

[35] Topping K. Peer tutored paired reading: outcome data from ten projects. Edu Psychol: Int J Exp Edu Psychol 1987b;7(2):133–45.

[36] Topping K. Peer tutoring and paired reading: combining two powerful techniques. The Reading Teacher 1989;42:488–94.

[37] Topping K. Paired, Reading, Spelling and Writing: The Handbook for Teachers and Parents. London: Cassell, 1995.

[38] Topping K. Paired reading: a powerful technique for parent use. The Reading Teacher 1987;40(7):608–14.

[39] Topping K. Peer tutoring and paired reading: combining two powerful techniques. The Reading Teacher 1989;42:488–94.

[40] Topping K. Peer tutored paired reading: outcome data from ten projects. Edu Psychol: Int J Exp Edu Psychol 1987b;7(2):133–45.

[41] Topping K. Paired, Reading, Spelling and Writing: The Handbook for Teachers and Parents. London: Cassell, 1995.

[42] Topping K. Paired, Reading, Spelling and Writing: The Handbook for Teachers and Parents. London: Cassell, 1995.

[43] Topping KJ, Lindsay GA. Paired reading: a review of the literature. Res Papers Edu 1992;7(3):199–246.

[44] Topping K, Wolfendale S. (Eds.) Parental involvement in children's reading. New York: Nichols, 1985.

[45] Morgan R, Lyon E. Paired reading — a preliminary report on a technique for parental tuition of reading retarded children. J Child Psychol Psychiatr 1979;20(2):151–60.

[46] Hewison J, Tizard J. Parental involvement and reading attainment. Edu Psychol 1980;50(3):209–15.

[47] Vanwagenen MA, Williams RL, Mclaughlin TF. Use of assisted reading to improve reading rate, word accuracy, and comprehension with ESL Spanish-speaking students. Perceptual Motor Skills 1994;79(1):227–30.

[48] Overett J, Donald D. Paired reading: effects of a parent involvement programme in a disadvantaged community in South Africa. Br J Edu Psychol 1998;68(3):347–56.

[49] Lam S, Chow-Yeung K, Wong BPH, Kiu Lau K, In Tse S. Involving parents in paired reading with preschoolers: Results from a randomized controlled trial. Contemp Edu Psychol 2013;38(2):126–35.

[50] Cadieux A, Boudreault P. The effects of a parent-child paired reading program on reading abilities, phonological awareness and self-concept of at-risk pupils (1). The Free Library. 2005 Project Innovation (Alabama) 24 Feb 2015. http://www.thefreeli-brary.com/The±effects±of±a±parent-child±paired±reading±program±on±reading...-a0142874180

[51] Hannon P, Jackson A, Weinberger J. Parents' and teachers' strategies in hearing young children read. Res Papers Edu1986;1(1):6–25.

[52] Ellis MG. Parent-child reading programs: Involving parents in the reading intervention process. ERIC Number: ED397377, 1996.

[53] Chomsky C. After decoding: what? Language Arts 1976;53(3):288–96.

[54] Carbo M. Teaching reading with talking books. The Reading Teacher 1978;32(3):267–73.

[55] Cadieux A, Boudreault P. The effects of a parent-child paired reading program on reading abilities, phonological awareness and self-concept of at-risk pupils (1). The Free Library. 2005 Project Innovation (Alabama) 24 Feb 2015. http://www.thefreeli-brary.com/The±effects±of±a±parent-child±paired±reading±program±on±reading...-a0142874180

[56] Wasik BA. Volunteer tutoring programs in reading: a review. Reading Res Quart 1998;33:266–92.

[57] Deegan J. Impress method. Downloaded from websites.pdesas.org/jamesdeegan/2013/9/12/520805/file.aspx, 2007.

[58] Morgan A, Wilcox BR, Eldredge JL. Effect of difficulty levels on second-grade delayed readers using dyad reading. J Edu Res 2000;94(2):113–9.

[59] Stahl SA, Heubach KM. Fluency-oriented reading instruction. J Literacy Res 2005;37(1):25–60.

[60] Homan SP, Klesius JP, Hite C. Effects of repeated readings and nonrepetitive strategies on students' fluency and comprehension. J Edu Res 1993;87(2):94–9.

[61] Shah-Wundenberg M, Wyse D, Chaplain R. Parents helping their children learn to read: the effectiveness of paired reading and hearing reading in a developing country context. J Early Childhood Literacy 2013;13(4):471500.

[62] MacDonald P. Paired reading: a structured approach to raising attainment in literacy. Support Learning 2010;25(1):15–23.

[63] Scarborough HS. Early identification of children at risk for reading disabilities: Phonological awareness and some other promising predictors. Specific Reading Disability: A View of the Spectrum 1998a;75–119.

[64] Scarborough HS. Predicting the future achievement of second graders with reading disabilities: contributions of phonemic awareness, verbal memory, rapid naming, and IQ. Anna Dyslexia 1998b;48(1):115–36.

[65] Scarborough HS. Developmental relationships between language and reading: reconciling a beautiful hypothesis with some ugly facts. In: Catts HW, Kamhi AG. (Eds.) The Connections between Language and Reading Disabilities. New Jersey: Lawrence Erlbaum, 2005, pp. 3–22.

[66] Scarborough HS. Connecting early language and literacy to later reading (dis)abilities: evidence, theory and practice. In: Fletcher-Campbell F, Soler J, Reid G. (Eds.) Approaching Difficulties in Literacy Development: Assessment, Pedagogy and Programmes. New York: Sage, 2009; pp. 23–38.

[67] Potter CS, Grasko D, Pereira C. Using spelling error patterns to identify children with learning difficulties. SAALED International Conference "Reading for All". Nelspruit, September, 2006.

[68] Potter CS, Fridjhon P, Grasko D, Pereira C, Ravenscroft G. Spelling error profiles: an index for evaluating the learning needs and progress of children in the classroom. Pretoria, ASEASA International Conference, July, 2008.

[69] Potter CS, Fridjhon P, Grasko D, Pereira C, Ravenscroft G. Identifying patterns of phonic errors in children with learning disabilities. Salt Lake City, UT: 46th International Conference of the Learning Disabilities Association of America, February, 2009.

[70] Shaywitz SE, Shaywitz BA, Pugh KR, Fulbright RK, Constable RT, Mencl WE, Gore JC. Functional disruption in the organization of the brain for reading in dyslexia. Proc Nat Acad Sci 1998;95(5):2636–41.

[71] Schulte-Körne G, Deimel W, Bartling J, Remschmidt H. Auditory processing and dyslexia: evidence for a specific speech processing deficit. Neuroreport 1998;9(2):337–40.

[72] Brunswick N, McCrory E, Price CJ, Frith CD, Frith U. Explicit and implicit processing of words and pseudowords by adult developmental dyslexics: a search for Wernicke's Wortschatz? Brain 1999;122(10):1901–17.

[73] Schulte-Körne G, Deimel W, Bartling J, Remschmidt H. Auditory processing and dyslexia: evidence for a specific speech processing deficit. Neuroreport 1998;9(2):337–40.

[74] Shaywitz SE, Shaywitz BA, Pugh KR, Fulbright RK, Constable RT, Mencl WE, Gore JC. Functional disruption in the organization of the brain for reading in dyslexia. Proc Nat Acad Sci 1998;95(5):2636–41.

[75] Brunswick N, McCrory E, Price CJ, Frith CD, Frith U. Explicit and implicit processing of words and pseudowords by adult developmental dyslexics: a search for Wernicke's Wortschatz? Brain 1999;122(10):1901–17.

[76] Klingberg T, Hedehus M, Temple E, Salz T, Gabrieli JDE, Moseley ME, Poldrack RA. Microstructure of temporo-parietal white matter as a basis for reading ability: Evidence from diffusion tensor magnetic resonance imaging. Neuron 2000;25(2):493–500.

[77] Burton MW. The role of inferior frontal cortex in phonological processing. Cognitive Sci 2001;25(5):695–709.

[78] Temple E, Poldrack RA, Salidis J, Deutsch GK, Tallal P, Merzenich MM, Gabrieli JDE. Disrupted neural responses to phonological and orthographic processing in dyslexic children: an fMRI study. Neuroreport 2001;12(2):299–307.

[79] Bentin S, Mouchetant-Rostaing Y, Giard M, Echallier J, Pernier J. ERP manifestations of processing printed words at different psycholinguistic levels: time course and scalp distribution. J Cognitive Neurosci 1999;11(3):235–60.

[80] Brown WE, Eliez S, Menon V, Rumsey JM, White CD, Reiss AL. Preliminary evidence of widespread morphological variations of the brain in dyslexia. Neurology 2001;56(6):781–3.

[81] Simos PG, Fletcher JM, Bergman E, Breier JJ, Foorman BR, Castillo EM, Davis RN, Fitzgerald M, Papanicolaou AC. Dyslexia-specific brain activation profile becomes normal following successful remedial training. Neurology 2002;58(8):1203–13.

[82] Shaywitz BA, Shaywitz SE, Blachman BA, Pugh KR, Fulbright RK, Skudlarski P, Mencl WE, Constable RT, Holahan JM, Marchione KE, Fletcher JM, Lyon GR, Gore JC. Development of left occipitotemporal systems for skilled reading in children after a phonologically-based intervention. Biol Psychiatr 2004;55(9):926–33.

[83] Maurer U, Brem S, Kranz F, Bucher K, Benz R, Halder P, Steinhausen H, Brandeis D. Coarse neural tuning for print peaks when children learn to read. Neuroimage 2006;33(2):749–58.

[84] Shankweiler D, Mencl WE, Braze D, Tabor W, Pugh KR, Fulbright RK. Reading differences and brain: cortical integration of speech and print in sentence processing varies with reader skill. Develop Neuropsychol 2008;33(6):745–75.

[85] Poldrack RA. A structural basis for developmental dyslexia: evidence from diffusion tensor imaging. In: Wolf M.Ed.) Dyslexia, Fluency, and the Brain. Baltimore, MD: York Press, 2001; pp. 3–17.

[86] Shaywitz BA, Shaywitz SE, Blachman BA, Pugh KR, Fulbright RK, Skudlarski P, Mencl WE, Constable RT, Holahan JM, Marchione KE, Fletcher JM, Lyon GR, Gore JC. Development of left occipitotemporal systems for skilled reading in children after a phonologically-based intervention. Biol Psychiatr 2004;55(9):926–33.

[87] Poldrack RA. A structural basis for developmental dyslexia: evidence from diffusion tensor imaging. In: Wolf M. (Ed.) Dyslexia, Fluency, and the Brain. Baltimore, MD: York Press, 2001, pp. 3–17.

[88] Fields D. Myelination: an overlooked mechanism of synaptic plasticity? Neuroscientist 2005;11(6):528–31.

[89] Hasan KM, Molfese DL, Walimuni IS, Stuebing KK, Papanicolaou AC, Narayana PA, Fletcher JM. Diffusion tensor quantification and cognitive correlates of the macrostructure and microstructure of the corpus callosum in typically developing and dyslexic children. NMR in Biomedicine 2012;25(11):1263–70.

[90] Vandermosten M, Poelmans H, Sunaert S, Ghesquière P, Wouters J. White matter lateralization and interhemispheric coherence to auditory modulations in normal reading and dyslexic adults. Neuropsychologia 2013;51(11):2087–99.

[91] Shaywitz SE, Shaywitz BA, Pugh KR, Fulbright RK, Constable RT, Mencl WE, Gore JC. Functional disruption in the organization of the brain for reading in dyslexia. Proc Nat Acad Sci 1998;95(5):2636–41.

[92] Brunswick N, McCrory E, Price CJ, Frith CD, Frith U. Explicit and implicit processing of words and pseudowords by adult developmental dyslexics: a search for Wernicke's Wortschatz? Brain 1999;122(10):1901–17.

[93] Temple E, Poldrack RA, Salidis J, Deutsch GK, Tallal P, Merzenich MM, Gabrieli JDE. Disrupted neural responses to phonological and orthographic processing in dyslexic children: an fMRI study. Neuroreport 2001;12(2):299–307.

[94] Frost SJ, Landi N, Mencl WE, Sandak R, Fulbright RK, Tejada ET, Jacobsen L, Grigorenko EL, Constable RT, Pugh KR. Phonological awareness predicts activation patterns for print and speech. Anna Dyslexia 2009;59(1):78–97.

[95] Vellutino FR, Fletcher JM, Snowling MJ, Scanlon DM. Specific reading disability (dyslexia): what have we learned in the past four decades? J Child Psychol Psychiatr 2004;45(1):2–40.

[96] Shaywitz BA, Shaywitz SE, Blachman BA, Pugh KR, Fulbright RK, Skudlarski P, Mencl WE, Constable RT, Holahan JM, Marchione KE, Fletcher JM, Lyon GR, Gore JC. Development of left occipitotemporal systems for skilled reading in children after a phonologically-based intervention. Biol Psychiatr 2004;55(9):926–33.

[97] Simos PG, Fletcher JM, Bergman E, Breier JJ, Foorman BR, Castillo EM, Davis RN, Fitzgerald M, Papanicolaou AC. Dyslexia-specific brain activation profile becomes normal following successful remedial training. Neurology 2002;58(8):1203–13.

[98] Shaywitz BA, Shaywitz SE, Blachman BA, Pugh KR, Fulbright RK, Skudlarski P, Mencl WE, Constable RT, Holahan JM, Marchione KE, Fletcher JM, Lyon GR, Gore JC. Development of left occipitotemporal systems for skilled reading in children after a phonologically-based intervention. Biol Psychiatr 2004;55(9):926–33.

[99] Maurer U, Brem S, Kranz F, Bucher K, Benz R, Halder P, Steinhausen H, Brandeis D. Coarse neural tuning for print peaks when children learn to read. NeuroImage 2006;33(2):749–58.

[100] Scarborough HS. Developmental relationships between language and reading: Reconciling a beautiful hypothesis with some ugly facts. In: Catts HW, Kamhi AG. (Eds.) The Connections between Language and Reading Disabilities. New Jersey: Lawrence Erlbaum, 2005, pp. 3–22.

[101] Galaburda AM. Ordinary and extraordinary brain development: Anatomical variation in developmental dyslexia. Anna Dyslexia 1989;39(1):65–80.

[102] Poldrack RA. A structural basis for developmental dyslexia: evidence from diffusion tensor imaging. In: Wolf M. (Ed.) Dyslexia, Fluency, and the Brain. Baltimore, MD: York Press, 2001, pp. 3–17.

[103] Stein J. Dyslexia: the role of vision and visual attention. Curr Develop Disord Rep 2014;1(4):267–80.

[104] Ahissar M, Lubin Y, Katz HP, Banai K. Dyslexia and the failure to form a perceptual anchor. Nat Neurosci 2006;9(12):1558–64.

[105] Ahissar M. Dyslexia and the anchoring-deficit hypothesis. Trend Cogn Sci 2007;11(11):458–65.

[106] Scarborough HS. Connecting early language and literacy to later reading (dis)abilities: evidence, theory and practice. In: Fletcher-Campbell F, Soler J, Reid G. (Eds.) Approaching Difficulties in Literacy Development: Assessment, Pedagogy and Programmes. New York: Sage, 2009, pp. 23–38.

[107] Scarborough HS, Dobrich W. Development of children with early language delay. J Speech Language Hearing Res 1990;33(1):70–83.

[108] Galaburda AM. Ordinary and extraordinary brain development: anatomical variation in developmental dyslexia. Anna Dyslexia 1989;39(1):65–80.

[109] Poldrack RA. A structural basis for developmental dyslexia: evidence from diffusion tensor imaging. In: Wolf M. (Ed.) Dyslexia, Fluency, and the Brain. Baltimore, MD: York Press, 2001, pp. 3–17.

[110] Stein J. Dyslexia: the role of vision and visual attention. Curr Develop Disord Rep 2014;1(4):267–80.

[111] Witton C, Talcott JB, Hansen PC, Richardson AJ, Griffiths TD, Rees A, Stein JF, Green GGR. Sensitivity to dynamic auditory and visual stimuli predicts nonword reading ability in both dyslexic and normal readers. Curr Biol 1998;8(14):791–7.

[112] Farmer ME, Klein RM. The evidence for a temporal processing deficit linked to dyslexia: a review. Psychonom Bull Rev 1995;2(4):460–93.

[113] Stein J, Walsh V. To see but not to read; the magnocellular theory of dyslexia. Trend Neurosci 1997;20(4):147–52.

[114] Hari R, Renvall H. Impaired processing of rapid stimulus sequences in dyslexia. Trend Cogn Sci 2001;5(12):525–32.

[115] Amitay S, Ben-Yehudah G, Banai K, Ahissar M. Disabled readers suffer from visual and auditory impairments but not from a specific magnocellular deficit. Brain 2002;125(10):2272–85.

[116] Talcott JB, Witton C, Hebb GS, Stoodley CJ, Westwood EA, France SJ, Hansen PC, Stein JF. On the relationship between dynamic visual and auditory processing and literacy skills: Results from a large primary-school study. Dyslexia, 2002;8(4):204–25.

[117] Cohen-Mimran R, Sapir S. Auditory temporal processing deficits in children with reading disabilities. Dyslexia 2007;13(3):175–92.

[118] Ziegler JC, Pech-Georgel C, Dufau S, Grainger J. Rapid processing of letters, digits and symbols: what purely visual-attentional deficit in developmental dyslexia? Develop Sci 2010;13(4):F8–14.

[119] Lervåg A, Hulme C. Rapid automatized naming (RAN) taps a mechanism that places constraints on the development of early reading fluency. Psychol Sci 2009;20(8):1040–8.

[120] Temple E, Poldrack RA, Salidis J, Deutsch GK, Tallal P, Merzenich MM, Gabrieli JDE. Disrupted neural responses to phonological and orthographic processing in dyslexic children: an fMRI study. Neuroreport 2001;12(2):299–307.

[121] Gaab N, Gabrieli JDE, Deutsch GK, Tallal P, Temple E. Neural correlates of rapid auditory processing are disrupted in children with developmental dyslexia and ameliorated with training: an fMRI study. Restor Neurol Neurosci 2007;25(3–4):295–310.

[122] Stein J. Dyslexia: the role of vision and visual attention. Curr Develop Disord Rep 2014;1(4):267–80.

[123] Lovegrove B. Dyslexia and a transient/magnocellular pathway deficit: the current situation and future directions. Austral J Psychol 1996;48(3):167–71.

[124] Stein J, Walsh V. To see but not to read; the magnocellular theory of dyslexia. Trend Neurosci 1997;20(4):147–52.

[125] Stein J, Walsh V. To see but not to read; the magnocellular theory of dyslexia. Trend Neurosci 1997;20(4):147.

[126] Salmelin R, Kiesilä P, Uutela K, Service E, Salonen O. Impaired visual word processing in dyslexia revealed with magnetoencephalography. Annal Neurol 40(2):157–62.

[127] Livingstone MS, Rosen GD, Drislane FW, Galaburda AM. Physiological and anatomical evidence for a magnocellular defect in developmental dyslexia. Proc Nat Acad Sci 1991;88(18):7943–7.

[128] Vidyasagar TR, Pammer K. Dyslexia: a deficit in visuo-spatial attention, not in phonological processing. Trend Cogn Sci 2010;14(2):57–63.

[129] Vidyasagar TR. Attentional gating in primary visual cortex: a physiological basis for dyslexia. Perception 2005;34(8):903–11.

[130] Sireteanu R, Goebel C, Goertz R, Wandert T. Do children with developmental dyslexia show a selective visual attention deficit? Strabismus 2006;14(2):85–93.

[131] Misra M, Katzir T, Wolf M, Poldrack RA. Neural systems for rapid automatized naming in skilled readers: unraveling the RAN-reading relationship. Sci Stud Reading 2004;8(3):241–56.

[132] Vidyasagar TR, Pammer K. Dyslexia: a deficit in visuo-spatial attention, not in phonological processing. Trend Cogn Sci 2010;14(2):57–63.

[133] Amitay S, Ben-Yehudah G, Banai K, Ahissar M. Disabled readers suffer from visual and auditory impairments but not from a specific magnocellular deficit. Brain 2002;125(10):2272-85.

[134] Ramus F, Rosen S, Dakin SC, Day BL, Castellote JM, White S, Frith U. Theories of developmental dyslexia: insights from a multiple case study of dyslexic adults. Brain 2003;126(4):841–65.

[135] Ziegler JC, Pech-Georgel C, Dufau S, Grainger J. Rapid processing of letters, digits and symbols: what purely visual-attentional deficit in developmental dyslexia? Develop Sci 2010;13(4):F8–14.

[136] Schulte-Körne G, Deimel W, Bartling J, Remschmidt H. Auditory processing and dyslexia: evidence for a specific speech processing deficit. Neuroreport 1998;9(2):337–40.

[137] Stein J. Dyslexia: the role of vision and visual attention. Curr Develop Disord Rep 2014;1(4):267–80.

[138] Brennan A, Worrall L, McKenna K. The relationship between specific features of aphasia-friendly written material and comprehension of written material for people with aphasia: an exploratory study. Aphasiology 2005;19(8):693–711.

[139] Martelli M, Di Filippo G, Spinelli D, Zoccolotti P. Crowding, reading, and developmental dyslexia. J Vision 2009;9(4):article 14.

[140] Legge GE, Bigelow CA. Does print size matter for reading? A review of findings from vision science and typography. J Vision 2011;11(5):article 8.

[141] Spinelli D, De Luca M, Judica A, Zoccolotti P. Crowding effects on word identification in developmental dyslexia. Cortex 2002;38(2):179–200.

[142] O'Brien BA, Mansfield JS, Legge GE. The effect of print size on reading speed in dyslexia. J Res Reading 2005;28(3):332–49.

[143] Yu D, Cheung S, Legge GE, Chung STL. Effect of letter spacing on visual span and reading speed. J Vision 2007;7(2):article 2.

[144] Chung STL. The effect of letter spacing on reading speed in central and peripheral vision. Investig Ophthalmol Visual Sci 2002;43(4):1270–6.

[145] Yu D, Cheung S, Legge GE, Chung STL. Effect of letter spacing on visual span and reading speed. J Vision 2007;7(2):article 2.

[146] De Luca M, Burani C, Paizi D, Spinelli D, Zoccolo Z. Letter and letter-string processing in developmental dyslexia. Cortex 2010;46(10):1272–83.

[147] Arditi A, Knoblauch K, Grunwald I. Reading with fixed and variable character pitch. J Optics Soc Am 1990;7(10):2011–15.

[148] Di Filippo G, Brizzolara D, Chilosi A, De Luca M, Judica A, Pecini C, Spinelli D, Zoccolotti P. Naming speed and visual search deficits in readers with disabilities: evidence from an orthographically regular language (Italian). Develop Neuropsychol 2006;30(3):885–904.

[149] De Luca M, Burani C, Paizi D, Spinelli D, Zoccolo Z. Letter and letter-string processing in developmental dyslexia. Cortex 2010;46(10):1272–83.

[150] Martelli M, Di Filippo G, Spinelli D, Zoccolotti P. Crowding, reading, and developmental dyslexia. J Vision 2009;9(4):article 14.

[151] Spinelli D, De Luca M, Judica A, Zoccolotti P. Crowding effects on word identification in developmental dyslexia. Cortex 2002;38(2):179–200.

[152] Lerner JW. Children with learning disabilities: theories, diagnosis, teaching strategies. Boston: Houghton Mifflin, 1976.

[153] Lerner JW. Educational interventions in learning disabilities. J Am Acad Child Adolesc Psychiat 1989;28(3):326–31.

[154] Lerner JW. Attention deficit disorders: assessment and teaching. Pacific Grove CA: Brooks/Cole, 1995.

[155] Shaywitz SE, Escobar MD, Shaywitz BA, Fletcher JM, Makuch R. Distribution and temporal stability of dyslexia in an epidemiological sample of 414 children followed longitudinally. New Eng J Med 1992;326:145–50.

[156] Elliott JG, Grigorenko EL. The dyslexia debate (No. 14). Cambridge MA: Cambridge University Press, 2014.

[157] Potter CS. Using informal phonic inventories to identify spelling error patterns in children with learning difficulties. Johannesburg: University of the Witwatersrand, International Conference on Learning Disabilities, Division of Continuing Medical Education, July, 1979.

[158] Potter CS. The Phonic Inventories: an ipsative instrument for analysing the error patterns of children. Johannesburg: University of the Witwatersrand, Department of Psychology, 1996.

[159] Potter CS. The Phonic Inventories: Test Administration Manual Version One (South African Edition). Johannesburg: University of the Witwatersrand, Department of Psychology, 2009a.

[160] Potter CS. Information for test users of the Phonic Inventories Version One (South African Edition). Johannesburg: University of the Witwatersrand, Department of Psychology, 2009b.

[161] Rebolo C. Phonic inventories: a comparison of the development of spelling patterns and errors of normal and dyslexic children in grades one to seven. Honours research dissertation. Johannesburg: University of the Witwatersrand, Department of Psychology, 2002.

[162] Els K. The use of mental imagery in improving the English spelling, reading and writing abilities of Grade IV learners with learning disabilities. Honours research dissertation. Johannesburg: University of Witwatersrand, Department of Psychology, 2003.

[163] Els K. The Use of Mental Imagery in Improving the Simultaneous and Successive Processing Abilities of Grade V Learners with Learning Disorders of Reading and Written Expression. Unpublished Masters thesis. Johannesburg: University of Witwatersrand, 2005.

[164] Grasko D. The Phonic Inventories. Unpublished Masters thesis. University of the Witwatersrand, Johannesburg, 2005.

[165] Pereira C. An analysis of the short and long-term validity of the Phonic Inventories. Unpublished Masters thesis. Johannesburg: University of the Witwatersrand, 2008.

[166] Potter CS, Grasko D, Pereira C. Using spelling error patterns to identify children with learning difficulties. SAALED International Conference "Reading for All". Nelspruit, September, 2006.

[167] Potter CS, Fridjhon P, Grasko D, Pereira C, Ravenscroft G. Spelling error profiles: An index for evaluating the learning needs and progress of children in the classroom. Pretoria, ASEASA International Conference, July, 2008.

[168] Potter CS, Fridjhon P, Grasko D, Pereira C, Ravenscroft G. Content, construct, predictive, pragmatic and viable validity: Evaluating a test's conceptual properties and utilisation potential. Johannesburg: University of the Witwatersrand, Programme Evaluation Group, Virtual Conference on Methodology in Programme Evaluation, 2010, http://wpeg.wits.ac.za

[169] Potter CS, Fridjhon P, Grasko D, Pereira C, Ravenscroft G. The Phonic Inventories: A Technical Manual. Johannesburg: University of the Witwatersrand, Department of Psychology.

[170] Callander A. Using Phonic Inventories to identify children with learning disorders or barriers to learning. B.Ed Honours research report. Johannesburg: University of the Witwatersrand, Department of Psychology, 2007.

[171] Mazansky K. Using Phonic Inventories to identify children with learning disorders/ barriers to learning with specified spelling difficulties in a mainstream Grade 6 classroom in South Africa. B.Ed Honours research report. Johannesburg: University of the Witwatersrand, Department of Psychology.

[172] Ravenscroft G, Potter CS, Fridjhon P. Using Information and Communication Technology (ICT) to identify error patterns amongst children and guide their remedial intervention. Barcelona, Proceedings International Conference ICERI 2009, pdf 1294, November, 2009.

[173] Kruger M. A comparison of reading and spelling test scores and frequency of phonic errors in a remedial and a mainstream high school. Honours research dissertation. Johannesburg: University of Witwatersrand, Department of Psychology, 2011.

[174] Sfetsios N. The Use of Mental Imagery in the Treatment of a Child with Severe Learning Difficulties. Honours research dissertation. Johannesburg: University of Witwatersrand, Department of Psychology.

[175] Sfetsios N. The Use of Mental Imagery in the Treatment of a Child with Severe Learning Difficulties. Honours research dissertation. Johannesburg: University of Witwatersrand, Department of Psychology, 2002, pp. 82–3.

[176] Sfetsios N. The Use of Mental Imagery in the Treatment of a Child with Severe Learning Difficulties. Honours research dissertation. Johannesburg: University of Witwatersrand, Department of Psychology, 2002, pp. 83–4.

[177] Dr Graeme Maxwell, neurosurgeon, Sandton Clinic, Johannesburg, telephone conversations 1995, 1996, 1997 on child Q, 2013 and 2014 on child A; diagnosis checked by reading draft of this chapter 2015.

[178] Dr Graeme Maxwell, neurosurgeon, Sandton Clinic, Johannesburg, telephone conversations 1995, 1996, 1997, 2013 and 2014; conclusions checked by reading draft of this chapter 2015.

[179] Gillingham A, Stillman BW. The Gillingham manual: remedial training for students with specific disability in reading, spelling, and penmanship. Toronto and Cambridge MA: Educators Publishing Service, 1997.

[180] Caroline, Sister M. Breaking the Sound Barrier. New York: Macmillan, 1956.

[181] Lindamood PC, and Ages PDLA. LiPS: The Lindamood phoneme sequencing® program for reading, spelling, and speech. Globe 1998;864:288–3536.

[182] Geschwind N, Levitsky W. Human brain: left-right asymmetries in temporal speech region. Science 1968;161:186–7.

[183] Schulte-Körne G, Bruder J. Clinical neurophysiology of visual and auditory processing in dyslexia: a review. Clin Neurophysiol 2010;121(11):1794–809.

[184] Stein J. Dyslexia: the role of vision and visual attention. Curr Develop Disord Rep 2014;1(4):267–80.

[185] Spinelli D, De Luca M, Judica A, Zoccolotti P. Crowding effects on word identification in developmental dyslexia. Cortex 2002;38(2):179–200.

[186] Martelli M, Di Filippo G, Spinelli D, Zoccolotti P. Crowding, reading, and developmental dyslexia. J Vision 2009;9(4):article 14.

[187] O'Brien BA, Mansfield JS, Legge GE. The effect of print size on reading speed in dyslexia. J Res Reading 2005;28(3):332–49.

[188] Brennan A, Worrall L, McKenna K. The relationship between specific features of aphasia-friendly written material and comprehension of written material for people with aphasia: an exploratory study. Aphasiology 2005;19(8):693–711.

[189] Martelli M, Di Filippo G, Spinelli D, Zoccolotti P. Crowding, reading, and developmental dyslexia. J Vision 2009;9(4):article 14.

[190] Levi DM. Crowding—An essential bottleneck for object recognition: a mini-review. Vision Res 2008;48(5):635–54.

[191] Legge GE, Bigelow CA. Does print size matter for reading? A review of findings from vision science and typography. J Vision 2011;11(5):article 8.

[192] Stein J. Dyslexia: the role of vision and visual attention. Curr Develop Disord Rep 2014;1(4):267–80.

[193] Sireteanu R, Goebel C, Goertz R, Wandert T. Do children with developmental dyslexia show a selective visual attention deficit? Strabismus 2006;14(2):85–93.

[194] Lervåg A, Hulme C. Rapid automatized naming (RAN) taps a mechanism that places constraints on the development of early reading fluency. Psychol Sci 2009;20(8):1040–8.

[195] Chomsky C. After decoding: what? Language Arts 1976;53(3):288–96.

[196] Shaywitz BA, Shaywitz SE, Blachman BA, Pugh KR, Fulbright RK, Skudlarski P, Mencl WE, Constable RT, Holahan JM, Marchione KE, Fletcher JM, Lyon GR, Gore JC. Development of left occipitotemporal systems for skilled reading in children after a phonologically-based intervention. Biol Psychiatr 2004;55(9):926–33.

[197] Legge GE, Bigelow CA. Does print size matter for reading? A review of findings from vision science and typography. J Vision 2011;11(5):article 8.

[198] Fuchs LS, Fuchs D, Hosp MK, Jenkins JR. Oral reading fluency as an indicator of reading competence: A theoretical, empirical, and historical analysis. Sci Stud Reading 2001;5(3):239–56.

[199] Stein J. Dyslexia: the role of vision and visual attention. Curr Develop Disord Rep 2014;1(4):267–80.

[200] Scarborough HS. Connecting early language and literacy to later reading (dis)abilities: evidence, theory and practice. In: Fletcher-Campbell F, Soler J, Reid G. (Eds.) Approaching Difficulties in Literacy Development: Assessment, Pedagogy and Programmes. New York: Sage, 2009, pp. 23–38.

[201] Ramus F, Rosen S, Dakin SC, Day BL, Castellote JM, White S, Frith U. Theories of developmental dyslexia: Insights from a multiple case study of dyslexic adults. Brain 2003;126(4):841–65.

[202] Ziegler JC, Pech-Georgel C, Dufau S, Grainger J. Rapid processing of letters, digits and symbols: what purely visual-attentional deficit in developmental dyslexia? Develop Sci 2010;13(4):F8–14.

[203] MacDonald P. Paired reading: a structured approach to raising attainment in literacy. Support for Learning 2010;25(1):15–23.

[204] Morgan A, Wilcox BR, Eldredge JL. Effect of difficulty levels on second-grade delayed readers using dyad reading. J Edu Res 2000;94(2):113–9.

[205] Potter CS. Vision, intention, policy and action: dimensions in curriculum evaluation. J Edu Eval 1999;8:1–29.

[206] Potter CS. Programme evaluation. In: Terreblanche M, Durrheim K. (Eds.) Research Methodology in the Social Sciences in Southern Africa, 2nd edition, Cape Town: University of Cape Town Press, 2006, pp. 209–26.

[207] Potter CS. Multimethod research. In: Wagner C, Kawulich B, Garner M. (Eds.) Doing Social Research: A Global Context. Maidenhead, Berkshire: McGrawHill, 2012, pp. 161–74.

[208] Gillingham A, Stillman BW. The Gillingham manual: Remedial training for students with specific disability in reading, spelling, and penmanship. Toronto and Cambridge MA: Educators Publishing Service, 1997.

[209] Caroline, Sister M. Breaking the Sound Barrier. New York: Macmillan, 1956.

[210] Lindamood PC, Ages PDLA. LiPS: The Lindamood phoneme sequencing® program for reading, spelling, and speech. Globe 1998;864:288–3536.

[211] Schulte-Körne G, Bruder J. Clinical neurophysiology of visual and auditory processing in dyslexia: a review. Clin Neurophysiol 2010;121(11):1794–809.

[212] Stein J. Dyslexia: the role of vision and visual attention. Curr Develop Disord Rep 2014;1(4):267–80.

[213] Spinelli D, De Luca M, Judica A, Zoccolotti P. Crowding effects on word identification in developmental dyslexia. Cortex 2002;38(2):179–200.

[214] Martelli M, Di Filippo G, Spinelli D, Zoccolotti P. Crowding, reading, and developmental dyslexia. J Vision 2009;9(4):article 14.

[215] Hewison J, Tizard J. Parental involvement and reading attainment. Edu Psychol 1980;50(3):209–15.

[216] Stahl SA, Heubach KM. Fluency-oriented reading instruction. J Literacy Res 2005;37(1):25–60.

[217] Topping KJ. Peer tutored paired reading: outcome data from ten projects. Edu Psychol: Int J Exp Edu Psychol 1987b;7(2):133–45.

[218] Topping KJ. Tutoring. Genf, Switzerland: International Academy of Education, 2000.

[219] Topping KJ. Trends in peer learning. Edu Psychol 2005;25(6):631–45.

[220] Fisher CW, Berliner DC. (Eds.) Perspectives on instructional time. New York: Longman, 1985.

[221] Hiebert EH, Fisher CW. Fluency from the first: what works with first graders. In: Rasinksi T, Blachowicz CLZ, Lems K. (Eds.) Fluency Instruction: Research-based Best Practices. New York: Guilford Press, 2006, pp. 279–95.

[222] Hiebert EH, Martin LA. Repetition of words: the forgotten variable in texts for beginning and struggling readers. Finding the right texts: what works for beginning and struggling readers, 2007, 47–69.

5

Support for Learning of Dynamic Performance of Electrical Rotating Machines by Virtual Models

Viliam Fedák and Pavel Záskalický

Additional information is available at the end of the chapter

Abstract

The undergraduate electrical machines course belongs to basic courses in electrical engineering. It is especially crucial for the students studying continuing subjects like electrical drives and control of electrical drives. Thus, a good knowledge of the behavior of electrical machines in various control modes and various supply and the changeable parameters of machines is needed to understand the behavior of machines. This chapter deals with the development of virtual models of two electrical machines in MATLAB GUIDE: an one-phase motor and a stepper motor. It serves as a guide for similar applications; only the necessary explanation of the machines operation and their mathematical models is presented, which creates a core of developed virtual models. The graphical user interfaces contribute in modernizing the electrical machines course and in enriching their attractiveness by a fast and comfortable visualization of the machine performance at their changeable control modes and parameters. They also serve as an introduction to the measurement of real machines in the laboratory. Of course, the teacher is expected to clarify the obtained graphical results and phenomena running in real machines corresponding to the machine behavior.

Keywords: Virtual model, one-phase induction motor, stepper motor, MATLAB GUI, simulation

1. Introduction

An electrical machine is a complex device being multidomain by nature, involving electromagnetic, mechanical, and thermal phenomena. Thus, the subject of electrical machines is highly multidisciplinary and holds a significant position in engineering education. The knowledge obtained in the electrical machines subject presents a starting point in the whole series of subjects like electrical drives, controlled drives, motion control, control of robots, control of mechatronic systems (industrial lines), etc.

This is why the subject Electrical Machines requires a solid understanding of energy conversion and a good knowledge of physics and physical thinking, supported by mathematical background. Here a student learns the principles of motion and the operation of various types of electrical machines in order to evaluate the influence of various changeable parameters on the performance of the machine. The contribution describes one of possibilities how to improve training methods from the subject of electrical machines.

The main objective of practical training from the subject Electrical Machines is to verify theoretical knowledge from the lectures. It is required that the students should have a good knowledge about the machine construction and its behavior before they enter the laboratory to measure to investigate the machine. There they learn how to understand deeper the substance of the measured machines, to avoid any damage of equipment, and to maintain safety of the work. Classical lectures and printed materials cannot offer students enough possibility to prepare themselves satisfactory for the labs. They give theoretical explanation, but the deep understanding of the machine behavior can be grasped through hands-on experimentation. Also, the time and the space available within courses on electrical machines are not elastic for the verification of various modes and for checking the influence of changeable parameters of a machine on its performance and characteristics.

Various animation models used for the explanation of the phenomena usually do not offer the required variety of a virtual experimentation to get information about the real data of the machine. By contrast, various simulation models offer a possibility to verify the machine performance, but a problem arises here-the learner should master a simulation program. Moreover, a possibility of obtaining false results is very high, not speaking about any user-friendly changing parameters of the machine and other optional parameters to change machine dynamics.

Like pointed out by Dongmei et al in [1], the verification of static and dynamic properties of electrical machines by the application of virtual models, where the mathematical and simulation models are hidden and working in the background, is becoming a key element of modern electrical engineering school. The readiness of the application of virtual dynamical models of electrical machines and drive systems for their analyzing is not disputable (not speaking about cost and time saving). Nice application of using simulation techniques applied to the learning of Electrical Machines is shown in Djeghloud et al in [2]. An example of simulation of a synchronous generator based on it a remote access to the electrical machines remote lab has been published by Martis et al in [3].

MATLAB GUI (graphical user interface) in connection with the Simulink program (and also with some special toolboxes like SimPowerSystems, SymbolicMath toolbox and Control toolbox) presents an extremely suitable tool for the development of purpose-oriented virtual model of any dynamical system. Easy and comfortable change of parameters by control elements, such as push and radio buttons, text boxes, and visualization of results, enables the operation of virtual models either without any deep knowledge of their substance or without any complex programming and debugging of the models.

The proposed chapter presents an extension of the knowledge presented in a series publications by Fedak et al. [5-7] and a continuation of the development of the teaching aids by the application of the virtual models to more specialized topics not described there – a single-phase machine and a stepper machine, including their supply and modes of the operation. This chapter is more-or-less technically oriented and presents a practical guide for the development of a whole series of virtual models of electrical machines to be utilized in the teaching process.

This chapter is organized as follows: for each motor, it starts with its brief description and some peculiarities of motor starting, followed by mathematical and simulation models, and continued by a series of graphs from the simulation to document the behavior and correctness of the model. The simulation model creates a core of the virtual model. The screen of the virtual model was carefully designed from a pedagogical point of view, having in mind easy operation and well arrangement of input (sliders, buttons, and text boxes) and output elements (graphs). Finally, the experience of using the virtual models in teaching several subjects is described, and an evaluation of questionnaires is presented.

2. Methodology of virtual models design of electrical machines

In designing successful virtual models, it is necessary to preserve some basic rules, especially in designing the screen, which are as follows:

- The model should be easy to operate, without any special guide.

- The screen should contain the basic information and cannot be overcrowded by supplementary information taking the learner's attention and concentration. For example, the parameters of the machine that input into the solution in the beginning of any simulation should be hidden, usually on the second screen.

- A proper ergonomic arrangement of the elements upon the screen should be kept. It covers the placement of:

  o controlling elements like buttons, sliders, etc.

  o edit/text boxes (input data, system parameters, and various scales), and

  o output information to display-graphs, number, texts, and figures.

Basic rules to place the control, input, and output elements as well as the procedures were published in previous publications [5-7].

3. Virtual model development of a single-phase induction machine

Single-phase induction motors are widely used in applications, and they excel in its simplicity, undemandingness, and reliability. They are also affordably priced. Usually, they are of smaller powers, approximate in the range of tens of watts to kilowatts units, and typically they are used in household appliances (because usually the single-phase supply system is available in the home distribution of electrical energy).

3.1. Principle of operation

The mechanical construction of the single-phase induction motor does not differ much from the three-phase one. Different is the way of arrangement of the stator winding and supply: one winding in the stator of the single-phase induction motor cannot create rotating magnetic field necessary for running the machine, but it produces only a vibrant field. The rotor will not start without any auxiliary winding. This is why the motor has two stator windings – the main and the auxiliary ones. The motor power is transmitted through the main winding, which is stored in two-thirds of the stator slots and is supplied directly from the single-phase network. The auxiliary winding is rated for lower current than the main winding. In interactivity having the main winding, its aim is to develop rotating magnetic field with the form approaching as the most to the circular shape.

The single-phase induction motors are distinguished by the structure of the rotor motor with wound rotor and squirrel cage rotor. The cage motor is used only for small performances.

3.2. Modes of starting

To get the rotating magnetic field, the current in the auxiliary winding shall be displaced by 90° from the current in the main winding. This is achieved by connecting an inductor or a capacitor in series with the auxiliary winding and parallel connection of the circuit to the main winding connected to the supply. For this reason, a suitable reactance is connected into the auxiliary winding (Figure 1). Here we recognize the following:

a.   Starting with inductor (Figure 1a). This is seldom used (it results in a lower efficiency)

b.   Starting with capacitor (Figure 1b): connected full time or by a double capacitor.

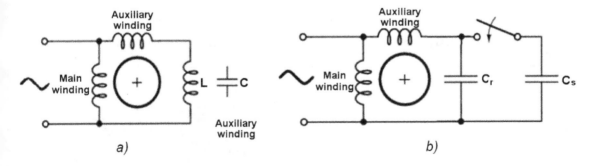

Figure 1. Starting modes of one-phase induction machine.

The capacitor C_r connected into the auxiliary phase is optimally calculated according to the following equation:

$$C_r = 2200 \frac{P_N}{U_N^2} \left[\mu F; \ W, \ V \right] \tag{1}$$

The one-phase induction motor is supplied by an alternating sinusoidal harmonic voltage that is generated by a simple harmonic oscillator in the model, having on its output the signal of harmonic voltage with the amplitude U_{1n} and frequency f_1 corresponding to the supply net. To achieve the starting torque, which is equal to the nominal, two to three times larger capacitor C_s is required, i.e.,

$$C_s = (2 \div 3) C_r \tag{2}$$

3.3. The one-phase induction motor model

The motor mathematical model consists of models of electrical and mechanical parts. The electrical part is represented by the scheme in Figure 2.

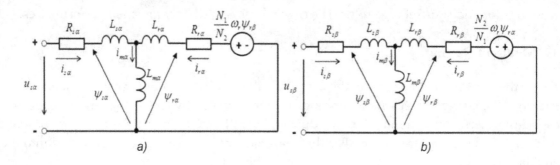

Figure 2. Equivalent circuits: (a) the main winding and (b) the auxiliary winding.

Based on the equivalent circuits and dynamic equation of the motor, the mathematical equations with their representations are shown in Table 1.

Equation for	Mathematical model (equations)	Simulation model in Simulink
stator magnetic flux	$\psi_{s\alpha} = L_{s\alpha} i_{s\alpha} + L_{m\alpha} i_{r\alpha}$	
	$\psi_{s\beta} = L_{s\beta} i_{s\beta} + L_{m\beta} i_{r\beta}$	A similar simulation scheme to the previos one with corresponding parameters and variables

Equation for	Mathematical model (equations)	Simulation model in Simulink
rotor agnetic flux	$\psi_{r\alpha} = L_{m\alpha} i_{s\alpha} + L_{r\alpha} i_{r\alpha}$	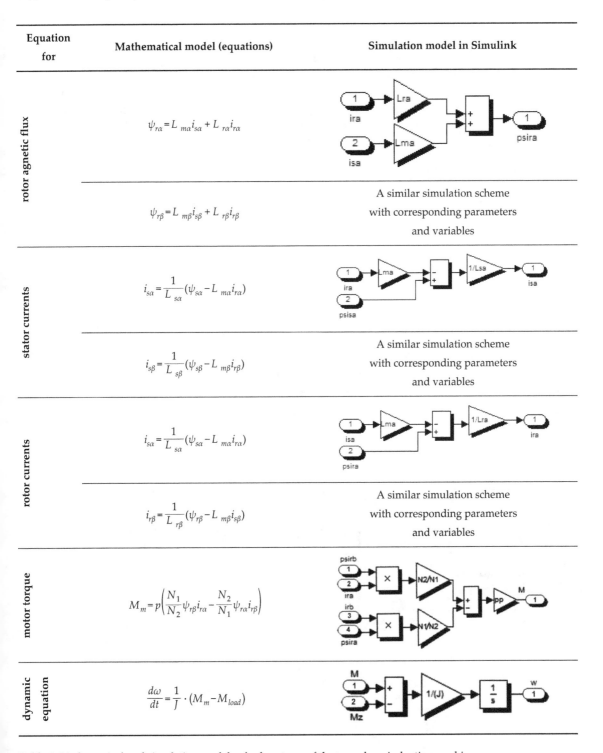
	$\psi_{r\beta} = L_{m\beta} i_{s\beta} + L_{r\beta} i_{r\beta}$	A similar simulation scheme with corresponding parameters and variables
stator currents	$i_{s\alpha} = \dfrac{1}{L_{s\alpha}}(\psi_{s\alpha} - L_{m\alpha} i_{r\alpha})$	
	$i_{s\beta} = \dfrac{1}{L_{s\beta}}(\psi_{s\beta} - L_{m\beta} i_{r\beta})$	A similar simulation scheme with corresponding parameters and variables
rotor currents	$i_{s\alpha} = \dfrac{1}{L_{s\alpha}}(\psi_{s\alpha} - L_{m\alpha} i_{r\alpha})$	
	$i_{r\beta} = \dfrac{1}{L_{r\beta}}(\psi_{r\beta} - L_{m\beta} i_{s\beta})$	A similar simulation scheme with corresponding parameters and variables
motor torque	$M_m = p\left(\dfrac{N_1}{N_2}\psi_{r\beta} i_{r\alpha} - \dfrac{N_2}{N_1}\psi_{r\alpha} i_{r\beta}\right)$	
dynamic equation	$\dfrac{d\omega}{dt} = \dfrac{1}{J}\cdot(M_m - M_{load})$	

Table 1. Mathematical and simulation models of subsystems of the one-phase induction machine

Combining all schemes together, we get the block diagram of the motor (Figure 3), which presents a core of the virtual model enabling deeper understanding of the phenomena in the motor at various modes of operation and supply.

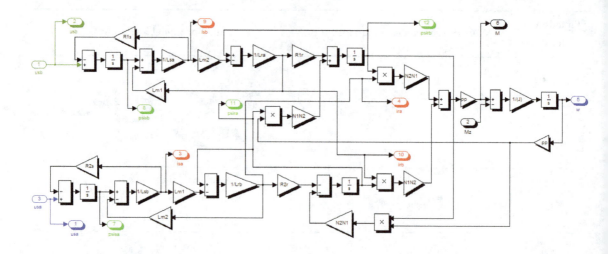

Figure 3. Simulink block diagram of one-phase induction motor.

In investigating various modes of starting and operation, it is suitable to complete the model by supplementary blocks, like harmonic oscillator generating sinus and cosinus voltages, by the switches switching the capacitors according to the chose mode of operation, and by block generating the load torque in the optional time instant of loading the machine. The final scheme, used for the virtual model, is shown in Figure 4.

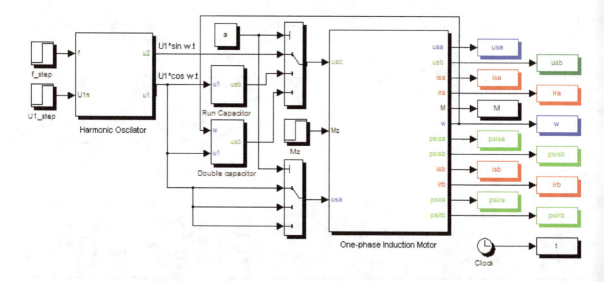

Figure 4. The model of the motor with connected inputs and outputs enabling to simulate capacitor run and double capacitor starting the motor.

3.4. Verification of the motor model with permanently connected capacitor

The speed can be changed by the frequency, by changing the number of poles, and-in a small scale-by change of the voltage or value of the capacitor. The change of the direction of rotation is simply done by the pole change of the auxiliary winding.

Time courses of the motor basic variables, motor torque, speed, and currents in both windings, are shown in Figure 5.

Simulation parameters:

$$U_1 = 230\ V, f_1 = 50\ Hz, M_{load} = 5\ Nm, C_r = 32\ \mu F, T_{sim} = 0.8\ s, T_{load} = 0.5\ s.$$

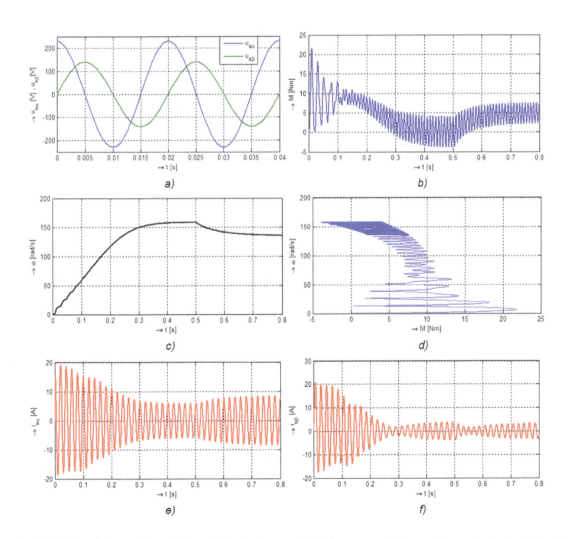

Figure 5. Time responses of the one-phase induction motor with the permanently connected capacitor in the stator reference frame $\{\alpha, \beta\}$ at starting and loading the motor in the time 0.5 s: (a) supply voltages $u_{s\alpha}$, $u_{s\beta}$ of the motor mode; (b) motor torque M ; (c) angular speed ω; (d) static characteristic of the motor ω/M; and (d) stator currents: torque producing component $i_{s\alpha}$ and magnetic flow component $i_{s\beta}$.

3.5. One-phase motor with a double capacitor

To improve the motor performance during start period, a higher capacity is required in the auxiliary phase circuit. This is done by a capacitor C_s connected in parallel to the existing one (Figure 1b) up to the time instant the motor runs by speed about 70% ω_N, which is followed by a centrifugal switch. After disconnecting, only the capacitor C_r of a lower value remains connected permanently. The next figure (Figure 6) shows performance graphs of the motor with double capacitor.

Simulation parameters: $U_1 = 230$ V, $f_1 = 50$ Hz, $M_{load} = 5$ Nm, $C_s = 53$ µF, $C_r = 32$ µF, $\omega_n = 110$ rad/s, $T_{sim} = 0.8$ s, and $T_{load} = 0.5$ s.

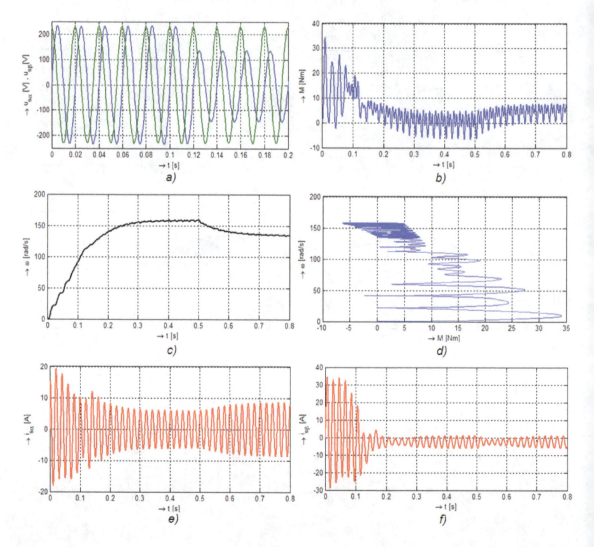

Figure 6. Time responses of the one-phase induction motor with the double-starting capacitor in the stator reference frame $\{\alpha,\beta\}$ while starting and loading the motor at time 0.5 s: (a) supply voltages $u_{s\alpha}$, $u_{s\beta}$ of the motor mode; (b) motor torque M ; (c) angular speed ω; (d) static characteristic of the motor $\omega = f(M)$; (e, f) stator currents: torque producing component $i_{s\alpha}$ and magnetic flow component $i_{s\beta}$

3.6. Comparison of the motor performance supplied by the voltages of different frequencies

To get the best motor performance, the constant stator flux must be preserved at various supply frequencies. From this condition, it follows up that U/f = const. (Figure 7).

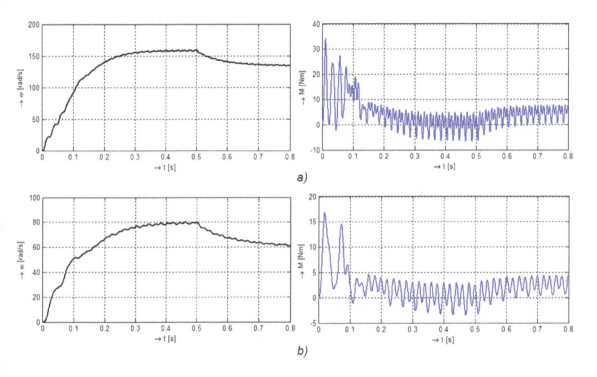

Figure 7. Time courses of the angular speed ω and motor torque at various frequencies of the supply voltage: (a) U = 230 V, f = 50 Hz, C_s= 53 µF C_r = 32 µF; (b) U = 115 V, f = 25 Hz, C_{sb} = 28 µF, C_r = 14 µF.

3.7. GUI application for the one-phase induction motor

After the verification of the mathematical model of the single-phase motor by simulation, we can design and develop the motor virtual model-graphical user interface in the MATLAB program. The application is designed so that the user is granted simple handling in adjusting motor parameters, and waveforms show typical values of the motor. Graphical user interface (GUI) allows you to visualize four different graphs: the input supply voltage, torque, angular velocity of the rotor, components of stator and rotor currents, and components of magnetic fluxes motor when starting the motor, during steady-state operation, and after loading it the chosen time. The ergonomics of handling and pedagogical respects should be strictly taken into consideration, as widely analyzed in the previous publications [1-3]. Moreover, these aspects of using the model should be also considered-they should be suitable.

1.   for explanation at lectures the phenomena and motor behavior during various operating modes and

2.   for preparation of the students for the experimentation in the labs.

3.8. GUI screen description

The developed GUI for the one-phase induction motor consists of two screens:

1. The first (auxiliary) screen (Figure 8) serves:

    a. for explanation – it displays equivalent diagram of the motor on the left side and its mathematical model on the right side. The basic differential equations describing the motor that are in boxes, the color of which corresponds to the color of the graphs

    b. for inputting the motor basic parameters.

2. The second (main) screen (Figure 9) shows the graphs of the motor variables and contains control elements for simulation models and displaying the graphs.

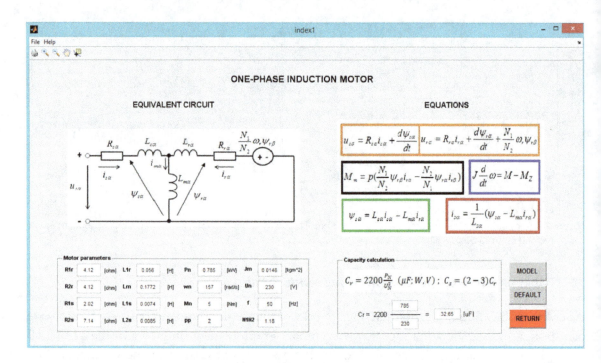

Figure 8. The screen for inputting parameters for the model of single-phase motor displaying motor equivalent diagram, equations of the model, and input motor parameters.

The panel *Motor Parameters* (Figure 10a) enable to input motor parameters and thus to verify and compare behavior of various motors. After pushing the return button, the main program starts model simulation with the actual parameters.

In the bottom-right corner, there are three buttons: the *model* button displays the motor model in the Simulink program, as shown in Figure 4 (and inside the block of the motor, the full scheme appears according to the Figure 3). The *default* button sets the preset values of the parameters, and the *return* button causes return to the second screen with the graphs, and immediately, the simulation starts with the set parameters.

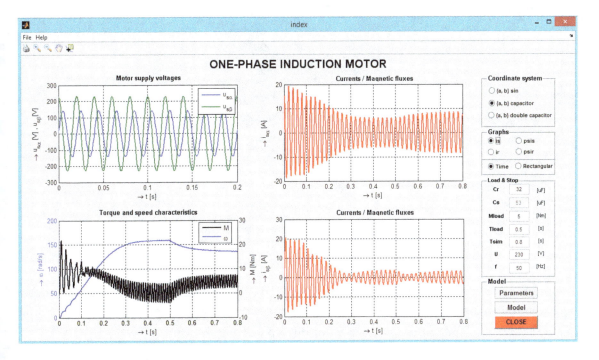

Figure 9. The GUI main screen with the graphs and control modes of calculation and visualization.

Figure 10. (a) The panel for input and changes basic parameters of the motor. (b) The panel for calculation of value of the capacitor connected into the auxiliary phase.

3.9. Description of the control panels

The panel *Coordinate system* (Figure 11a) contains three switches to choose the supply mode: (1) supply by the harmonic voltage in the $\{\alpha, \beta\}$ coordinate system connected with the stator, (2) supply with the permanently connected capacitor, and (3) supply with the double capacitor.

The panel *Graphs* (Figure 11b) consists of two parts: the upper one contains four buttons serving to choose the graphs to display stator/rotor currents or stator/rotor magnetic fluxes. By the buttons in the lower part, the time graphs ($i = f_1(t)$, $\psi = f_2(t)$) or mutual dependence of the variables is chosen ($i_\alpha = g_1(i_\beta)$, $\psi_\alpha = g_1(\psi_\beta)$). The variables of the motor we are intend to display (stator or rotor) are selected by the above-mentioned buttons.

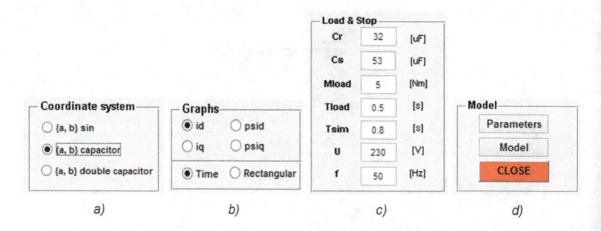

Figure 11. The GUI panels: (a) Coordinate system; (b) Graphs; (c) Load and Stop; (d) Model.

The panel *Load and Stop* (Figure 11c) shows the edit boxes for setting the values of the capacitors: permanently connected C_r, starting capacitor C_s, load torque M_{load}, time of loading T_{load}, time of simulation T_{sim}, and supply voltage U and its frequency f.

The panel *Model* (Figure 11d) contains the possibility to finish simulation and exit from the program (*Close*), displaying motor model in Simulink (*Model*), and after pushing the button *Parameters*, we switch to the screen with parameters (Figures 8 and 10a).

The panel of tools (Table 2) makes the work with the GUI comfortable. The *Tools* panel consists of five icons. The *Context* menu enables to set up line widths for the simulation courses (Line Width), to make a copy of the screen (screenshot) by saving it (Save), to run help (Help), and to close the graphical interface (Close).

🖨	**Print** - printing graphs	The context menu:
🖐	**Pan** - shifting the graph	
🔍₋	**Zoom out** - decreasing the graph	
🔍₊	**Zoom in** - zooming the graph	
⊞	**Data cursor** - showing coordinates of the points (by clicking on graph)	

Table 2. Panel of tools and menu of the graphical user Interface

4. Virtual model development of a stepper motor

Stepper motor is an asynchronous machine, the stator of which contains a control winding. The rotor is either fitted with a permanent magnet or made up of a toothed ferromagnetic magnetic circuit. The stepper motor is an impulse-excited electric machine, the movement of which is not continuous but is done stepwise. Its main advantage consists of motor performance without the necessity of any controllers, and when the motors are not overloaded, they can work without feedback. The precise control of position or rotation at a constant speed is done simply by counting steps.

According to the construction, the stepper motors are divided into three groups, [8]:

a.   Stepper motors with variable reluctance

b.   Stepper motors with permanent magnets

c.   Hybrid stepper motors

4.1. Hybrid stepper motor

The hybrid stepper motor accumulates benefits both of stepper motors with variable reluctance and permanent magnets. It has a very small step and high power per unit of weight. The arrangement of the stator winding is similar to this stepper motor with variable reluctance. It differentiates by the rotor that is made from a cylinder permanent magnet with mounted rotor poles along the circumference having teeth. The number of teeth determinates an angle step. Typically, the motors with 50 teeth are produced, in which one step is equal to the angle of 1.8°. In the stator of the hybrid stepper motor, there are usually two windings having terminals arranged as shown in Figure 12.

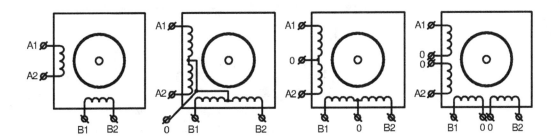

Figure 12. Twelve ways of arranging the stator windings of a two-phase hybrid stepper motor: (a) 4 wires-only start and end points are led to terminals; (b) 5 wires-also the common middle point is led out to terminals; (c) 6 wires-the middle point of each phase is led out to terminals; and (d) 8 wires-the phases are divided into the halves and the start and end points are led to the terminals.

4.2. Control of stepper motors

According to the types of the windings, the stepper motors are divided into the unipolar stepper motor and the bipolar one. Similarly, the control of the stepper motors is divided into the following:

- Unipolar control, which is mostly used for a four-phase stepper motor with variable reluctance or for hybrid stepper motors.

- Bipolar control, which is used for stepper motors with permanent magnets of for hybrid stepper motors. In this type of control, the current flows through the windings are placed opposed.

4.2.1. Four-tact control magnetizing one phase

In a simple drawing (Figure 13), the rotor is replaced by a rotating permanent magnet having the north pole (red) and the south pole (blue). By switching the stator winding phases in the in the opposite coils, the north and the south poles are also excited.

The principle of the control consists of exciting (and magnetizing) one phase only. According to the cyclogram in Figure 13a, the sequence of excitation A1-B1-A2-B2 ensures the rotation of the magnetic field in the positive direction. The change of the direction is done through reverse switching of the motor phases. Here the current flows through one winding only.

In case of bipolar control (Figure 13b), the current flows simultaneously through two opposite coils. This means the current is twice higher in comparison with the unipolar type. The bipolar control differs by the necessity of change the current direction.

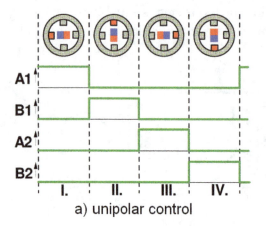 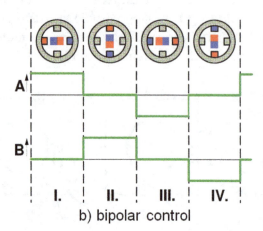

Figure 13. Cyclogram of four-tact control magnetizing one phase of a hybrid stepper motor.

4.2.2. Four-tact control magnetizing two phases

When two neighboring coils are excited simultaneously, according to the cyclogram in Figure 14, the motor torque is $\sqrt{2}$ times higher. The position of the rotor will follow the vector sum of magnetic fluxes of both phases. At this type of control, the current flows through all four windings. This type of control is used the most often.

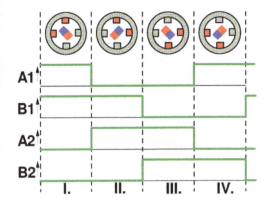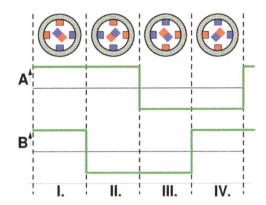

Figure 14. Cyclogram of four-tact control of a hybrid stepper motor.

4.2.3. Eight-tact control

Combining the previous two control algorithms leads to doubling the number of stable states (cyclogram in Figure 15). Consequently, an increase of positioning accuracy is achieved (called "soften up"), without changing the structural adjustment. The previous commutation (four-tact control) was the symmetrical one, and the asymmetrical eight-tact commutation causes doubling of the number of rotor steps.

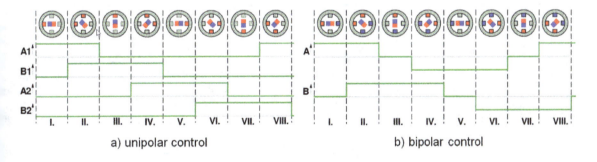

Figure 15. Eight-tact control of a hybrid stepper motor: (a) unipolar control; (b) bipolar control.

4.2.4. Further modes of the control

Other ways of controlling hybrid stepper motors exist, but due to simplification, we do not deal with them in detail here (although the modes are also included into the virtual model):

- Vector control. The commutation consists in simultaneous supplying both phases by different voltages. This enables to rotate the stator magnetic field vector by a softer step.

- Microstepper. This is done by commutation at supplying the coils by harmonic voltages that are mutually shifted by $\pi/2$. This causes a smooth, continuous movement of the rotor.

4.3. Simulation model of the hybrid stepper motor

The model of the motor consists of the electrical part (Figure 16) and mechanical part, described by the dynamic equation.

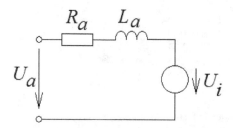

Figure 16. Equivalent circuit diagram of hybrid bipolar stepper motor for phase A; L_a presents the inductance, R_a is the resistance of phase A winding, and U_i is the electromotive force depending on the angle of the rotor.

The mathematical models of all motor subsystems together with corresponding simulation schemes are displayed in Table 3.

Equation for	Mathematical model (equations)	Simulation model in Simulink
phase currents	$$\frac{di_a}{dt} = \frac{U_a}{L_a} - \frac{R_a}{L_a} \cdot i_a + \frac{K_m}{L_a} \cdot \omega \cdot \sin(N_r \cdot \theta)$$	
phase currents	$$\frac{di_b}{dt} = \frac{U_b}{L_b} - \frac{R_b}{L_b} \cdot i_b - \frac{K_m}{L_b} \cdot \omega \cdot \sin(N_r \cdot \theta - \pi/2)$$	A similar simulation scheme with corresponding parameters and variables
phase torques	$$M_a = -K_m \cdot i_a \cdot \sin(N_r \cdot \theta)$$	
phase torques	$$M_b = -K_m \cdot i_b \cdot \sin(N_r \cdot \theta - \pi/2)$$	A similar simulation scheme with corresponding parameters and variables
aretating torque	$$M_d = -T_{dm} \cdot \sin(N_r \cdot \theta)$$	

Equation for	Mathematical model (equations)	Simulation model in Simulink
Total motor torque	$M_c = M_a + M_b + M_d$	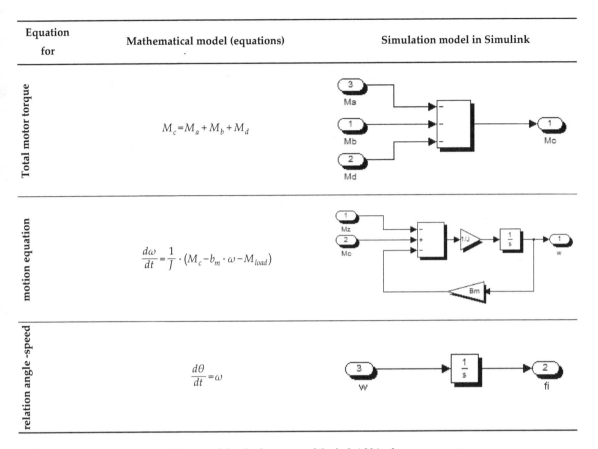
motion equation	$\dfrac{d\omega}{dt} = \dfrac{1}{J} \cdot (M_c - b_m \cdot \omega - M_{load})$	
relation angle -speed	$\dfrac{d\theta}{dt} = \omega$	

Table 3. Mathematical and simulation models of subsystems of the hybrid bipolar stepper motor

Figure 17 shows the complete simulation scheme consisting of the schemes of subsystems.

4.4. Simulation results of hybrid bipolar stepper motor at various control modes

A series of experiments before developing the GUI was done in order to verify correctness of the developed motor simulation model.

The hybrid bipolar stepper motor parameters used for simulation are as follows: $L_a = L_b = 0.058$ H, $R_a = R_b = 30\ \Omega$, $S_a = 1.8°$, $N_r = 50$, $K_m = 0.8$ Nm/A, $T_d = 0$ Nm, $b_m = 8.10^{-4}$ Nms/rad (damping coefficient), $M_{load} = 0.1$ Nm, $U = 12$ V, and $J = 6.10^{-6}$ kg m^2.

The motor simulation schemes were completed by schemes of simplified voltage sources, enabling control of the chosen stepper motor by whether the full step, half step, reduced (or shortened) step, or microstep.

Just note that the time courses in Figures 18-22 were obtained from the graphical user interface of the hybrid bipolar stepper motor (explained in detail later, in the subchapter 4.5). The graphs display the motor torque M, the angular speed ω, and the angle of displacement θ, and there are courses of the current and supply voltage at the bottom.

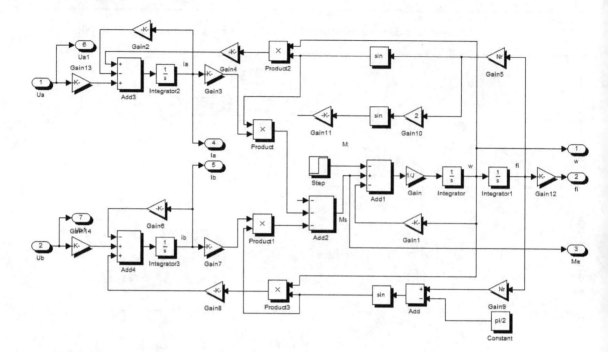

Figure 17. Simulation model of a hybrid bipolar stepper motor in Simulink

4.4.1. Motor control at full step and magnetizing one phase only

The angular displacement starts after the voltage is connected to phase B (Figure 18). The angular step displacement is 1.8° (i.e., 90/50). The load torque influence on the angular displacement is very small.

4.4.2. Motor control at full step and magnetizing two phases

The step displacement in this control mode control comes to a half in comparison with the previous case 0.9° (Figure 19). Also, the load torque has lesser influence on the angular displacement like in the previous case.

4.4.3. Motor control at the half step

Interchange of active coils results in a varying torque and angular velocity, as shown in the simulation results of half-step (Figure 20). The angle displacement step is 0.9°.

4.4.4. Vector control of the motor

In the vector control, two phases are supplied by different voltages (Figure 21). This allows the rotation of the vector of the stator magnetic field. In our case, the nominal value of the voltages U_1 and the second one has the value that ensures the constant step. In this case, this is $U_2 = 0.4U_1$.

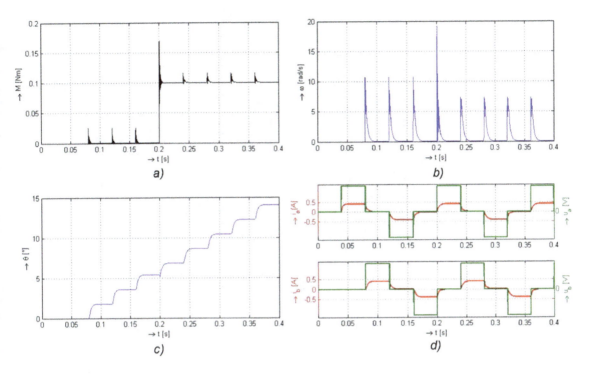

Figure 18. Time courses of the hybrid bipolar stepper motor at full step and magnetizing one phase.

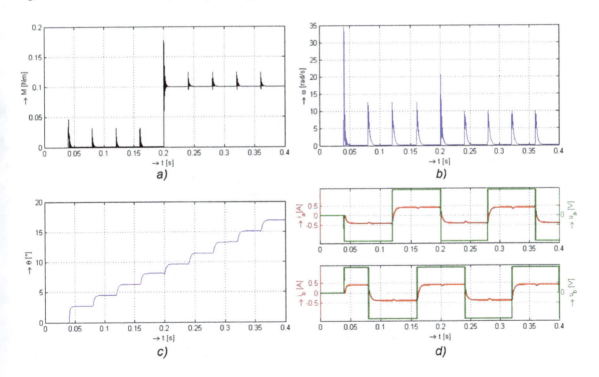

Figure 19. Time courses at the full step and magnetizing both phases.

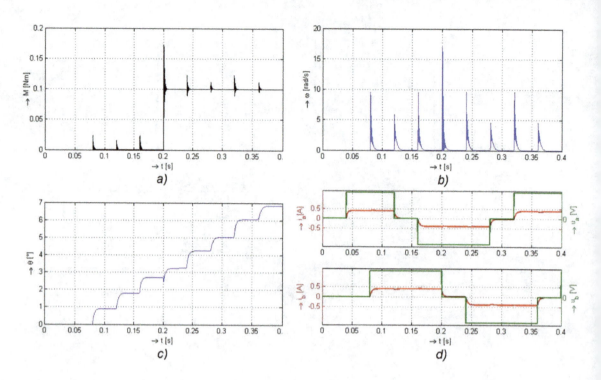

Figure 20. Time courses for the chosen half step.

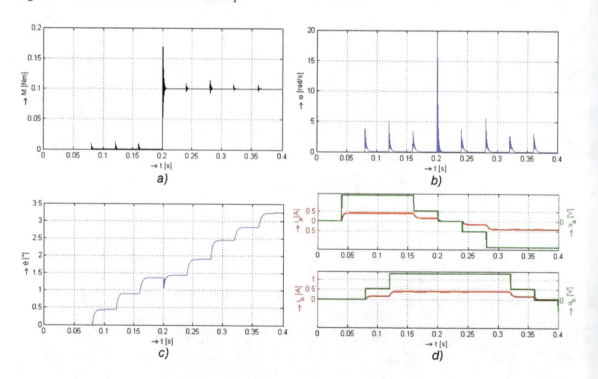

Figure 21. Time courses for vector control and step equal to 0.45°

4.4.5. Microstepper of the motor

At microstepper, one phase is supplied by the sine voltage and the second phase by the cosine voltage (Figure 22). It is possible to replace the harmonic voltage by a discrete course with a low frequency of 1.5 Hz. The achieved final step is 0.21°.

4.5. GUI for the hybrid stepper motors

Similarly, like in the previous case, GUI application was developed for analyzing both the bipolar and unipolar hybrid stepper motors. The chosen supply mode is selected by a button. The application allows to implement a simple change of parameters to choose the mode of the motor run to load the motor and to visualize results in four basic charts: for the motor torque, angular speed, the angle of the rotation of the rotor and the line voltage, and the currents in the respective phases.

4.5.1. Description of the screen with graphs

The GUI screen (Figure 23) displays the motor torque M, the angular speed ω, the angle of displacement θ, and there are courses of the current and supply voltage at the bottom.

The panel *Type of Motor* (upper right) contains two buttons: Bipolar SM and Unipolar SM, where the user selects the mode of basic control of the stepper motor. After selecting the chosen mode, the button turns green.

The panel *Control Mode* (Figure 24a) contains three further subpanels. In the subpanel *Direction*, a direction of rotation is chosen; in the subpanel *Step Modes*, a value of the step is chosen from the choice: full step, half step, reduced or shortened step for the vector control, and, the last choice, microstep. In the last subpanel *Power Supply Phase*, it is possible to choose either the active one or both phases of the motor (this possibility is available only when the full step is chosen).

In the panel *Other Simulation Parameters* (Figure 24b), the user inputs further information required by some modes of control. Here the first panel box is accessible only if a reduced step is chosen in the control mode panel. This gives a possibility to choose a reduced step divided into four parts or into eight. The next panel box is available when the microstep is chosen. The choice gives a possibility to change the frequency of the input sinus-cosinus signals. By the Slider Step Size, it is possible to soften the step size. In the last panel box, it is possible to change the time of simulation T_s, and the parameter T_v is related to the microstepper (the text box is available only when the microstepper mode is chosen).

The tools panel and the context menu have similar meaning like in the previous case (see Table 2). At the mentioned step choice, the user can change the direction of rotation of the motor to select other cyclogram of motor supply, to choose the length of each cyclogram (by the parameter T_v), to change the frequency of a voltage supply at the microstepper, and to choose the step size when the movement of the rotor is continuous.

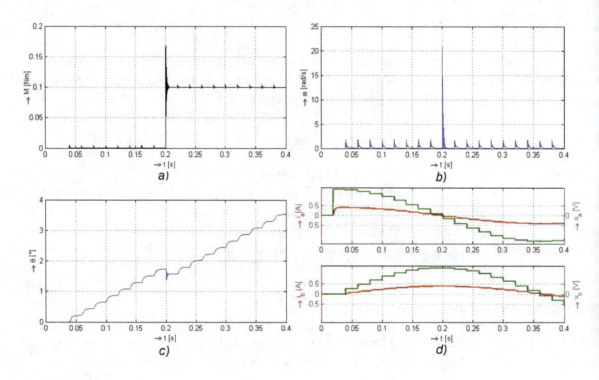

Figure 22. Time courses at the microstepper with the step 0.21°.

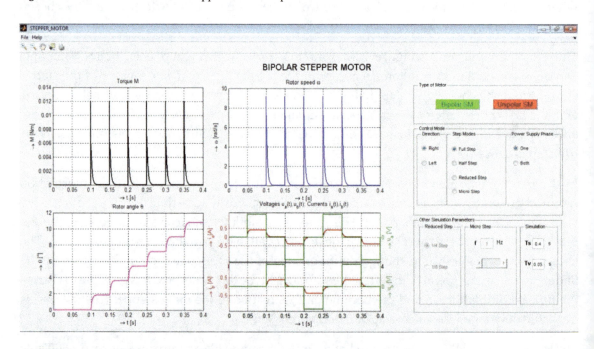

Figure 23. GUI screen for the stepper motor.

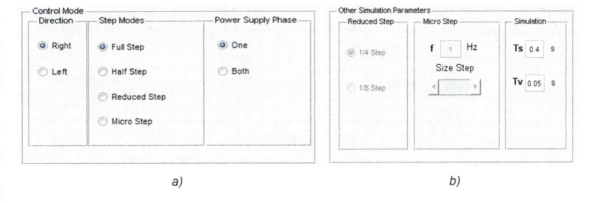

a)   b)

Figure 24. The panels (a) for selection of the stepper motor control mode and (b) for inputting control and simulation parameters.

4.5.2. The screen for inputting parameters of the bipolar stepper motor

The GUI screen enables easy change of parameters of a chosen stepper motor. This GUI screen (Figure 25) appears after choice of bipolar motor-the button *Bipolar SM* in the panel *Type of Motor* (see the GUI main screen in Figure 23). The screen also displays differential equations of the mathematical model of the bipolar stepper motor and equivalent diagram of the motor one phase.

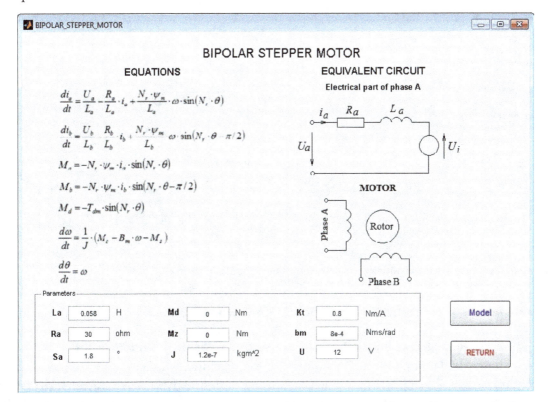

Figure 25. The GUI screen for inputting parameters for the model of bipolar hybrid stepper motor.

The parameters for any arbitrary bipolar motor are set in the bottom panel *Parameters*. After clicking the model, the Simulink model of the motor is displayed. Pushing the return button causes switch over the main screen.

4.5.3. The screen for inputting parameters of the unipolar stepper motor

After choosing the unipolar stepper motor (the button **Unipolar SM** in the main screen, Figure 22), a screen for inputting unipolar stepper motor parameters is displayed (Figure 26).

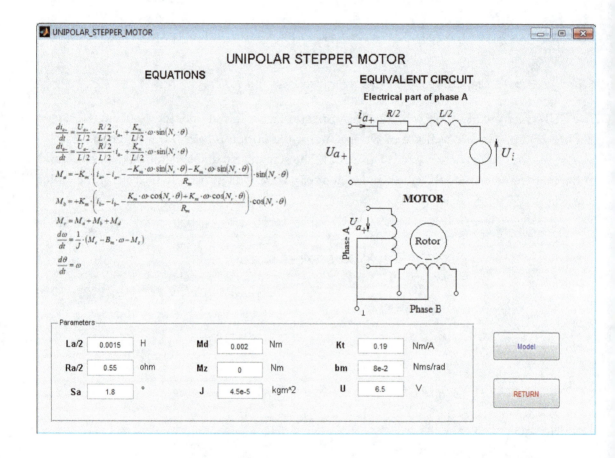

Figure 26. The GUI screen for inputting parameters for the model unipolar hybrid stepper motor.

4.6. Integration of the realized virtual models into virtual laboratory of electrical machines

The subject electrical machines taught in the second year of the undergraduate course is devoted to the explanation of the phenomena in the machine, which is supported by various animation models. During lectures, when explaining static and dynamic characteristics of each machine by presentation of demo pictures, animations, videos, and of course using the blackboard for derivation of the dependencies, the virtual models are briefly introduced. The students have a free access to the models through the institutional LAN (the access is also available in the student hostels).

In the laboratory, they measure the characteristics of the motors and compare them with those from virtual models. They also discuss and explain in detail the motor behavior and the influence of motor parameters on the characteristics.

The work with the virtual models saves time at virtual experimentation, but it requires a careful and detailed explanation and analysis of the obtained characteristics by the teacher-how and why is the behavior of the motor corresponding to the form of the characteristics. Otherwise, the students do not fully understand the graphs.

To get feedback from the students and their opinion of introducing the virtual models in the regular teaching, inspired by a questionnaire presented in [9] for Electrical Drives subject we have applied the questionnaire for the Electrical Machines subject and evaluated it (Table 4). Altogether, 36 full-time students of the bachelor study in four groups answered the questions.

#		A	B	C	D	E
Q1	My background knowledge is sufficient to understand working with of the virtual models	11	18	5	2	0
Q2	I need the help of instructor to understand graphs	16	13	3	2	2
Q3	Working with models helped me to understand better experimentation in the laboratory	27	5	2	2	0
Q4	I gained new knowledge when working with virtual models (they helped me to understand better the phenomena in electrical machines)	29	4	2	1	0
Q5	The virtual models of electrical machines are useful and I recommend to continue with their development	30	5	1	0	0
Q6	I would recommend development of similar virtual models also in other subjects	30	4	2	0	0

Evaluation criteria: A - strongly agree, B - agree, C - neutral, D - disagree, E - strongly disagree

Table 4. Questionnaire statements and their evaluation

The student ratings on the evaluation of incorporating the virtual models into teaching – both into lectures and prior laboratory work – are generally positive. It was observed that majority of students found it useful, interesting, and contributing to increasing knowledge about the subject.

The students works with the virtual models also in the following years in the subjects like:

- The subject Electrical Drives where the dynamic characteristics and the influence of parameters on the motor behavior are analyzed in connection with the power electronic converter.

- The subject Controlled Drives, for which specialized virtual modules for the subject were developed, which facilitate the calculation and verification of controllers and enable to analyze the influence of the controller parameters on the dynamic behavior of the controlled electrical drives. Of course, a connection with the practical realization is pointed out at each utilization of the virtual model.

5. Conclusion

The aim of this study was to present the methodology and results in the development of virtual models of two types of electrical machines in the MATLAB graphical development environment: the one-phase induction motor used in home applications and the stepper motor used widely in automation.

The MATLAB GUIDE, on the one hand, presents a comfortable tool enabling the development of GUI in a very easy and understandable way. On the other hand, it limits the utilization of virtual models by the necessity of the MATLAB program purchase. We do consider it as a limitation because MATLAB is widely distributed and presents a standard tool at the universities. Another solution is to use MATLAB server features through the Internet, which enables registered users (students) to utilize the developed interfaces for free. In the boundary case, a stand-alone .exe program can also be developed, but here, some special features of the MATLAB program are lost (Simulink, SymbolicMath toolbox, Animation toolbox, and some other specialties), and they are replaced by bothersome programming.

The two developed GUIs of the one-phase induction motor and of the stepper motor complete the series of virtual modules developed earlier [5] for the subject of electrical machines, like the virtual models of the DC motor, the three-phase AC motors, and the BLDC motor. The virtual models show system performance in various working points and analyze the influence of variable system parameters, modes of supply, and control parameters on system behavior.

The virtual dynamical models, on one hand, contribute to the e-learning support of teaching and, on the other hand, serve for preparation of students before entering the laboratory experimentation. Their utilization also supports and makes more attractive lectures and considerably enhances the explanation of properties of machines.

Acknowledgements

The financial support of the Slovak Grant Agency VEGA under the contract VEGA 1/0121/15 is acknowledged. The research was also supported by the project VEGA No 1/0464/15 "Research of New Principles and Methods for Design of Electrotechnical Systems".

Author details

Viliam Fedák* and Pavel Záskalický

*Address all correspondence to: Viliam.Fedak@tuke.sk

Department of Electrical Engineering and Mechatronics, Faculty of Electrical Engineering and Informatics, Technical University of Košice, Slovakia

References

[1] Dongmei Wang, Lingshun Liu, Yan Li. Discussion on teaching reform of electric machinery and drive course. In: 30-31 July 2011; Singapore. p. 1-3. DOI: ISBN 978-1-4577-0859-6

[2] Djeghloud H, Larakeb M., Bentounsi A.. Virtual labs of conventional electric machines. In: 2012 IEEE International Conference on Interactive Mobile and Computer Aided Learning (IMCL); 6-8 Nov. 2012; Amman. IEEE; 2012. p. 52-57. DOI: ISBN 978-1-4673-4924-6

[3] Martis C.S., Hedesiu H.C., Szabo L., Tataranu B., Jurca F., Oprea C.. Electrical machines virtual laboratory: grid connection of a synchronous generator. In: 12th Power Electronics and Motion Control Conference, EPE-PEMC 2006; Portoroz, Slovenia. p. 1709-1714.

[4] Mehmet Dal. Teaching electric drives control course: incorporation of active learning into the classroom. IEEE Transactions on Education. Nov. 2013;56(4):459-469.

[5] Fedak V., Balogh T., Zaskalicky P.. Dynamic simulation of electrical machines and drive systems using MATLAB GUI. In: Dr. Sergio Kofuji, editor. E-Learning. Book 4 ed. Rijeka, Croatia: INTECH-Open Access publisher of Scientific Books and Journals; 2012. p. 317-342. DOI: ISBN 979-953-307-774-0

[6] Fedak V., Durovsky F., Keusch P.. E-learning in mechatronic systems supported by virtual experimentation. In: Dr. Sergio Kofuji, editor. E-Learning. Book 4 ed. Rijeka, Croatia: INTECH-Open Access publisher of Scientific Books and Journals; 2012. p. 84-106. DOI: ISBN 979-953-307-774-0

[7] Fedak V., Balogh T., Ismeal G.A.. Virtual models of dynamic systems: design, methodology, applications, and experiences in learning of mechatronics. In: Jakab F., editor. 10th IEEE International Conference on Emerging eLearning Technologies and Applications; 8-9 Nov. 2012; StaráLesná, High Tatras, Slovakia. 2012: IEEE, Budapest; 2012. p. 111-116. DOI: ISBN 978-1-4673-5123-2

[8] Zaskalicky P.,. Krokový motor/Stepper motor. Košice: C-PRESS Košice; 2007. 97 ISBN 978-80-8073-778-8

[9] Mehmet Dal. Teaching Electric Drives Control Course: Incorporation of Active Learning Into the Classroom. IEEE Transactions on Education. Nov. 2013;56(4): 459-469.

6

Differences in Perceived Benefit, Use, and Learner Satisfaction between Open Source LMS and Proprietary LMS

Ahmad Rafi, Khairulanuar Samsudin and
Hafizul Fahri Hanafi

Additional information is available at the end of the chapter

Abstract

Currently, many institutions are using expensive proprietary learning management systems (LMSs). Open source LMSs have been introduced to offer affordable solutions; however, these solutions have not been fully embraced. The researchers undertook a study to examine the differences between these two types of LMSs. This study used a survey to collect data pertaining to perceived benefit, LMS use, and learner satisfaction. The survey sample comprised 608 information technology (IT) major undergraduates from two Malaysian universities. Two groups were set up based on the LMSs used, where the first group ($n = 290$) and the second group ($n = 318$) used the proprietary and open source solutions, respectively. Students were asked to fill out a questionnaire to elicit their opinions concerning constructs *perceived benefit*, *use*, and *learner satisfaction*, and data were analyzed using SPSS (ver. 19). Independent sample t-tests were performed, indicating that there were significant differences in the three constructs, which favored the open source solution. Correlational analysis showed that each construct correlated significantly with each other, suggesting that each contributes to the overall effectiveness of the system. These findings reinforce the imperative of deploying open source learning solutions that are not only affordable but also effective to support students' needs for effective online learning.

Keywords: Learner satisfaction, open source LMS, perceived benefit, proprietary LMS, use

1. Introduction

Today's educational realm is witnessing an ongoing tremendous transformation in the teaching and learning process as the result of the continual advancement of technology. For decades, learners were immersed in learning settings that were dictated by physical learning tools (which was naturally cumbersome), confined learning spaces, and the presence of the teacher. Then, this learning landscape changed to a better setting, with the introduction of the then technology – the monochrome television (TV). The teacher, on certain occasions, showed students the scheduled broadcast over the educational channel containing pre-recorded teaching topics relevant to the current learning objectives. In the same period, many public universities that offered distance-learning courses began to conduct such learning classes by broadcasting live lectures to students in their designated classes, which were geographically spread across the country. Even though this type of learning environment was not exactly perfect, many students managed to learn quite effectively with minimum cost. Later, this learning setting morphed into a revolutionized teaching and learning environment in response to the advancement of the personal computing platform together with the introduction of the Internet, especially the World Wide Web. Hence, the birth of electronic learning (e-learning) was inevitable, bringing in tremendous benefit to the educational, social, and economical spheres. From the educational perspective, students' independent learning becomes more intense with more online materials and contents being delivered over the Internet and Intranet. This intensification of independent learning has shifted the role of instructors – from being the teacher to the facilitator, especially in collaborative learning classes.

Given the enormous economic and educational potential of e-learning, many solutions have been introduced since the late 1990s. These solutions assume many different terms or names, such as course management system (CMS), learning content management system (LCMS), virtual learning environment (VLE), virtual learning system (VLS), learning portal, or e-learning platform, which reflects the many flavors of their functionalities. Among these, LMS is the dominant term commonly used in the educational sphere that focuses on learners rather than learning contents. The literature is quite replete with many definitions of LMS. For example, an LMS is "[a] comprehensive, integrated software [application] that the development, delivery, assessment, and administration of courses in traditional face-to-face, blended, or online learning environments" [1]. In a similar tone, Ref. [2] defined an LMS as "... as a software application for the administration, documentation, tracking, reporting and delivery of e-learning education courses or training programs."

Many learning management system (LMS) companies have entered the market to provide online learning solutions to many institutes of higher learning (IHLs). Invariably, these proprietary LMSs were, and still are, prohibitively expensive to other branches of educational sphere, such as public schools, colleges, and training institutions. The licenses of the LMSs are notoriously exorbitant, ranging from tens of thousands to hundreds of thousands (depending on the scale of users). In fact, the costing of LMS covers not only the cost of acquisition, but installation, customization, and maintenance costs as well. To highlight the impact of the preceding factors, the finding of a survey by eLearning Guild survey [3] involving 909 of its members serves as a guideline for any prospective organizations that decide to implement these learning solutions. Depending on the scale and needs of an organization, the cost of acquisition, installation, and customization can range from as low as $10,000 to more than $1 million. On top of this cost, the maintenance of such a system will incur additional cost, ranging from $10,000 to more than $250,000 annually. Clearly, the overall cost of running these learning management systems is quite staggering, especially for small organizations. Despite these cost constraints, many institutions still prefer to use proprietary LMSs because of several factors, such as ease of upgrades, security, downtime, and support, which are relatively better handled by proprietary systems [4].

In view of the high initial cost of implementation, many non-profit organizations, such as the open source software (OSS) community (which consists of dedicated individuals or teams) have begun developing their own version of LMS, with considerable degree of success. According to a white paper by Ref. [5], "[o]pen-source solutions are software for which the source code is provided under a license that permits users to access, change, and improve it." Likewise, Ref. [6] defined open source software solutions as "... computer solutions or applications that are developed, tested, updated, and distributed among the community members." The development of open source LMSs entails the utilization of open source platforms, such as PHP/MySQL, Java, Python, Ruby on Rails, or on open source content management systems (CMS), such as Joomla and Drupal [7]. In addition, open source LMSs, such as Moodle, Sakai, and Wordpress, are built on content management systems, such as Joomla and Drupal. Initially, open source systems were built for education, but now they have been adopted by both educational organizations and some companies as well [7].

From the initial outlay perspective, "several OSS systems can help mitigate the ever-increasing licensing fee of commercial providers" [8]. In fact, in certain functionalities, they may have surpassed certain performances of the proprietary LMSs. For example, better customization, intuitive navigation, "simple chat tool" [9] and "highly interactive" [10] are some of the features of the OSS systems that users found to be appealing. "Ample evidence can be gleaned from the relevant literature that supports the use of affordable OSS systems to help improve student leaning" [9,11,12]. Then again, the superiority of one system over the others may no longer hold true when the latter may have made further improvements, far exceeding the former. Nonetheless, there are bound to be intrinsic differences between OSS and licensed LMSs, which cover a range of features, functionalities, and characteristics. These differences in functionalities or features could make – depending on the background of a range of stakeholders, such as the end user (e.g., students and lecturers) and the system administrator – certain LMS systems more preferable compared to others. For example, the end user would naturally prefer an LMS system that is easy to use, while the system administrator would desire an LMS system that is easy to maintain. Irrespective of the types of LMSs, these learning solutions should be able to perform the following core functions for educational purposes as follows [2]:

- Centralize and automate administrative functions

- Use self-service and self-guided services

- Assemble and deliver learning content rapidly

- Consolidate training initiatives on a scalable web-based platform

- Support portability and standards

- Personalize content and enable knowledge reuse

Figure 1 shows a snapshot of the learning materials interface of an LMS system indicating available lecture and presentation notes to registered students of a particular course, serving as the third core function (i.e., Assemble and deliver learning content rapidly) of any LMS systems as mentioned above.

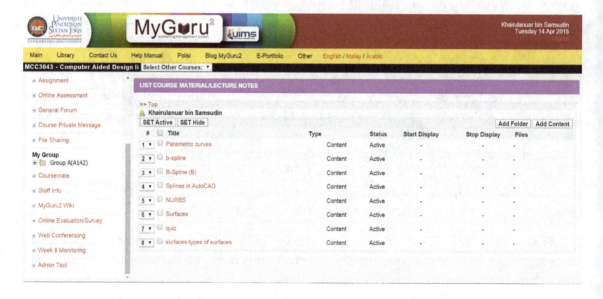

Figure 1. A snapshot of a learning materials interface

Implementing LMSs for learning purposes that involves audiences consisting of students, teachers, and administrators would entail the following features [13]:

- Registration and Enrollment options to teachers and students.

- Adding/Deleting Courses by the University/Educational Bodies.

- Setting the different User Roles and user account.

- Setting the course calendar.

- Uploading and Retrieving Assignment and Resources

- Forum module

Figure 2 shows a snapshot of the group forum interface of an LMS system that can setup to facilitate discussion among a group of students involved in a project or an assignment. Through this online forum, students will be able to discuss their ongoing work without the usual constraints faced by face-to-face discussion, namely, time and place. At any time, at any place every member of the group can compose and post comments to collaborate on that work.

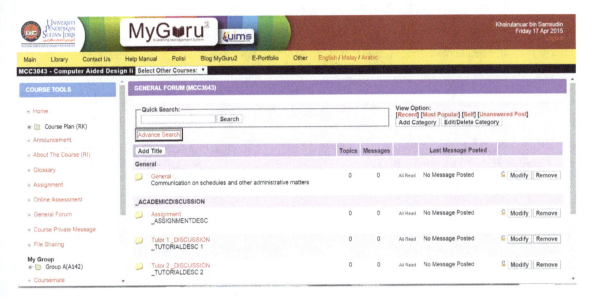

Figure 2. A snapshot of a group forum interface

In general, there are two main categories of learning management system, namely Education LMS and Corporate LMS [7]. The former primarily focuses on learners and learning facilities, launching and monitoring of online learning, and keeping record of learning activities. On the other hand, even though the latter shares similar functionalities as the former, corporate LMS is also equipped with e-Commerce capability, regulatory compliance, competency, performance, human capital, and talent management [7]. For Education LMS, there are two categories: a) commercial (proprietary) Education LMS, and b) open source Education LMS. In fact, there is another category involving systems (which is small in number) that were developed by the universities themselves. Examples of the university-built systems include Brigham Young University, Maryland University, University of Phoenix, Western Governors University, and the Oberta University in Catalonia, among others. Currently, there are about 214 commercial Education LMSs available. In contrast, for open source Education LMSs, the number is about 60, and this number is expected to grow enormously as they become more technically mature over the years, enabling improved installation and customization. Table 1 shows some examples of both types of Education LMSs commonly used by universities worldwide.

Leading commercial Education LMS include Blackboard Learn (Blackboard Inc.), Desire2Learn (D2L) Brightspace, Edmodo (Edmodo LLC), Instructure Canvas (Instructure Inc.), Pearson LearningStudio, and Schoology (Schoology, Inc.). For open source Education LMS, popular systems include ATutor (University of Toronto), eFront (Epignosis Ltd.), ILIAS 4 e-Learning, Instructure Canvas (Instructure Inc.), Moodle (open source), OpenOLAT, Sakai, and Chamilo. Clearly, commercial Education LMSs still dominate the educational landscape

No.	Commercial Education LMS	Open source Education LMSs
1	Blackboard Learn (Blackboard Inc.)*	ATutor (University of Toronto)*
2	Desire2Learn (D2L) Brightspace *	eFront (Epignosis Ltd.)*
3	Edmodo (Edmodo LLC) *	ILIAS 4 e-Learning*
4	Instructure Canvas (Instructure Inc.) *	Instructure Canvas (Instructure Inc.)*
5	Pearson LearningStudio	Moodle (open source)*
6	Schoology (Schoology, Inc.) *	OpenOLAT*
7	CourseWebs (Case Consulting, LLC)	Sakai*
8	Collaborise Classroom (DemocraSoft)	Chamilo*
9	AdrennaLearn (Adrenna Inc.)	CourseWork (Stanford University)
10	Academic Systems LMS	LMS Global BusinessLMS
11	Destiny One (Destiny Solutions Inc.)	Google Classroom
12	Education Elements HLMS	JoomlaLMS (JoomlaLMS)
13	eScholar (eScholar LLC)	Open LMS
14	FrogLearn (FrogEducation Ltd.)	EctoLearning (Ecto, LLC)
15	Helix LMS (Helix Education)	Sensei (Woothemes)
16	InYourClass (InYourClass.com)	Uzity (Foradian Technologies)
17	JoomlaLMS (Joomla LMS)	Metacoon Metastudy
18	Krawler LMS (Krawler Networks)	OpenSWAD
19	McGraw-Hill Connect	Whiteboard Courseware System
20	Top Scholar (Top Scholar)	WeBWorK

* Leading, popular LMS

Table 1. Some examples of commercial and open source Education LMSs used by universities

compared to open source Education LMSs. This is not surprising given the former's earlier adoption by many major corporations for the training of their personnel. However, open source Education LMSs are tailing closely behind their commercial counterparts for reasons as explained earlier. With greater effort by the open source movement, this type of learning systems is poised to make greater inroad in online learning environments in the near future.

In general, IHLs can adopt two categories of LMSs – either licensed (proprietary) systems or non-licensed (OSS) systems. WebCT, Blackboard, MyGuru, eCollege, and LearningSpace are some of the examples of the former category; on the other hand, Moodle, ILIAS, ATutor, and Claroline represent some of the latter systems. Undisputedly, deciding on which one of the two will rely on many aspects, such as user acceptance, technical support, maintenance, training, servicing, and cost of ownership, which will have an overall significant impact on the use of the system.

For any technology implementations, the ultimate aim is to ensure that the intended users (e.g., students, executives, trainees, or personnel) will be able to improve their knowledge and skills after using such systems. More importantly, users must be made to realize that the systems are indispensable to the efforts to make them more competent. From the managerial perspective, it becomes the imperative of the instructors, teachers, or administrators to select and implement the right system in their organization lest the implementation will run into problems, which could be costly and damaging. To achieve a successful implementation of any LMS system will entail conditions that help users to appreciate the full potential of the solution. In other words, they should perceive the system to be highly beneficial to their training or leaning. Of course, there are interrelated factors that come into play in shaping the perceived usefulness or perceived benefit of such systems.

To explain the factors and their relations, several researchers have formulated a few models such as *Technology Acceptance Model (TAM)* [14], *Unified Theory of Acceptance and Use of Technology (UTAUT)* [15], *DeLone and McLean model (DL&ML)* [16], and *Educational Technology Model (ETM)* [17]. Invariably, some of the newer models were formulated based on older models, thus some having the same underlying constructs, such as system quality, service quality, course quality, learner satisfaction, LMS use, and *perceived benefit* [18]. In this paper, the constructs that were examined were learner satisfaction, LMS use, and perceived benefit given that the remaining constructs mainly deal with the technical aspects of the systems. According to Ref. [19], user (learner) satisfaction, which measures learner's attitude toward the system, is " the extent to which users believe the information system available to them meets their information requirements." Thus, if the user perceives the system to be poor, the system is rendered inferior. In contrast, higher learner satisfaction of the system will lead to higher "intention to use," which in turn improves usage [16].

Based on these interrelations, satisfied learners will perceive the system to be beneficial to their learning and will most likely use the system more persistently. "The construct LMS use measures the extent to which learners use the LMS, which in effect serves as a barometer that shows the success (or failure) of such a system implementation" [16]. With frequent use of the system, learners will be more likely to improve their knowledge and skills – the positive impact of which will resonate throughout the organization. Accordingly, measuring the net benefit of the system entails the evaluation of the system along with the purpose of the system. "One of the practical ways to measure the perceived net benefit is through eliciting learners' perception on the benefit of the system" [18]. In unison, all these factors will have a serious impact of the selection and use of such a LMS. Furthermore, the use of such a system will also be influenced by several mediating, notably demographic factors, which need to be considered when implementing online learning for students.

As with other computer-based solutions, both proprietary and non-proprietary systems are readily available. Given the availability of both types of the systems, undertaking a comparative study of these two systems will not only be interesting but purposeful, as the lessons to be learned will help universities' administrators to make an informed decision on the final choice of a particular system type to be used in their organizations. Such a choice will have an overwhelming impact on the learning and teaching process in the long term. Thus, three research questions that focus on perceived benefit, LMS use, and learner satisfaction were formulated to guide the study as follows:

a.   Is there a significant difference in perceived benefit between the open source LMS and the proprietary LMS as reported by the participants?

b.   Is there a significant difference in perceived LMS use between the open source LMS and the proprietary LMS as reported by the participants?

c.   Is there a significant difference in perceived learner satisfaction between the open source LMS and the proprietary LMS as reported by the participants?

Based on the three research questions, three corresponding research hypotheses were also formulated as follows:

a.   Perceived benefit of the open source LMS will differ significantly from the perceived benefit of the proprietary LMS.

b.   LMS use of the open source LMS will differ significantly from the LMS use of the proprietary LMS.

c.   Learner satisfaction of the open source LMS will differ significantly from the learner satisfaction of the proprietary LMS.

2. Research method

In this study, the researchers used a quantitative research method based on a survey to collect the required data from a group of students. Using this approach helped the researchers to test the preceding research hypotheses by employing relevant participants, research instruments, and procedure. The details of the research method are as follows.

2.1. Participants

The sample of the survey comprised a group of 608 undergraduates, who were majoring in information technology at two institutions of higher learning in Malaysia. In terms of gender composition, this sample consisted of 401 female undergraduates and 207 male undergraduates. Their mean age was 21.5 years, and, on average, they had been using the LMSs for more than 2 years. Their participation in this survey was based on voluntary basis.

2.2. Research instruments

The research instrument used in this study was mostly based on the questionnaire used by Ref. [18] to collect data pertaining to the constructs LMS use, learner satisfaction, and perceived benefit. There were 11 items in the questionnaire, which were split into three categories. The first category comprised four items to measure LMS use, the second category comprised three items to measure learner satisfaction, and the third category consisted of four items to measure perceived benefit. The participants were asked to state their opinions with regard to the three constructs along 5-Likert-type scales, ranging from "1" (*strongly disagree*) to "5" (*strongly agree*). Cronbach's alpha coefficients for construct reliability measurement of LMS use, learner satisfaction, and perceived benefit were 0.89, 0.88, and 0.91, respectively. These coefficients suggest that the internal consistency of the items are good, exceeding the acceptable value of 0.7 [20]. Table 2 summarizes the 11 items, constructs, and internal consistencies as reported in Ref. [18].

Item	Construct	Statement	Cronbach's alpha coefficients
1		I use LMS to help me to interact with my instructor.	0.79
2		I use LMS to access learning resources electronically	0.80
3	LMS use	I use LMS to communicate and share knowledge with my colleagues.	0.81
4		I use LMS to accomplish and submit my assignments.	0.77
5		I am pleased with the LMS.	0.69
6	Learner Satisfaction	I am very satisfied with the course content I access from LMS.	0.80
7		Overall, my interaction with LMS is very satisfying.	0.79
8		Using LMS has helped me to accomplish my learning tasks more quickly.	0.76
9	Perceived Benefit	Using LMS has made my learning activities become much easier than before.	0.82
10		My learning performance has enhanced since I started using LMS.	0.82
11		I find the system useful in my studies.	0.81

Table 2. Items, constructs, and internal consistencies

2.3. Procedure

Two groups of participants were formed based on their locations of study. The first group comprised 290 undergraduates (204 females, 86 males) of a private university, who used a proprietary (licensed) LMS. The second group comprised 318 undergraduates (197 females, 121 males) of a public university, who used use a non-proprietary (open source) LMS. The participation of the undergraduates was secured through personal contact of the researchers to allow them to send an online survey questionnaire to the students. This questionnaire also contained a brief introduction of the purpose of the survey and an assurance that their answers would remain confidential. Collected questionnaires were analyzed using Statistical Software for Social Science (Ver. 19.) The statistical procedures to address the research questions were a series of independent t-tests and Pearson correlation. The former procedure was used to examine any significant differences in the perceived constructs. The latter procedure was employed to examine the relations among the constructs. "Pearson correlation is commonly used in social science studies to examine the size and direction of the linear relationship between two continuous variables" [21].

3. Findings

Participants' responses to the questionnaire items were processed to produce the required descriptive statistics, namely, the mean scores, maximum scores, minimum scores, and standard deviations. The overall mean scores (standard deviations) of LMS use, learner satisfaction, and perceived benefit were 3.95 (.68), 3.97 (.69), and 3.78 (.65), respectively, as shown in Table 3.

Type of LMS	Construct (Measure)					
	LMS use		Learner Satisfaction		Perceived Benefit	
	Mean	SD	Mean	SD	Mean	SD
Open source (n = 318)	4.02	0.62	4.04	0.64	3.85	0.52
Proprietary (n = 290)	3.86	0.73	3.87	0.72	3.72	0.76
Overall (N = 608)	3.95	0.68	3.97	0.69	3.78	0.65

Table 3. Mean scores and standard deviations of the three constructs

An independent-samples t-test indicated that LMS use's mean scores were significantly higher for the group that used open source system (M = 4.02, SD = 0.62) than for the group that used the proprietary systems (M = 3.86, SD = 0.73), $t(606)$ = 2.91, p < 0.05. The same test also indicated that learner satisfaction's mean scores was significantly higher for the group that used open source system (M = 4.04, SD = 0.64) than for the group that used the proprietary systems (M = 3.87, SD = 0.72), $t(606)$ = 2.77, p < 0.05. Similarly, the perceived benefit's mean score was significantly higher for the group that used open source system (M = 3.85, SD = 0.52) than for the group that used the proprietary systems (M = 3.72, SD = 0.76), $t(606)$ = 2.32, p < 0.05.

Bivariate correlations between pairs of constructs were also computed using the Pearson correlation procedure. Perceived benefit and LMS use were significantly correlated, $r(606)$ = 0.11, p < 0.05. Likewise, perceived benefit and learner satisfaction were also significantly correlated, $r(606)$ = 0.12, p < 0.05. For constructs LMS use and learner satisfaction, their correlation was found to be strong and highly significant, $r(606)$ = 0.95, p < 0.001. Table 4 summarizes the correlations among perceived benefit, LMS use, and learner satisfaction.

Construct (Measure)	1	2	3
1. Perceived benefit	—		
2. LMS use	0.112*	—	
3. Learner satisfaction	0.120*	0.95**	—

*$p <.05$, $p < 0.001$

Table 4. Pearson correlations among perceived benefit, LMS use, and learner satisfaction

4. Discussion and conclusion

One of the major findings of the independent-samples t-test indicates that the participants who used the open source LMS rated the perceived benefit of their LMS significantly higher than their counterpart who used the proprietary LMS. In other words, the difference in perceived benefit between the two types of LMSs as reported by the participants was significant. Thus, this finding supports the first research hypothesis of the study. Similarly, the LMS use of the open source LMS was observed to differ significantly from the LMS use of the proprietary LMS, which lends support for the second research hypothesis of the study. Likewise, another finding of the independent-samples t-test indicates that the participants who used the open source LMS tended to rate Learner satisfaction significantly higher than those who used the proprietary LMS. There was a significant difference between the two groups in this measure, thus supporting the third research hypothesis of the study.

Given the support of all research hypotheses, there is growing evidence to suggest that learning management solutions developed by the open source community might have matured to a level that is on par with licensed solutions – or, as demonstrated in this case, the former might have surpassed the latter in terms of perceived benefit, LMS use, and learner satisfaction. Clearly, when these measures are perceived to be important by users, it can be inferred that the implementation of such a leaning management system is successful to a certain extent. Undisputedly, "there are numerous technical and socio-psychological factors" [22,23,24] "involving all the stakeholders that can determine the success (or failure) of LMSs" [25]. In this study, the perceived benefit (perceived usefulness), learner satisfaction, and LMS use of the open source LMS were highly rated. In addition, based on the correlational analysis, all the three factors were also significantly correlated with each other. More notably, the significant positive association between learner satisfaction and perceived benefit is consistent with earlier findings. This finding reinforces the contention that users will accept an LMS to be beneficial when they "are satisfied with the performance of such a system" [26]. This significant positive relation will in turn make users utilize the system more often and readily to support their learning process. Continued use of such systems will not only benefit students and instructors but administrators as well. In view of this revelation, it is important for both teaching staff and academic administrative personnel to institute several initiatives to high-light the benefits of LMS to their students. Through such initiatives, students will be able to recognize and appreciate the immense potential of an LMS. With the right frame of mind, students, especially the freshmen, will be primed to adapt to new, novel learning environment.

Interestingly, in this study, perceived benefit, LMS use, and learner satisfaction of an open source LMS were rated higher than the proprietary LMS. This finding suggests that solutions developed by the open source organizations or individuals have a promising future in providing online learning opportunities to a wide spectrum of users. Though the proprietary LMS entered the educational landscape much earlier than the open source LMS and dominated the online learning environment, the ongoing and relentless efforts by the open source community have made the latter system a formidable solution on par with the former system. Given its relatively inexpensive outlay, many institutions, especially cash-strapped schools, can now afford to implement open source, non-proprietary learning solutions. As demonstrated in this study, the open source LMS was rated high by students who used it to support their learning, especially outside the classroom. The high ratings of the perceived benefit, LMS use, and learner satisfaction strongly suggest that "features and functionalities of open source LMSs to support online independent learning have improved over the years to provide the essential teaching and learning needs" [27].

Despite the many advantages of open source LMSs, some factors may hinder successful implementation of such systems. Even though the acquisition of open source LMSs are almost without cost, a highly trained personnel (e.g., a system analyst) is required to manage the systems, which encompasses a wide range of technicalities. Without proper system management, the solution put in place will ultimately become inefficient and ineffective. Like any other database systems, LMSs require constant monitoring, updating, and maintenance over time as the number of users is growing. In addition, there is concern that some of the open source LMSs do not provide the level of security that is needed by certain educational institutions. Hence, important information could be comprised, which is detrimental to the organizations' reputation. Of course, there are other factors as well that can make an open source implementation challenging, but these two factors represent the major concern that can make such adoption either a success or a failure. Given these issues, adopting an open source solution entails appropriate planning that holistically focuses on all aspects pertaining to technical, training, and cost considerations.

In this study, even though the open source Education LMS was highly rated higher than the proprietary Education LMS in terms of the three constructs, the researchers strongly believe that the success of any LMS system – irrespective of being either proprietary or open source – will rely on technical, managerial, institutional, and attitudinal aspects. For example, at the institutional level, universities should not view LMS as a mere technological tool, but more importantly, this system should be implemented with careful, comprehensive planning. To plan such an implementation would entail a rigorous review of existing infrastructure, current teaching and learning practices, and policies. Failure to factor in these aspects in the planning process could make the system underutilized. The researchers opine that for any universities to embark on an LMS project, a dedicated team drawn from various and relevant background should be set up to plan all the necessary details to help guide the selection, installation, testing, and full deployment of a proper LMS system. Ideally, these team members should work in a unit, which may be called (as an example) an e-learning unit under the ambit of the academic affairs department.

This team should be given sufficient empowerment to study, formulate, and deploy strategies for effective LMS deployment. This team should examine existing infrastructure to help determine the capabilities of available hardware to support the proposed learning management system. Having the knowledge of the performance of this hardware would help IT personnel to carry out appropriate upgrading or retrofitting work to run the proposed learning management system. It is worthy to note that implementing learning management system is not only about the software per se, but the hardware to run the system is equally important. In other words, the importance of the symbiotic relation between software and hardware to operate such a learning management should not be downplayed. Thus, a thorough review of existing equipment and IT tools is not only important but also mandatory. Likewise, a review of existing teaching and learning practice of a university should be performed with utmost importance. After all, the main aim of deploying LMS is to improve the existing process of teaching and learning, thus this review would help identify weak spots or areas that require redress. Problems associated with teaching and learning in many universities worldwide have increased without respite given the ever-increasing number of students enrolling in diverse academic programs. Face-to-face lectures have become a serious problem to many educational institutions as infrastructure is stretched to its limits, putting great constraint on it capability. Naturally, lectures have to be complemented by other means, notably online learning to cater vast student populations. Nowadays, many universities have adopted blended learning as a solution to handle the teaching needs and learning needs of lecturers and students, respectively.

In addition, the introduction of learning management systems in institutes of higher learning would entail a sound, appropriate policy to make their implementations a success. Ultimately, these systems would be deemed worthwhile and beneficial if all the stakeholders (students, lecturers, and administrators) could fully utilize these solutions. For example, a part of the policy may contain provisions to necessitate (or to enforce) all lecturers to use the LMS in the following teaching activities: a) uploading lecture notes on LMS, b) making online announcements, c) setting up online discussion groups, d) conducting online quizzes and tests, e) providing online feedback of students performance, and f) posting online information and news. With all these teaching activities performed on the learning management system, students would be more prone to partake in online learning activities to complement their face-to-face learning. Hence, the use of the system would be more intense, leading students to perceive the system to be highly beneficial. Sustaining this level of teaching and learning activities would in the end make the adoption of the LMS a success.

Overall, the findings of this study provide some assurances that open source education learning management systems are on par with their proprietary counterparts for the constructs learner satisfaction, LMS use, and perceived benefit. In fact, the latter system has been demonstrated to be rated higher than the former system for the three constructs. However, this finding is informative in terms of the continually increasing capability of open source education learning management systems, but not conclusive to stake claim that these open source systems are better than proprietary systems. Many factors are involved in making the adoption of learning management systems a success; thus, the interpretation of this finding should be embraced with caution as this study was based on students' opinions. Other stakeholders' opinions and feedback are needed to ascertain the performance of any learning management systems with some degree of certainty.

In summary, open source education learning management systems are beginning to be seriously viewed as an effective, efficient learning solution from the student perspective. Now, more learning opportunities will be made available to a greater pool of learners across the nation to help them pursue their academic programs in an environment that suits today's educational landscape – more precisely, digital landscape in which more and more contents and materials are in electronic form. Therefore, it is incumbent on the management of universities, training centers, and institutions that are currently using expensive learning solutions to seek affordable solutions, which are equally effective, to further enhance their students' online learning experiences. More importantly, schools, especially the public ones, which do not have such systems in place, should try to learn from others that have successfully implemented the open source education learning management systems so that their pupils can experience online learning at the early age.

Author details

Ahmad Rafi[1*], Khairulanuar Samsudin[2] and Hafizul Fahri Hanafi[2]

*Address all correspondence to: rafi@mmu.edu.my

1 Faculty of Creative Multimedia, Multimedia University, Cyberjaya, Selangor, Malaysia

2 Computing Department, Faculty of Art, Computing and Creative Industry, Sultan Idris University of Education, Tanjung Malim, Perak, Malaysia

References

[1] Wright, C.R., Lopes, V., Montgomerie, C., Reju, S.A., & Schmoller, S. Selecting a learning management system: Advice from an academic perspective. EDUCAUSE review, April 21, 2014. Available from: http://www.educause.edu/ero/article/selecting-learning-management-system-advice-academic-perspective [2015-03-17].

[2] Ellis, R.K. Field Guide to Learning Management Systems. Alexandria: ASTD Learning Circuits, 2009.

[3] Shank, P. Learning management systems, the eLearning guild. 2010. Available from: http://www.elearningguild.com/research/archives/index [2015-03-17].

[4] Kano-Bower, E. Open source vs. commercial learning platforms: Total cost of owner-ship and total cost of effective use. 2010. Available from: http://www.itslearning.net/Websites/itstest/Images/Documents/TCO.pdf [2015-03-17].

[5] Monarch Media, Inc. Open-source learning management systems: Sakai and Moodle. Monarch Media, Inc., Business White Paper. 2010.

[6] Feller, J., & Fitzerald, B. A framework analysis of the open source software develop-ment paradigm University College Cork Ireland. 2000. Available from: http://www.josephfeller.com/publications/ICIS2000.pdf [2000-02-10].

[7] McIntosh. D. Vendors of learning management and e-learning products. Available from: http://www.trimeritus.com/vendors.pdf [2015-04-10].

[8] Wheeler, B. The open source parade. EDUCAUSE Review. 2004; 39 (5): 68–69.

[9] Hotrum, M., Ludwig, B., & Baggaley, J. Open source software: Fully-featured vs. "the devil you know." International Review of Research in Open and Distance Learning. 2005; 6 (1). Available from: http://cde.athabascau.ca/softeval/reports/R430410.pdf [2015-03-17].

[10] Beatty, B., & Ulasewicz, C. Online teaching and learning transition: Faculty perspec-tives on moving from Blackboard to Moodle learning management system. Tech-Trend. 2007; 50 (4): 36–45.

[11] Awang, N., & Darus, M.Y. Evaluation of an open source learning management sys-tem: Claroline. Procedia – Social and Behavioral Sciences. 2012; 67: 416–426.

[12] Cavus, N., Uzunboylu, H., & Ibrahim, D. Assessing the success of students using a learning management system and together with a collaborative tool in web based teaching of programming languages. Journal of Education Computer Research. 2007; 36 (3): 301–321.

[13] Ankita, S., & Vatta, S. Role of learning management systems in education. Interna-tional Journal of Advanced Research in Computer Science and Software Engineering. 2013; 3 (6): 997–1002.

[14] Davis, F.D., Bagozzi, R.P., & Warshaw, P.R. User acceptance of computer technology: A comparison of two theoretical models. Management Science. 1989; 35 (8): 982–1003.

[15] Venkatesh, V., Morris, M.G., Davis, G.B., & Davis, F.D. User acceptance of informa-tion technology: Toward a unified view. MIS Quarterly. 2003; 27 (3): 425–478.

[16] DeLone, W.H., & McLean, E.R. The DeLone and McLean model of information sys-tems success: A ten-year update. Journal of Management Information Systems. 2003; 9: 9–30.

[17] Almarashdeh, I.A., Sahari, N., Zin, N.A.M., & Alsmadi, M. The success of learning management system among distance learners in Malaysian universities. Journal of Theoretical and Applied Information Technology. 2010; 12 (2): 80–91.

[18] Mtebe, J.S., & Raisamo, R. A model for assessing learning management system success in higher education in Sub-Saharan countries. The Electronic Journal of Information Systems in Developing Countries. 2014; 61 (7): 1–17.

[19] Ives, B., Olson, M., & Baroudi, J.J. The measurement of user information satisfaction. Communications of the ACM. 1983; 26: 785–793.

[20] DeVon, H.A., Block, M.E., Moyle-Wright, P., Ernst, D.M., Hayden, S.J., Lazzara, D.J. et al. A psychometric toolbox for testing validity and reliability. Journal of Nursing Scholarship. 2007; 39 (2): 155–164.

[21] Goodwin L.D., & Leech, N.L. Understanding correlation: Factors that affect the size of r. The Journal of Experimental Education. 2006; 74 (3): 251–266.

[22] Abrahams, D. Technology adoption in higher education: A framework for identifying and prioritising issues and barriers to adoption of instructional technology. Journal of Applied Research in Higher Education. 2010; 2 (2): 34–49.

[23] Al-Busaidi, K., & Al-Shihi, H. Key factors to instructors' satisfaction of learning management systems in blended learning. Journal of Computing in Higher Education. 2012; 24: 18–39.

[24] Liaw, S., Huang, H., & Chen, G. Surveying instructor and learner attitudes toward e-learning. Computers & Education. 2008; 49: 1066–1080.

[25] Naveh, G., Tubin, D., & Pliskin, N. Student LMS use and satisfaction in academic institutions: The organisational perspective. Internet and Higher Education. 2010; 13: 127–133.

[26] Sun, P., Tsai, R., Finger, G., Chen, Y., & Yeh, D. What drives a successful e-learning? An empirical investigation of the critical factors influencing learner satisfaction. Computers & Education. 2008; 50: 1183–1202.

[27] Fariha, Z. & Zuriyati, A. Comparing Moodle and eFront software for learning management system. Australian Journal of Basic and Applied Sciences. Special Issue 2014; 8 (4): 158–162.

7

Physics Learning in Primary and Secondary Schools with Computer Games—An Example — Angry Birds

Robert Repnik, Dominik Robič and Igor Pesek

Additional information is available at the end of the chapter

Abstract

In this paper, we discuss how we can make physics lessons more interesting with the use of information and communications technology (ICT). We explain why physics teachers need to be ICT competent and which ICT tools teachers can use to improve their lessons. Nowadays, many learners spend their free time playing computer games that use basic physics laws for game mechanics. One of our goals was to find out which computer games would be appropriate for learning physics and how to include those games in the learning process. We also show an example how to teach physics using the computer game *Angry Birds*, where we take into account primary and secondary school curriculum. Finally, we analyze how teaching physics with computer games affect students and what are the benefits and weaknesses using this method. In addition, we conduct a survey to gain insight on the opinion of physics teachers about the appropriateness of the computer game *Angry Birds* for teaching physics in elementary and high school. Surprisingly, the teachers find the game more appropriate for the teaching of physics in elementary school, despite of the fact that there are physics themes mostly from high school physics included in the game.

Keywords: ICT, Angry Birds, computer games, physics, teaching, e-learning, curriculum

1. Introduction

The fast penetration of information and communication technology (ICT) into our lives and society is causing how, when, and where we work and study. School-aged children nowadays spend their free time immersed in a media-rich, ubiquitous, always-connected world where most of the time they usually play computer games. For two decades, scientists were trying to figure out why are computer games so motivating and why children spend so much time playing them [1]. The results of research were three features: challenge, fantasy, and curiosity. The same three features are also very important aspects in learning. Challenge helps us to stay motivated to achieve our goal, fantasy helps us to better imagine how things should work, and curiosity drives us to figure out things that we did not know.

Educators around the world in the last 50 years try to incorporate ICT and computers into the education system. Four threads have been identified [2]. The first thread, computer-assisted instruction (CAI) and lately intelligent tutoring systems (ITS), has promised a new way of how learners would learn but never gained much attention. Second thread, computer science and computer programming, is gaining momentum lately as few countries are bringing them as obligatory subjects in school curriculum. The third thread is cognitive development and problem solving skills, which are getting much of attention as problem solving is one of the key competencies for 21st century citizen. The fourth thread is Internet use for gathering information and as a tool for improving problem solving skills. Perhaps the greatest potential for ICT in education is the improvement of traditional teaching with the inclusion of different tools in the classrooms.

The next generation of jobs will be characterized by increased technology use, extensive problem solving, and complex communication [3]. These are the skills that go beyond typical reading, writing, and arithmetic of years past. It is not only what students need to learn that is shifting but also how and when they learn. Students of today are growing up with laptops, tablets, cell phones, and video call, and they expect to use this technology in their daily interactions [4].

One area of significant promise in this regard is a movement toward the use of educational computer games as learning tools in schools [5]. We will tackle this area in subsequent sections.

This chapter is structured as follows, we first categorize computer and educational games, and then we introduce the computer game *Angry Birds* and describe how *Angry Birds* can be used in physics curriculum. Next we explain which computer programs and how to use them with *Angry Birds* in the classroom. We conclude this chapter with the survey on how teachers would use *Angry Birds* in classrooms.

2. Computer and educational games

For the purposes of this paper, we will define a game as a system in which players engage in artificial conflict, defined by rules, that results in quantifiable outcome [6]. A definition of digital game requires a game system to incorporate technology. Simulations, augmented reality, and traditional computer games meet the requirement. However, purely virtual worlds, such as Second Life, would not be games because there is no quantifiable outcome [5].

The different types of computer games are as follows [7]:

- **Card games**—Its computerized version of typical card games and games where game mechanics involves playing with cards where graphics can make card more alive in the virtual world. Examples *Poker, Solitaire*, and *Black Jack*.

- **Board Games**—These are virtual presentation of classic board games like *Chess, Monopoly, and Backgammon*.

- **Puzzles**—These are games that are mostly evolved around problems. In these games, the player must figure out a solution for the given problem using different in-game tools to solve an enigma. Good examples are *Tetris, Mastermind, Brain Age, Ilomilo*.

- **Maze**—The basic mechanics of this is evolved by problem of navigation, where a player's main objective is to get out of the maze. Examples are *Pack Man, Doom, Wolfenstien 3D*.

- **Fighting**—Fighting games involve characters who usually fight hand-to-hand in one-on-one combat situation. Examples are *Street Fighter* and *Avengers* [7].

- **Action**—These types of games involve control of a character who proceeds through story and shoots to objects and enemies. Nowadays, we can also refer to this type of games as first-person shooter (FPS) games. These are very popular and can be played online against other players. Examples are *Counter-Strike, Call of Duty, Unreal Tournament*, and *America's Army*.

- **Adventure**—Adventure games are similar to action games, but they evolve more around the story and mystery behind it. Players are often placed in historical environment where they try to solve a mystery. Examples are *Zork: Grand Inquisitor, Quest for Glory IV, Grim Fandango*, and *Gone Home*.

- **Role playing**—In role-playing games, players can choose between different types of character. Play style depends from what type of character you have chosen. Characters may differ from gender, abilities, races, specializations, profession, and other specifics that games have to offer. When a character is chosen, you can adventure in the virtual world where you can go on a quest where you deal with different problems and adversaries. During quests, you upgrade your character in agility, strength or magic. This type of game is very popular nowadays, and it is mostly played online. This type of game is called massively multiplayer online role-playing game (MMORPG). Examples are *Diablo, Titan Quest, World of Warcraft*, and *Skyrim*.

- **Strategy**—strategy games emphasize on involving a strategy to defeat your opponent. In this game, players need to resolve a problem of resources, economy, defense, and attack. Most known strategy games are *Age of Empires, Warcraft, Civilization, Europa Universalis, Total War*, and *Stronghold*.

- **Sports**—These games are mostly a virtual presentation of real-life sports, where the player picks a team or individual and compete in sport discipline. Most known are *FIFA, NHL*, and *NBA*, among others.

- **Simulation**—There are two types of simulation games, training and management. At training simulation game, designers try to simulate a real-world environment, where you can practice. Good examples of training simulation games are games *Wheels of Steels, Flight Simulator*, and *Ship Simulator*. Management simulation games are about managing community and economy. Good examples of these games are *Tycoon* series, *The Sims, and SimCity.*

These games are mostly a product of big entertainment companies, which can provide enough funding for game designers and programmers to develop new games and to sustain old ones up to date. If we can compare these games with didactic games, we can surely get to the conclusion that designers of nondidactical games put more effort to make games fun and graphically appealable and, in this case, also more playable. Another factor is freedom of game designers at nondidactical computer games. They do not need to evolve game around lessons that should be learned in certain stage of game, but they have more freedom at designing environment details and effects. Also, they put more focus on playability of the game rather than learning a certain lesson. That gives nondidactical computer games advantage in popularity.

Research in the United States has shown that majority of children and adolescents nowadays are playing computer games for at least 1 hour per day [6]. This indicates that computer games take a great part not only in children's but also in adolescents' everyday life. Many parents are worried that playing games to much could lead to addiction, violence, and depression of their children, but they mostly overreact because they fail to see the positive effects of playing computer games and are mostly mislead by media. Computer games changed dramatically, and they became much more complex, diverse, and social in nature, which means that they offer much more to players than they did in a previous decade. Let us check what we can gain and what the benefits at playing computer games are. Research has shown that computer games can improve cognitive brain functions. Numerous studies has shown that computer games can help at faster and more accurate attention allocation, higher spatial resolution in visual processing, and enhanced mental rotation abilities. It is also interesting that spatial skills can be trained relatively quickly and skills like this can be easily transferred in real-life usage. Preliminary research has also demonstrated that these cognitive advantages manifest in measurable changes in neural processing and efficiency, which means that players of computer games can filter irrelevant information much faster than nonplayers. However, we must say that these benefits do not apply to all genres of games but mostly to games where 3D environment is included.

Great benefit can be also gained with problem solving skills, which is dependent on game complexity. It seems that nowadays children have evolved around the aspect of problem solving. We rarely see someone reading a manual, but they mostly learn by trial and error, which can also be related to computer games where game designers often offer very little instructions how to solve a problem. A final cognitive benefit from playing computer games is enhanced creativity. Another benefit from playing video games also shows up in the motivation of players. It seems that many computer games are stimulating just enough frustration that players stay highly motivated to solve the problem and take great pleasure succeeding. It seems that challenge in games provides enough motivation and fun for players to play the game, and that makes a positive effect on them in a way to attain better motivation and persistence, which can also lead to better marks at school if the same can be applied to learning. Another benefit from playing computer games is on the emotional state of a player. Gaming may be among the most efficient and effective means by which children and youth generate positive feelings. Puzzle games like for instance *Angry Birds*, which has minimal interfaces, short-term commitments, and high-degree of accessibility can improve player moods, promote relaxation, and ward off anxiety, which can also result in higher self-esteem and better grades in school. If playing a game can make a person happier, then this is a great factor that we can gain from playing games and may result in various positive effects such better inspiration and connectivity. Computer games stimulate not only positive emotions but also negative ones, which may not be as grim as it sounds. By stimulating just enough negative emotions such anger, anxiety, frustration, and sadness, we are able to take control of those feelings and learn how to react on them, which can also lead to better adaptive behavior. Playing computer games also improves our social skills. We already said that games changed a lot from last decade, and they also changed in social prospective. Majority of players nowadays play computer games with their friends and rarely alone, which also indicates that they must obtain certain social skills to be able to communicate with friends. Nowadays, some online games provide players with lots of social possibilities where they chat and even send emoticons to each other. Game designers also enforce collaboration between them, so players have to work together to defeat greater adversaries, and that mostly requires good communication skills and coordination [8]. Due to all of benefits that we can gain from computer games, why not use them as a teaching material.

Computer games that were designed for learning are called educational games [2]. What makes games "educational" are specific characteristics [1]. Educational games should also have appropriate methods for learning contents, which depends on nature of contents. For example, we must distinguish between learning of knowledge, processes, procedures, and casual principles. Each of those requires different learning methods that depend on content's complexity. Methods that are used for learning also affect game structure and game mechanics. Finally, what every educational game should have is a feedback system that provides players with information of learning success. We described key characteristics of educational games, where we found out that game structure and game mechanics depend on game content and methods of learning [5]. On the other hand, we need to ask ourselves why children prefer playing classic computer games than educational computer games. The key element is that educational games are not primarily designed for fun only, and major software companies do not develop educational games. Those companies have expert knowledge in computer graphics and game designs, but they have discovered that educational games are not commercially successful and revenue is too small for them. So to get good learning results in computer games, we should either design and develop better educational games or find those computer games that are popular and could be used for educational purposes.

At this point, we must also mention game-based learning, which is defined as "an innovative learning approach derived from the use of computer games that possess educational value or different kinds of software applications that use games for learning and education purposes such as learning support, teaching enhancement, assessment and evaluation of learners" [9].

Some computer games are using actual physics as their game mechanics, and children are very eager to spend hours playing them. So why don't we use those as a teaching tools for physics? One of those games that are using actual physics as their game mechanics is the very popular computer game *Angry Birds* but is not specifically made for teaching.

3. Computer games and physics

Nowadays, a lot of pupils at the end of their secondary school are discouraged to go to study physics. If we would ask them, why is that so, we would get a common answer that physics is boring, hard to understand, and not interesting. This response from pupils mainly results from physics teacher's old-fashioned methods of teaching. Most of teachers are using mainframe (or traditional) method, teaching by telling, which seems to be less effective and boring for students than inquiry-oriented teaching [1]. A great help for this method is the use of information and communications technology (ICT). To use all these, the physics teacher needs to be e-competent [10]. It means that the physics teacher should be able to successfully use ICT as tool for teaching. The use of ICT gives us access to a lot of information, and it is also essential for the support and development of functional skills required in life. It is also a great motivational factor because many of the pupils have highly developed skills of using ICT, and it allows pupils to maintain their concentration longer [10,11]. With the use of ICT, we can effectively collect, display, and introduce data to pupils, and it is also a great tool to deepen knowledge. Teacher priority should not be only to teach physics and deliver information to pupils but also to teach them how to find this information (collecting information) and define which information are correct and useful for them (selecting information).

Learners are not always aware that the game that they are playing is using basic physics laws for game mechanics. Consequently, we could use these games as a didactical tool to teach them physics and make physics lessons more interesting for them. All we need is a computer and a software that measures and shows analyzed data from computer game. There is a variety of games that can be used for experiment. A well-known game and still very popular is the game *Super Mario Bros*. It can be used with problem-based approach for calculating basic kinematics and studying different problems within Mario world [12]. A very interesting game for learning physics is also *Scorched 3D*. In this game, a player must set the power, angle, direction of a projectile to hit another tank while considering the wind affecting the projectile course. In this game, we can learn the physics of projectile motion and introduce it clearly to the students [13]. Sometimes you have to fail in game to figure out how to complete the mission. A game that is made on this concept is called *Angry Birds* [14], where you use different birds as projectiles to destroy green pigs. We can use this game to teach various concepts in physics. Next, we present an example of how to provide physics teaching with *Angry Birds*.

4. Angry Birds

Angry Birds games are a product of a Finnish company called Rovio entertainment. The first game was released in year 2009 for Apple's iOS Android, Symbian, and Windows Phone operating systems. Since then, Rovio entertainment upgraded the game that can also be used on PCs and game consoles. Its addictive gameplay, comical design style, and low price has made the game very popular in almost any age-group. Its popularity also encouraged the company to make new sequels with different themes. From the first game *Angry Birds* to latest sequel *Angry Birds Transformers*, eight more sequels are listed, with different themes and game mechanics [14].

4.1. Game insight

The basic story of *Angry Birds* is about evil green pigs called "bad piggies," which are constantly stealing unwatched eggs from birds, desiring to cook and eat them. The pigs are under the command of King Pig, who commands his army of pigs to construct as many structures as possible to keep the birds from reaching him. The main protagonists of the game are the birds, which are trying to get their eggs back before the evil pigs can eat them. Red (Bird) is the main character of the *Angry Birds* series and also the leader of the flock. He does not have any special abilities and has appeared in every version except *Angry Birds Stella*. There are also Chuck the yellow bird, who has the ability to drastically accelerate; Jay, Jack, and Jim called "The Blues" with the ability to separate in three same-sized birds; Bomb the black bird, who has the ability to explode; and Matilda the white bird, whose ability is to drop one egg on the pigs. There is also Hal the boomerang, who can be seen as the green bird in many sequels and has the ability is to fly back like a boomerang. Bubbles the orange bird is also one of the flock crew members. He has the ability is to drastically expand and push all obstacles away. The newest member of the flock is Stella. She has different abilities like trapping objects into bubbles, speeding up when screen is tapped, and rebounding of walls [15].

4.2. Game mechanics and materials

In the game, a slingshot is used to shoot birds in a way to eliminate all green pigs that may be protected with different materials, which can be destroyed easier with a specific bird's ability. The game is also designed wherein you gain difficulty in every level, and sometimes it requires you to do the same level many times before you finish it. With difficulty scaling with every level, it also motivates and drags you to play the game. When you successfully complete a level, you can also keep track of the score that you achieved, which is measured by the stars that you gain. The final mark of how you preformed in a specific level is dependent on how many objects you destroyed and how many birds you used to eliminate green pigs [14]. We already mentioned that we have different materials (Figure 1) in the game, and we know that different materials have different properties, and it is also the same in *Angry Birds*. The basic materials in the game are stone, wood, and glass [15].

Figure 1. *Angry Birds* gameplay showing an example how to shoot a bird to destroy pigs hiding inside the walls. Stone, wood, and glass are the basics materials. How hard are they to destroy is not always dependent on the material but also on the shape of the material. Small square-shaped blocks are mostly harder to destroy than long square-shaped blocks.

5. Why is physics not popular?

Physics is not very popular among students, and consequently, the educators all over the world are facing the same problem in stimulating students to study physics (Figure 2). Most of the countries have shortage of physics teachers and scientists. The question is why is physics so unpopular among the students? The common beliefs that we encounter about physics are that physics is not an easy subject, it requires a high degree of dedication, and it is mostly meant for intelligent people who are sometimes socially discriminated, and because of that, they are discouraged to study physics. The most common replies that we get about physics when we ask people who finished high school or are still studying are as follows: "physics is boring," "physics is difficult," "physics is for boys," and "physics is strange and only crazy people are doing it" [16]. Why are most responses so negative? What is the problem? It seems that pupils in elementary school show big interest in physics when you ask them about topics that can be found in physics curricula like, for example, electricity, magnetism, force, universe, and others. However, it seems that interests are greatly lowered in high school when they are actually faced with a higher degree of knowledge about them, which includes the use of mathematic at higher degree and this causes students difficulties at understanding physics and also discourage them [17].

It seems that teaching methods and math involvement at a higher degree of education are the origin why students get lack of interest in physics. The question is What can we change to motivate students and to show them that physics is one of the essential science disciplines that not only brings great results at developing technologies but also gives us understanding how nature is working? Also, physics teachers often do not enjoy teaching physics. The main reason may be hidden behind physics curricula, which give really small flexibility at lesson distribution during the year, and the teacher really does not have time to improve their lessons because they have to deal with the lesson schedule for the year. There seems to be two crucial problems.

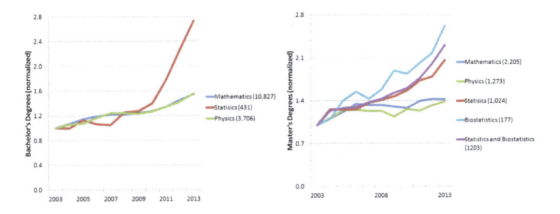

Figure 2. We can see from the ASA Community research that physics is far behind other science disciplines in master's degree. On the left chart, we can see that physics and mathematics bachelors who finished the degree are rising very slow compared to statistics. On the right chart, the number of students who finished master's degree is far behind other disciplines like biostatics and statistics [18].

One of them is a problem on how to introduce knowledge to students in that they will find it interesting, which is basically the problem of teaching methods. The other problem is physics curricula. It seems that physics curricula in many countries is not flexible enough for teachers and, as a result, is unfriendly to students. The solution to this problem would be to redesign physics curricula in a way to give the teacher more flexibility and hereby also relieve teachers from pressure so they could actually enjoy teaching physics and give full dedication to more attractive lessons. A great solution for teaching methods could be to include physics in other subjects such as computer science, where students could solve physics problem with the use of ICT. Games are also a great solution, where students could learn parts of physics simply by playing games and gain necessary knowledge. One of appropriate computer games from which students could learn physics is *Angry Birds*. We present which themes from physics curricula could be appropriate to teach concepts of physics.

6. Physics curricula and *Angry Birds*

All over the world in every school, teachers must follow a teaching plan called curriculum. In every curriculum, there are mandatory themes that consist of subthemes that are building the whole teaching process in certain order. How this process consists may differ from country to country. We may also say that the system of learning physics is concentric (Figure 3). Each physics curriculum is constructed from basic themes. The most important difference between curricula in different countries is in subthemes and their order. In physics, cores of concentric circles are the main themes, which are mechanics, matter, waves and optics, thermal physics, electricity and magnetism, modern physics, and astronomy [19].

The basic themes of physics curriculum are defined, so we studied which of those we may find in the computer game *Angry Birds* and which of them we can analyze.

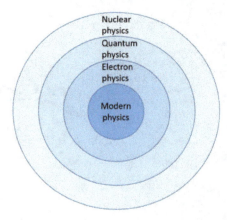

Figure 3. Example of concentric circle in physics. Outer layers may differ in number of subthemes and variety of sub-themes titles, but the core stays the same.

7. Mechanics

7.1. Forces and Newton's law, collision, and explosion

We know that when we launch a bird from the slingshot, the only force that is affecting the bird is the force of gravity $\vec{F_g}$. The air resistance force is in the game excluded. We also know that when the bird will collide with a wooden wall, it will be affected with the force of wall $\vec{F_w}$ that is resisting bird's movement in the opposite direction of its movement (Figure 4). Children can monitor and watch examples of collisions and explain how forces are working on the observed object. We already mentioned that black bird has an ability to explode from which we could observe effects of explosion to teach children the basic physics behind it.

Figure 4. We can see that the force of gravity $\vec{F_g}$. is the only force that affects the bird in the flight. Also, we can predict that when the bird hits the wall, it will slow down because the force of the wall is resisting the bird's motion.

7.2. Friction and motion

With the help of *Angry Birds*, we can also explain friction. After finishing the flight, the bird is touching and then rolling on the ground with some speed in the direction of the vector of velocity $\vec{v}$. The bird is slowing down because of friction $\vec{F_f}$, which is working on the bird in opposite direction and causing the bird eventually to stop (Figure 5). With this example, we could explain how friction is working on a (rolling) bird.

Figure 5. We can see that force friction is working in the opposite direction of the bird, causing the bird to slow down.

7.3. Circular motion and gravity

We mentioned before that Rovio entertainment released many sequels. One of much known sequel is called *Angry Birds Space* (Figure 6), where the game environment is in space and the gravity of objects affects the bird's flight. In designing this sequel, Rovio Entertainment worked with NASA, which helped at programming gravity effects and also tested them in actual space. In the game, we could learn the effects of gravity. Also, we can learn the basics of circular motion if we launch the bird in the angle where the bird would circle around the small planet, which is affecting the bird with its microgravity.

Figure 6. We can see that the force of gravity is pointing in the center of the small planet's mass, therefore also affecting the path of the bird's movement, which would circle for longer time if the force of gravity would be smaller or the velocity of the bird would be higher.

7.4. Work, energy, and power

We know that birds are moving with certain velocity $\vec{v}$ when we launch them. We also know that they change height when they are launched (Figure 7). From that aspect, we can also explain the change of kinetic and potential energy, where potential energy is changing according to change of height:

$$E_p = mgh,\tag{1}$$

Figure 7. If we know height and velocity, we can determine potential and kinetic energy; therefore, we can also know how much work and power the birds need when we shoot them.

where E_p is the potential energy, m is the mass of bird, g is the gravitational acceleration, and h is the height where the bird is located in correspondence to the ground. We could also explain the change of kinetic energy as follows:

$$E_k = \frac{1}{2}mv^2,\tag{2}$$

where E_k is the kinetic energy of bird and v is its velocity. We can also determine work as a result of energy change as follows:

$$W = \Delta E,\tag{3}$$

where W is work and ΔE is change of energy. From that, we can also determine average power as follows:

$$P_{avg} = \frac{\Delta W}{\Delta t},$$

(4)

where P_{avg} is the average power, and ΔW is the change of work in time interval Δt [20].

We can see that with the computer game *Angry Birds*, we can cover and explain most of the mechanics. Other themes are not so well covered, but we can still can find something. For example, we can explain buoyancy.

7.5. Buoyancy

We can explain that buoyancy is upward force $\vec{F}_b$ exerted by a fluid that opposes the weight of an immersed object, which is shown by gravity force $\vec{F}_g$. We can also see that one piggy is floating, which is the result of comparison of the average density of piggy to density of liquid in which piggy is located. For floating of the piggy, its density has to be smaller (Figure 8).

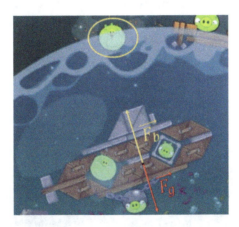

Figure 8. Here we can see an example where force buoyancy is working in the opposite direction as gravity force, causing the material and the pigs to float to the surface [21].

We showed some examples where we could use the computer game *Angry Birds* as a didactical tool for main topics in physics curriculum. However, we did not talk about experimental work and measurement, which is the main topic in following chapter.

8. Teaching with *Angry Birds*

We described some topics where the computer game *Angry Birds* could be appropriate for teaching physics. It contains many mandatory topics of physics curriculum, and it can either be used as a motivational tool, where children could get more comfortable with physics while using ICT or it can be used as an experiment to show children simulation of actual physics. From the experiment, we could define exercises where children could get basic knowledge about physics and calculus behind it. In this chapter, we show an example of how we can teach the physics of projectile motion using the computer game *Angry Birds*. Before we can explain the physics of *Angry Birds*, we have to make footage of *Angry Birds* gameplay, and after that, we can analyze data in that footage. For that, we need some additional programs appropriate for classroom usage, for which we present some examples.

8.1. LioLo Game Recorder

The recommended software for making gameplay footage is a program called LoiLo Game Recorder. You can download it for free from their website [22] and install the program on your computer. LoiLo Game Recorder is a program that enables us to record game sessions. It also supports Motion-JPEG file format that provides with the best balance between file size and image quality. For our purpose, we recorded full-HD videos, and file size is still manageable. When you downloaded and installed the program, simply start the program and the game in which you want to make a recording. Before you start to play, press F6 on keyboard and program will start recording (Figure 9). After you finish playing, press key F6 again and the program will stop recording and save the footage in your PC's video directory. Now you can use the footage for analysis. To minimize the measurement errors at analysis of gameplay, the footage must be smooth and without delays [22]. We will do our analysis in program called Tracker.

Figure 9. This is the LoiLo Game Recorder's user interface where we can see options available in program. We can also see an example of the footage that we made in *Angry Birds*.

8.2. Tracker

Tracker is a free video analysis and modeling tool built on the open source physics (OSP) Java framework. It is designed to be used in physics education and can be easily run from USB drive. Requirements for using Tracker are small, and it only requires that you have installed Java 1.6 or higher. It has a variety of tools to help user to analyze the data from recording where we can read what happened with physical quantity on the graphs (Figure 10). To analyze data from recording, we simply start the program Tracker in which we can open video that we have made with the program Loilo and start the measurements with different tools [23]. Before we can acquire the measurements for discussing physics problem, we need to set starting point to place our bird in space. We do that with calibration tool where we set the coordinate system in the foot of slingshot, which will be our starting point. We also need our measuring unit, which in our case will be the slingshot size. When we determined starting point and basic measuring unit, we use tracking tool to track bird's movement in the footage. When tracking is finished, we see all measurements in the graphs, which we can analyze with measurement analyzing tool. The program Tracker also has a video-analyzing tool where we can depart video frame by frame. For final results, we use measurement-analyzing tools where the data are displayed in different graphs.

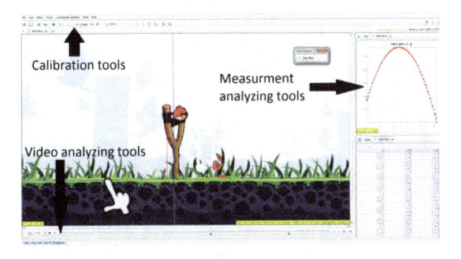

Figure 10. The program has many tools to offer; the most essential of them are the calibration tool, which we can find at the top; the measurement analyzing tools at the right; and the video analyzing tool at the bottom of program interface.

8.3. Physics of *Angry Birds*

When we have analyzed the data with the program Tracker, we can start talking about physics in games. Projectile motion is a case of motion which we can describe it as motion in two dimensions: vertical and horizontal. In this particular case, we can neglect air resistance because the game was not designed to include air resistance in projectile motion. We know that when we shot a bird slingshot, its initial speed ($\vec{v}_0$) is

$$\vec{v}_0 = (v_{0x},\ v_{0y}),$$ (5)

where v_{0x} is the size of the horizontal component of initial velocity and v_{0y} is the size of the vertical component of initial velocity [20]. The only force that is affecting the bird during the flight is gravitational force. That is why acceleration of bird is equal to the gravitational acceleration.

We also know that the horizontal component of velocity is not changing in size because acceleration only got vertical component. That is why we can define the movement of bird in time t:

$$x_{finished} = \left(v_{0x} \cos\theta\right)t + x_{starting},\tag{6}$$

where $x_{finished}$ is the location where bird has finished movement in time t in his horizontal path and $x_{starting}$ is the initial location from where bird has started moving in horizontal path. θ is the angle by which we shot the bird from slingshot [19]. As a result, we get Figure 11, which shows us that the body was moving in horizontal direction with constant velocity v_{0x} equal to 3.31 U/s [24].

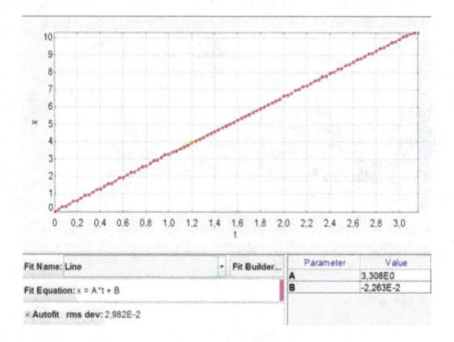

Figure 11. From the measurement, we can read that the horizontal component of velocity (A) is 3.31 U/s, and we can see that dependency position from time is linear.

For motion in vertical direction, we know that acceleration is constant. That is why we can define motion in vertical direction as

$$y_{highest} = (v_{0y} \sin\theta)t - \frac{1}{2}gt^2 + y_{starting},\tag{7}$$

where $y_{starting}$ is the starting height from which the birds was shot in vertical direction from angle θ and $y_{highest}$ is the maximum height that the birds will reach in at time t. We also see that acceleration is equal to gravitational acceleration g if our game is happening on Earth. From the measurement, we see that vertical motion fits to quadric equation (Figure 12), which also shows us that acceleration in vertical direction is constant and is equal to –1.9 U/ s² [25].

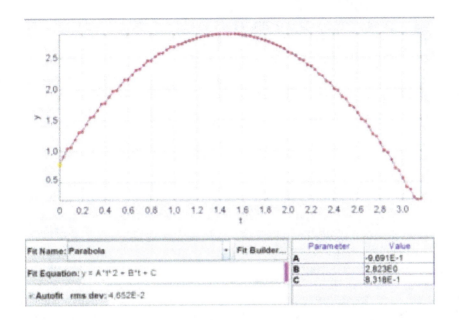

Figure 12. From Equation (7), we can see that acceleration (A) in vertical direction is $a/2$, which gives us a result acceleration equal to 1.9 U/ s². From the measurement, we can also read the vertical component of velocity (B), which is 2.8 U/s, and height (C), which is 0.8 U.

From the result, we wanted to determine what was the size of our basic unit. We measured acceleration in vertical direction as 1.9 U/ s². We placed our experiment on Earth so acceleration should be equal to gravitational acceleration, which is 9.8 m/ s² [24,25]. From that, we can calculate what was the size of our basic unit, and we get the result that our slingshot was 5.1 m high because the size of the slingshot was set as our basic unit. When we get our basic unit, we can calculate our velocity in vertical and horizontal directions so that we simply multiply our measured values with 5.1 m, and as result, we get that v_{0y} is 14.2 m/s and v_{0x} is 16.7 m/s. From this point, we can calculate initial velocity as follows:

$$v_0 = \sqrt{v_{0x}^2 + v_{0y}^2}, \tag{8}$$

and we get that v_0 is 21.9 m/s. From these measurements, we can also calculate our starting height $h_{starting}$, which is 4.2 m. When we obtain the starting height, we can also calculate the maximum height as follows:

$$h = \frac{v_{0y}^2}{2g} + h_{starting}. \tag{9}$$

We get that the maximum height h is 14.5 m. It is also interesting to know from which angel did we shoot the bird:

$$\theta = \tan^{-1}(\frac{v_{0y}}{v_{0x}}) \tag{10}$$

As a result, we get $\theta = 40.4°$. When we all needed information, we can also calculate the range d of the bird's flight using the following equation:

$$d = \frac{v_0}{g}\sqrt{v_0^2 + 2gh_{starting}}, \tag{11}$$

where we get range corresponding to value 52.8 m. We get a similar result when the range is 10.5 U, which is 53.0 m. We see that the range that we calculated is not the same as the range that we measured. We can explain that as an error in measurements.

8.4. Use of example in classroom

We have seen how we can analyze physics with the red angry bird, which does not have any special abilities. This type of analysis and understanding would be more appropriate for pupils in secondary school, in which pupils could use this particular experiment to determine the actual size of birds and the actual size of the slingshot, like we have shown in our example. We can also use experiment for teamwork, where we could divide pupils in two groups. the first group would have to explain the physics of vertical motion, and the second group would have to explain the physics of horizontal motion. At the end of the experiment, both explanations can be merged, and the physics of projectile motion can be explained. Our example can be also used in primary school, where we would have to lower the difficulty of tasks for pupils. We could teach them how to use the programs LoiLo and Tracker for simple analysis not only in *Angry Birds* but also in any other experiment footage. With this experiment, they can get familiar with graphs and errors in measurement. We also know that there is much more physics that can be explained with the use of *Angry Birds* for physics lessons. For additional work, students could explore the initial acceleration and midair acceleration of the yellow angry bird when we use his special ability. It would be also interesting to check the physics background of the blue angry bird, where students could check what is happening with momentum when he splits into three same-sized birds and if the mass of all three birds is the same. We already mentioned materials that show up in the game. For additional project work, students could analyze how different angry birds affect the same material.

9. Research

We showed an example of an experiment that could be used in the class. However, the question is if teachers would even use *Angry Birds* as a didactical tool. That is why we started research where we wanted to see teachers' responses on the proposal of teaching with *Angry Birds*. Our targeted group of teachers was mostly middle-aged teachers (age 36 years and older). We know that the use of ICT is in average a bigger problem in older teachers rather that new young teachers. That is why the middle-aged group is much more interesting. On the question if they know the computer game *Angry Birds*, 35% of the teachers answered yes (Figure 13), which is actually impressive according to age-group that was questioned.

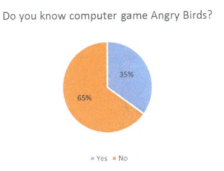

Figure 13. Chart where we can see how many teachers know the computer game *Angry Birds*.

With this, we have determined our group of teachers who actually know the game. Later on, we wanted to know how well they know the game. Hence, we set some common questions about the effects of the birds in the game and which of the physical content they see in the game is also included in physics curriculum. As a result, we learned that teachers who played *Angry Birds* know the game pretty well; 83% knew the effects of the birds in the game. The more interesting part comes when they had to determine the physical contents they found in the game, and the result was amazing. We found that physics teachers have noticed 9 different physics themes (Figure 14) in the computer game *Angry Birds*, which shows us that game really is suitable for physics class.

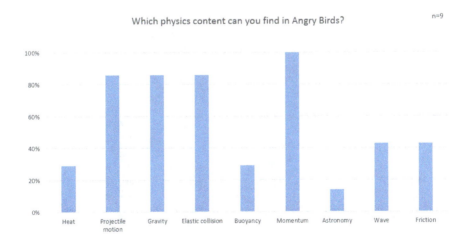

Figure 14. In the chart, we can see what teachers have found in the game *Angry Birds*: heat, projectile motion, gravity, elastic collision, buoyancy, momentum, astronomy, wave, and friction. The vertical axis shows the percentage of teachers who found certain physics content in the game. The horizontal axis shows the different physics contents.

We figured out that teachers can definitely see that game contains content for teaching physics. We also wanted to gain insight what teachers think about the suitability of the game in teaching physics in elementary and high school. Thus, we asked them how appropriate do they find the computer game *Angry Birds* for teaching physics in elementary school. None of teachers evaluated the computer game *Angry Birds* as inappropriate, and more than half of them find it appropriate for teaching physics (Figure 15).

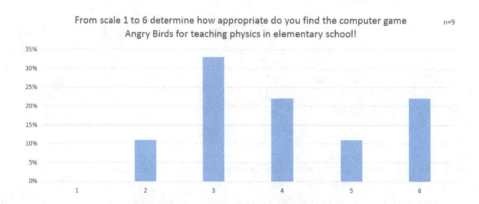

Figure 15. On the vertical axis, there is percentage of teachers who evaluated suitability for elementary school from 1 to 6, where 1 indicates completely inappropriate and 6 indicates perfectly suitable for teaching physics in elementary school, which could be found on the horizontal axis. We see that more than half of teachers found the computer game *Angry Birds* for teaching in elementary school as appropriate; 22% of them found it also perfectly suitable for teaching physics in elementary school.

We also asked them how they would evaluate the suitability of the computer game *Angry Birds* for lessons in physics in high school (Figure 16). We got results that more than half of teachers find it appropriate for teaching physics in high school.

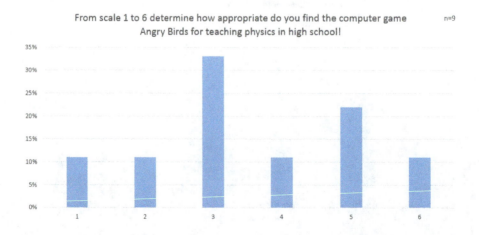

Figure 16. On the *y* axis, there is a percentage of teachers who evaluated suitability for high school from 1 to 6, where 1 indicates completely inappropriate and 6 indicates perfectly suitable for teaching physics in elementary school, which could be found on the *x* axis; 11% of them found it also perfectly suitable for teaching physics in high school.

In our survey, we also asked if the computer game *Angry Birds* is appropriate as a motivational tool in lessons in elementary and high school. As a result, 78% of the teachers find the computer game *Angry Birds* as a great motivational tool for both elementary and high school. The most impressive result was when we asked them if they would use the game for teaching physics. All of the teachers that know the computer game *Angry Birds* would use it for teaching physics.

9.1. Methodology

For our research, we used free online survey tool 1ka.si [26]. The tool offers many options to design an electronic survey. We took into account all basic rules of making survey where we limited the number of questions per page on 5 and separated the different topics of question in separate pages so the survey itself was not too harsh for respondents. In the survey, we also made a break point where we eliminated teachers who do not know the computer game *Angry Birds*. If they answered "no" on a question where we asked them if they know the computer game *Angry Birds*, the survey was finished; if they answered "yes," they could continue with the survey. We sent our survey through e-mail. The results that we introduced were analyzed in Excel table, where we merged our results in charts appropriate for the type of data that we got. In the research, we included 41 physics teachers who finished their study between the year 2005 and 2015 at our faculty and students of educational physics study. We got the response of 26 persons, 9 of them ware familiar with the game *Angry Birds*.

10. Conclusion

In this article, we determined that the use of ICT in learning is a skill that every teacher should acquire during his education. If we look in the present and, even more important, if we look in the future, ICT will be a main tool for learning. We also learn what the difference is between EG and fun CG. We found out that some computer games like *Angry Birds* could be more appropriate material for teaching because if its motivational fun factor. In educational game, designers mostly forget about it because their main point is focused on teaching, and game mechanics are obstructed by learning processes, in which most children forget that learning new things can also be fun. We become familiar with two new programs LoiLo Game Recorder and Tracker, which can be used for analysis. We also show an example of how we could use *Angry Birds* for teaching projectile motion where we explain the physics of *Angry Birds*. At the end, we also check the applicability of *Angry Birds* and how it can be used for further courses. We also conducted one research where we found out that most of the teachers think that Angry Birds is appropriate for teaching physics in high school and elementary school.

Author details

Robert Repnik[1*], Dominik Robič[1] and Igor Pesek[1,2]

*Address all correspondence to: robert.repnik@um.si

1 Faculty of Natural Sciences and mathematics, University of Maribor, Maribor, Slovenia

2 Institute E-um, Ptuj, Slovenia

References

[1]   Wenning C.J. Why the resistance to inquiry-oriented science teaching. Journal of Physics Teacher Education Online 2010; 5(3): 1–2. http://www2.phy.ilstu.edu/~wenning/jpteo/issues/jpteo5%283%29win10.pdf (accessed 8 December 2014).

[2]   Carnoy M. ICT in education: possibilities and challenges. In: Inaugural Lecture of the OUC 2004-2005, UOC, Barcelona; 2004

[3]   Levy F., Murnane R. J. The New Division of Labor: How Computers Are Creating the Next Job Market. Princeton University Press; 2004.

[4]   NCREL & Metiri Group. enGauge 21st Century Skills: Literacy in the Digital Age; 2003.

[5]   McClarty K.L., Orr A., Frey P., Dolan R., Vassileva V., McVay A. A Literature Review of Gaming in Education. Research report. Pearson; 2012.

[6]   Salen K., Zimmerman E. Rules of Play: Game Design Fundamentals. Cambridge MIT Press, 2003.

[7]   Wolf M. J. The Medium of the Video Game. Texas: University of Texas Press; 2002.

[8]   Granic I., Lobel A., Engels C.M.E. The benefits of playing video games. American Psychologist 2014; (69): 66–78.

[9]   Razak, A.A., Connolly M.T., Hainey T. Teachers' views on the approach of digital games-based learning within the curriculum for excellence. International Journal of Game-Based Learning 2012; 33: 33–51.

[10] Gruden B., Kreuh N., Možina Podbršcek I., Flogie A., Razbornik I., Trstenjak B. Path to E-Competency & E-Education Project: The Future of Education. Florence; 2013.

[11] Shan Fu J. ICT in education: a critical literature review and its implications. International Journal of Education and Development using Information and Communication Technology 2013; 9(1): 112–125.

[12] Nordine J. Motivating calculus-based kinematics instruction with *Super Mario Bros.* Physics Teacher 2011; 49: 380.

[13] Jurcevic J.S. Learning Projectile Motion with Computer Game "Schorched 3D." Physics Teacher 2008; 46: 48.

[14] Rovio Entertainment Ltd. *Angry Birds*. http://www.rovio.com/en/our-work/games/view/1/angry-birds (accessed 8 December 2014).

[15] Wikia Inc Angry Birds *Wiki*. http://angrybirds.wikia.com/wiki/Birds (accessed 21 March 2015).

[16] Pardhan H. Engagement enhance interest in physics. Alberta Science Education Journal 2003; 36(2): 25–30.

[17] Azuma T., Nagao K. An inquiry into the reproduction of physics-phobic children by physics-phobic teachers. Bulletin of Faculty of Education, Ibaraki University 2007; 56: 91–102.

[18] Pierson S. ASA Community, 20 December 2013 [Online]. http://community.amstat.org/blogs/steve-pierson/2013/12/20/statistical-science-degree-comparisons-updated-through-2012

[19] CERN. The Curricula of Various Countries. CERN and High School Teachers Programme, 18 July 2002 [Online]. http://teachers.web.cern.ch/teachers/materials/syllabus.htm#Belgium (accessed 21 March 2015).

[20] Haliday D., Resnick R., Walker J. Fundamentals of Physics 8th edition. Cleveland: John Wiley& Sons; 2007.

[21] S. Iyer. Angry Birds Space update splashes underwater with new Pig Dipper episode. NDTV Convergence Limited, 2013 [Online]. http://gadgets.ndtv.com/apps/news/angry-birds-space-update-splashes-underwater-with-new-pig-dipper-episode-316283 (accessed 21 March 2015).

[22] LoiLo. LoiLo Game Recorder. http://loilo.tv/us/ (accessed 8 December 2014).

[23] Douglas B. Tracker: Video analysis and modeling tool. http://www.cabrillo.edu/~dbrown/tracker/ (accessed 8 December 2014).

[24] Rodrigues M., Simeäo Carvalho P. Teaching physics with *Angry Birds*: exploring the kinematics and dynamic of the game. Physics Education 2013; 48: 431. http://iopscience.iop.org/0031-9120/48/4/431/article (accessed 8 December 2014).

[25] Condé Nast Digital. WIRED. Allain R. The physics of Angry Birds. http://www.wired.com/2010/10/physics-of-angry-birds/ (accessed 8 December 2014).

[26] Faculty of Social Sciences "1ka," University of Ljubljana; Faculty of Social Sciences, 2002–2009 [Online]. https://www.1ka.si/ (accessed 21 March 2015).

8

Increasing Access to Higher Education Through E-Learning

Susan L. Renes

Additional information is available at the end of the chapter

Abstract

Students with disabilities, rural students, students with parental responsibilities, and military students are populations who now have increased access to higher education due to E-Learning. Access limited by the location of the student, life circumstances that cannot be changed, or responsibilities that cannot be ignored, no longer act as barriers to higher education. This chapter examines how E-Learning benefits each of these populations and examines possibilities for international collaborations. The online environment has caused educators at all levels to re-examine how education might be delivered and who might benefit from this increased access.

Keywords: E-Learning, Access, Higher Education, Technology

1. Introduction

This chapter focuses on increased access to higher education that has resulted from E-Learning and reviews the literature addressing (a) students with disabilities, (b) rural students, (c) students with parental responsibilities, and (c) students currently serving in the military. A discussion of potential international collaborations that can occur thanks to the online environment is also included.

The National Center for Education Statistics [1] defined distance education as:

a formal educational process in which the instructor and the student are not in the same location. Thus, instruction might be synchronous or asynchronous, and it may involve communication through the use of video, audio, or computer technologies, or by correspond-ence (which may include both written correspondence and the use of technology such as CD-

ROM)...Hybrid/ blended online courses were defined as a combination of online and in-class instruction with reduced in-class seat time for students. (para. 1)

E-Learning in higher education has reached many unique populations. Students who have accessed higher education through E-Learning include (a) students with disabilities [2-7], (b) rural students who find it difficult to relocate [8-13], (c) parents with children [6, 14, 15], (d) military personnel [16-18], (e) students working full time [6, 19], and (f) urban students who find it easier to time-shift rather than space-shift [20, 21]. Renes and Strange [22] pointed out, "The National Center for Education Statistics reported in the 2006-07 academic year, 66 percent of the 4,160 2-year and 4-year Title IV degree-granting postsecondary institutions in the nation offered college-level distance education courses" (p. 204).

Students who have done well in E-Learning formats include:

(a) adult learners [23], (b) students who are self-directed learners [24], (c) students in rural areas [8, 25], (d) students who value interdependence [26], (e) students who must remain employed and require flexibility [25], and (f) students needed by their communities [8, 27]. [22, p. 204]

2. Students with disabilities

E-Learning has increased access to higher education for students with disabilities and allows many of these students to pursue their education in a place more suited to their needs than the college classroom. Some of the earliest work in distance education designed to meet the needs of these students occurred after World War II and the Korean War [28]. Texts were made available on tape; lectures were recorded; and students were taught using tutors, tape recorders, and the telephone. Herbert Rusalem was a pioneer who advocated for students with disabilities.

As Madeus [28] pointed out, in 1962 Rusalem wrote:

Physically handicapped college students requiring one or more special educational services are no longer a rarity on the American campus. Having the same goals as other students, they are enrolling in increasing numbers, encouraged by better public and private school preparation, improved rehabilitation services, the availability of scholarship funds, and a changing attitude toward disabled persons in our society. Since these sources of encouragement will probably become more influential in the future, in seems likely that the problems of educating the physically handicapped student will be receiving increasing attention. (p. 161)

Rusalem's [29] belief was that students with disabilities could achieve the high standards expected in higher education when certain modifications were made available.

In addition to students with visual or hearing impairments, students with disabilities who might benefit from E-Learning include students with cognitive or neurological disabilities (such as attention deficit disorder, autism, post traumatic stress disorder, traumatic brain injury, or memory impairments); physical disabilities (such as arthritis, repetitive stress injuries, quadriplegia, or paraplegia); and more temporary disabilities resulting from recent injuries or surgery [30].

There is currently momentum to evaluate and enforce the federal accessibility standards for online courses and this enforcement is significant, as it will allow students with or without disabilities to choose the learning delivery system that is most beneficial, given their particular circumstances [22, 30]. Three federal laws currently direct E-Learning programs with regard to accessibility standards: the Americans with Disabilities Act (ADA) and Section 504 and 508 of the Rehabilitation Act of 1973 [5, 28, 30-32]. Equal access to education is required by the ADA, and Section 504 provides for equal access to education but also stipulates that any educational institution receiving federal funding must ensure that web based programs, including E-Learning opportunities, are accessible to students with disabilities. Section 508 requires that types of technology are defined and include provisions that establish a minimum level of accessibility. The types of technology referred to in Section 508 include web-based and software applications, telecommunication products, and multimedia products [32].

E-Learning instructors often make their courses inaccessible without realizing it, as few instructors are trained to be aware of barriers for students with disabilities or barriers to accessibility in E-Learning courses [32]. However, it is the instructors' responsibility to make sure all students have access to course materials [33]. Courses designed to meet the needs of students with disabilities might also assist other students [34-36]. R. Mace in 1997 coined the term Universal Design for Learning (UDL) to describe a course design that improves the accessibility of course to students with different learning styles, different backgrounds, different abilities, and disabilities [32, 35, 37]. Far from being a "one size fits all," when done well, UDL offers various assignments and alternative learning tools to assist students. Roberts and colleagues [30] say students often do not want to disclose their disability for a variety of reasons and frontloading courses following UDL principles is especially helpful for these students. Tandy and Meachum [32] suggest that universal design helps "normalize" the experience of being disabled as UDL practices meet a variety of needs for students. For example, when an E-Learning instructor includes an audio and written description of the tools available to enhance watching a YouTube video, no student is singled out and all students might benefit from the enhancements in some way.

When designers follow UDL guidelines, physical environments, communication options, and the products developed are accessed by people with various characteristics including but not limited to:

age, race, ethnicity, gender, native language, and levels of ability to hear, see, move, and speak. When the range of characteristics of potential students is considered, distance learning course designers create learning environments where all students and instructors can fully partici- pate, just as architects design buildings that can be used by those who walk independently, walk with crutches, push baby strollers, and use wheelchairs. [37, p. 236]

Some of the more common tools include (a) captions for lived synchronized media, (b) insuring colored images are available in text format, (c) providing spoken versions of the text, and (d) lectures that can be repeatedly paused and restarted.

The technology required for E-Learning might take time for students with disabilities to learn [35]. However, the career commitment held by many persons with disabilities is often a key factor in their completion of a higher education program delivered in a distance format [38]. The number of students with disabilities desiring higher education is on the rise and addressing their needs could increase the number of students participating in E-learning courses [30, 33]. "An accessible course makes it possible for students or instructors with disabilities to interact with others in the class regardless of impaired mobility, speech, or vision" [32, p. 314].

3. Rural students

Information communication technology now available to a large number of rural students has increased the higher education opportunities for these students, but E-Learning for rural students is still challenged by significant barriers. The success of the rural student appears dependent on adequate preparation of (a) the faculty, (b) the rural student, and (c) the college or university supporting E-Learning. Lack of preparation by any one of these three potentially reduces the effectiveness of E-Learning. Owens and colleagues [9] interviewed 49 non-indigenous graduate and undergraduate students located in remote areas in Australia who completed distance education courses between 2003 and 2007. Three significant barriers were identified: (a) feelings of isolation, (b) the knowledge and attitude of the teaching staff, and (c) the ability to use the required technology. The quality of interaction between the student and the institution and the amount of communication was seen as the key to success. Communicating frequently with individuals who appeared caring and supportive deterred feelings of isolation, but the perception of not being treated as well as the students on campus undermined the distance learning experience. These conclusions are similar to what other studies have found [e.g., 39].

Training for faculty for e-learning online instruction in higher education varies significantly across institutions [2, 12, 40-43]. Faculty willing to accept the challenge, who are not overwhelmed by the expertise needed to both develop and then deliver a course in this manner, are often small in number [44]. Understanding rural students so instructors can teach in a culturally responsive way and improve the students' learning experiences requires another level of expertise [9, 45, 46]. Instructors serving rural students need to acknowledge the reasons their rural students do not want to leave their communities to attend school. Are they needed in their home communities and families to serve a vital role, are the travel costs prohibitive, are they hoping to avoid some of the discrimination and racism that exists on college campuses? Remaining sensitive to the needs of their rural students is vital for faculty serving rural students through E-Learning. Serving rural students from Indigenous communities will be more effective if the unique learning styles of the Indigenous people are understood and incorporated and if cultural and linguistic traditions including Indigenous knowledge are invited in to the E-Learning classroom [46].

Getting started in E-Learning can be challenging for rural or remote students due to possible insecurities about learning, potential disruptions to family life, and the financial cost of education [9, 11]. However, a strong desire on the part of rural students to pursue higher education has also been reported [13, 22, 44, 47], along with an understanding of the self-disciplined and self-regulated style required by E-Learning and an appreciation of the access to qualified or specialized instructors. The partial anonymity offered in E-Learning can actually make participation easier for rural students [25, 48].

The sense of isolation often felt by students engaged in E-Learning, including rural students, is well documented [22, 36]. Rural students, many who are first generation college students or members of other underrepresented groups in higher education, appreciate consistent and respectful communication with instructors and other members on the main college campus [47]. Prompt feedback from the instructor on how they performed on assignments is reported to reduce anxiety and the sense of isolation for rural students. Students are not generally looking for social interaction in the E-learning classroom but they do want to interact with their peers, their instructors, and the course content.

Institutional factors necessary to successfully launch and maintain e-learning programs are documented elsewhere [22, 25, 40, 49, 50], but a factor pertinent to successfully serving rural students is an understanding of the digital divide [11, 13, 41, 44, 51, 52]. The digital divide is a term used to describe economic and social inequality that exists for certain populations with regard to their access to, use of, or understanding of information and communication technologies [53]. In other words, who does or does not have fast, reliable Internet service and who is or is not able to use it. Higher education institutions hoping to serve rural students must appreciate the limitations of technology in both student access and student understanding of the technology. Many rural students do not have access to personal computers, requiring students to rely on the computers available in local schools or community centers, if available, and many rural students do not have access to computer training skills or access to a fast broadband connection [9, 13, 51]. Colleges and universities committed to (a) increasing student access to technology, (b) increasing student understanding of technology, and (c) improving the types of Internet access available are likely to see an increase in student enrollment and improve the chances for rural students to succeed in higher education.

4. Students with parental responsibilities

Students who are balancing student life, family life, and possibly job commitments often find E-Learning courses fit more easily in to their schedules. Like the students who live in urban environments, having the ability to time-shift rather than space-shift makes higher education more manageable [20, 21]. Specifically, women who have families and jobs, [14, 58], students parenting young children [6], and students who are pregnant [54] were found to benefit from E-Learning. Parents can see the task of getting to and from campus (with possibly a side trip to child care) as overwhelming when other responsibilities are looming. Another factor that makes E-Learning appealing for students with parental responsibilities is their experience of feeling "out of place" on a college campus, which can jeopardize their academic success [55]. The E-Learning environment often puts students who are parenting in touch with other students who are juggling the same responsibilities of wanting time to study, wanting to spend time with their children, and needing to earn a living [56].

The scheduled time for many face-to-face classes often conflicts with family responsibilities. However, parents who pursue higher education are often doing so for their children as much as for themselves, as they see themselves as role models for their children [56, 57]. Integrating their children in to the educational process by showing them the E-Learning platform, talking about assignments, and discussing successes as well as setbacks was reported to help with the flexibility parents need when completing college courses through E-Learning.

Students who are supporting families are part of the category of adult learners, defined as students age 25 and older who have multiple responsibilities, experiences that contribute directly to their learning, and goals based on well defined needs [58]. According to the National Center for Education Statistics (NCES), between 2008 and 2019, the number of students between the ages of 25 and 34 is projected to increase by 28 percent and for students 35 years of age and older, the projected increase is 22 percent. This compares to the 12 percent projected increase for "traditional" college students aged 18 to 24.

Following a critical review of the characteristics of adult students and adult learning theories, Cercone [23] determined that high quality E-Learning for adult students includes (a) collaboration and social interaction with peers, (b) the opportunity to connect new information with past experiences, (c) immediate application of the new knowledge, and (d) the opportunity for self-reflection and self-regulation of learning. Integrating these elements allows for what Majeski and Stover [10] describe as deep learning, a learning that is collaborative in nature, includes self-reflection, integrates new knowledge, and is directed toward an application. Deep learning moves learning from memorizing facts to integrating new knowledge with that which is already known, enriched by the fact that it occurs in a social environment.

5. Military populations

More than any group of soldiers in the past, current servicemen and servicewomen have the financial and technological resources to pursue higher education while still active in the military [17]. Even when remotely deployed, the E-Learning environment has made higher education accessible, making almost irrelevant the geographical requirements that used to exist for higher education. The current unparalleled availability of E-Learning along with an understanding of the benefits of higher education among prospective soldiers makes distance learning an effective tool for military recruitment. Prospective soldiers are aware of the benefits of higher education that will be available to them in their post military lives [17, 18]. Most men and women who are enlisted recruits do not have a college degree because, in general, they enlist before attending college [18]. However, approximately 90% of the recruits have a high school diploma or have obtained a GED, making recruits eligible to apply to colleges and universities.

While the structure of the E-Learning might fit well for military populations, the success of the military student will depend, in part, on the instructor's understanding of military culture [16,

59, 60]. Soldiers who are also students often work very hard and can set high standards in the E-Learning environment as they have been trained in the importance of duty and discipline. Students who are in the military often show great respect to the instructor, and are often willing to follow instructions and meet deadlines, as these have been reinforced in their daily lives as members of the military.

Higher education may support military students moving up the ranks and because their focus is "mission based," they often benefit from structure and well-defined goals with activities that lead directly to those goals [60]. The well-structured format along with clear and active communication between students and their instructors is essential when teaching distance students who might be unexpectedly taken away from the online environment or might be working in threatening and stressful environments. Letting students know ahead of time how TDY (Temporary Duty Yonder), PCS (Permanent of Station) or unexpected military assignments will be handled will be greatly appreciated by military students, as is constructive, consistent feedback from the instructor to let them know how they are performing in the class. Colleges and universities offering classes in an E-Learning environment to military students should understand that military students often do not complete their degrees until after their military service is done due to the threat, stress, and the unpredictability they might be dealing with [17].

6. International collaborations

International collaboration among students and instructors occurs easily in online formats [25]. With online international collaboration, learning is expanded beyond the local context. Including various cultural groups in the online format invites new ideas and views in to the learning community, potentially enriching the lives of the students and teachers involved [61-63]. The increased diversity that international collaborations offer in the E-Learning environment increases awareness of global and cultural issues and allows experts from other countries to participate and share their expertise. Online international collaborations that develop can be structured in a variety of ways and often develop from ordinary people taking on what Ife [64] describes as "globalization from below," an approach by interested local parties not driven by governments or institutions, that often result in international exchange that is more participatory in nature.

Students, teachers, schools, as well as institutions, and governments can benefit from international collaborations [61]. Leppisaari and Lee [65] investigated an international collaboration between students in Finland and Korea focused on environmental education. Leppisaari and Lee found that students in the study were enthusiastic about the subject matter; the students shared information and documented real world solutions to environmental problems using mobile phones and digital cameras. This sharing of information allowed students in both countries to view environmental problems from a new perspective, allowing them to better understand their own communities. Along with the subject matter, the students were also excited to learn about the culture and customs of another school. As the result of the pilot study, Leppisaari and Lee stated that the collaboration showed the possibilities of "cyber space pedagogy" (p. 244).

Colleges and universities hoping to increase diversity in both the face-to-face and E-learning classroom have entered in to agreements with developing countries that have a need for postsecondary education, resulting in networks of international education [61, 62]. These networks can result in aid for developing nations and academic publications and other academic acknowledgements for the faculty. Successful frameworks are now available and describe how to develop successful collaborations.

With the new opportunities now available for international collaboration come new caveats. When a classroom has an international community, the instruction coming from one culture might not follow the norms of the other students' cultures [66, 67] and questions asked from a western viewpoint might not be relevant to students living elsewhere [68]. Differences in communication styles and differences in teaching styles, both heavily influenced by the culture of the teacher and the student, make pedagogical sensitivity essential [69]. Part of this sensitivity includes an understanding of electronic colonialism [70], which means imposing western values on students from non-western cultures in E-Learning environments. Leppisaari and Lee [65] point out that while international learning communities develop around common interests, the pedagogy often has not caught up with the technology. Organization, continuous technical support, time allotted for development of the structure of the collaboration, and time allotted to develop trust between the collaborators are all key to successful collaborations [62, 63, 68].

The development of successful online collaborations requires that each group of collaborators understand their goals, hopes, fears, the time commitment involved in setting up and actually collaborating, and their beliefs about what will occur in the collaboration [71]. International collaboration can be a dynamic experience when there is sufficient planning and understanding among all the parties involved [68]. When teaching critical thinking skills and creative problem solving, it is essential that students examine situations from a variety of perspectives, and international collaborations in E-learning offer this environment. Mitroff and Linestone [72] stated, "because of long and arduous years involved in mastering a particular discipline, the academic/professional mind easily becomes the prisoner of a particular way of viewing the world" (p.34).

7. Conclusion

Information communication technology has increased the number of ways students and instructors interact with each other, the location of students who do the interacting, and the types of learning and student communities that can develop. The UDL principles that assist students with disabilities were found to improve the learning environment for all students. When working with rural students, understanding the digital divide and addressing these barriers will further increase their access to higher education. Understanding higher education as it relates to recruitment and rank in the military and understanding the military culture will allow better experiences for military personnel who choose to pursue higher education through E-Learning. Suspending the demand for a four-year completion rate now seen in higher education will ease the pressure on all of these populations, probably more for students with parental responsibilities than any other student group. Finally, while acknowledging the "cyber space pedagogy" [65, p. 244] that could develop as the result of international colonialism, the possibility of electronic colonialism described by Boshier and colleagues [70] must also be acknowledged and prevented.

Can E-Learning also be a platform that does not support oppression and allows education to be de-colonized, offering opportunities for all those who for various reasons have been denied the opportunity? In examining the new opportunities now available to students with disabilities, rural student, students with parental responsibilities, military populations, and the opportunities for international collaborations because of the E-learning environment, it is obvious that access to higher education can be increased due to E-Learning. The challenge now available for E-Learning is how to make this new learning environment less oppressive, more inclusive, and more collaborative than learning environments in the past. Successfully addressing this challenge will not only benefit the E-Learning but improve the face-to-face classroom environment as well.

Author details

Susan L. Renes

Address all correspondence to: slrenes@alaska.edu

School of Education, University of Alaska Fairbanks, Alaska

References

[1] National Center for Education Statistics. (2008). Distance education at degree-granting postsecondary institutions: 2006-07. Retrieved from http://nces.ed.gov/pubsearch/pubsinfo.asp?pubid=2009044

[2] Austin, G. A. (2010). Administrative challenges and rewards of online learning in a rural community college: Reflections of a distance learning administrator. *New Directions for Community Colleges, 150,* 27–36. doi: 10.1002/cc.402

[3] Crow, K. L. (2008). Four types of disabilities: Their impact on online learning. *TechTrends: Linking Research and Practice to Improve Learning, 52*(1), 51–55.

[4] McNab, L. (2005). Interview: Speaking personally with Chris Dede. *American Journal of Distance Education, 19*(2), 119–123.

[5] Musick, K. (2001). Distance education: Promoting access and equity for adult learners with disabilities. *Rehabilitation Education, 15*(1), 63–77.

[6] Nightengale, B. (2014). Teaching honors online at a public college. *Journal of the National Collegiate Honors Council, 15*(1), 61–62.

[7] Spaniol, M., Klamma, R., Springer, L., & Jarke, M. (2006). Aphasic communities of learning on the web. *International Journal of Distance Education Technologies, 4*(1), 31–45.

[8] Chaney, E., Chaney, J., Eddy, J., & Stellefson, M. (2008). Making the case for distance education in the health education and health promotion profession. *International Electronic Journal of Health Education, 11*(1), 5–18.

[9] Kawalilak, C., Wells, N., Connell, L., & Beamer, K. (2012). E-Learning access, opportunities, and challenges for aboriginal adult learners located in rural communities. *College Quarterly, 15*(2), 1–18.

[10] Majeski, R., & Stover, M. (2007). Theoretically based pedagogical strategies leading to deep earning in asynchronous online gerontology courses. *Educational Gerontology, 33*(3), 171–185. doi: 10.1080/03601270600850826

[11] Owens, J., Hardcastel, L., & Richardson, B. (2009). Learning from a distance: The experience of remote students. *Journal of Distance Education, 23*(3), 57–74.

[12] Ozdemir, Z. D., & Abrevaya, J. (2007). Adoption of technology-mediated distance education: A longitudinal analysis. *Information & Management, 44*(5), 467–479. doi: 10.1016/j.im.2007.04.006

[13] Philpott, D., Sharpe, D., & Neville, R. (2009). The effectiveness of web-delivered learning with aboriginal students: Findings from a study in coastal Labrador. *Canadian Journal of Learning and Technology/La Revue Canadienne de L'apprentissage et de La Technologie, 35*(3). Retrieved from http://www.cjlt.ca/index.php/cjlt/article/view/545

[14] Carnevale, D. (2002). Distance education attracts older women who have families and jobs, study finds. *The Chronicle of Higher Education, 49*(11), A33.

[15] Ke, F., & Xie, K. (2009). Toward deep learning for adult students in online courses. *Internet and Higher Education, 12*(1), 136–145. doi: 10.1016/j.iheduc.2009.08.001

[16] Garner, G., & Keynard, C. (2000). Serving the underserved--distance learning: An alternative for the military. *Community College Journal, 70*(5), 44–51.

[17] McMurry, A. J. (2007). College students, the GI bill, and the proliferation of online learning and contemporary challenges. *Internet & Higher Education, 10*(2), 143–150.

[18] Vardalis, J. J., & Waters, S. N. (2011). Factors influencing military police officers in their decision in selecting higher educational institutions. *Journal of Criminal Justice Education, 22*(4), 479–492. doi: 10.1080/10511253.2010.534487

[19] Talbert, J. J. (2009). Distance education: One solution to the nursing shortage? *Clinical Journal of Oncology and Nursing, 13*(3), 269–270.

[20] Whitaker, R. (2007). Teaching online in the Bronx: Local distance education. *On the Horizon, 15*(3), 145–156. doi: 10.1108/10748120710825031

[21] Zhao, J. J., Alexander, M. W., Perreault, H., Waldman, L., & Truell, A. D. (2009). Faculty and student use of technologies, user productivity, and user preference in distance education. *Journal of Education for Business, 84*(4), 206–212.

[22] Renes, S., & Strange, T. (2011). Using technology to enhance higher education. *Innovative Higher Education, 36*(3), 203–213. doi: 10.1007/s10755-010-9167-3

[23] Cercone, K. (2008). Characteristics of online learners with implications for online learning design. *Association for the Advancement of Computing in Education Journal, 16*(2), 137–159.

[24] Salinas, M. (2008). From Dewey to Gates: A model to integrate psychoeducational principles in the selection and use of instructional technology. *Computers & Education, 50*(3), 652–660. doi: 10.1016/j.compedu.2006.08.002

[25] Appana, S. (2008). A review of benefits and limitations of online learning in the context of the student, the instructor, and the tenured faculty. *International Journal on E-Learning, 7*(1), 5–22.

[26] Smith, K. A., Sheppard, S. D., Johnson, D. W., & Johnson, R. T. (2005). Pedagogies of engagement: Classroom-based practices. *Journal of Engineering Education, 94*(1), 87–101.

[27] Southernwood, J. (2008). Distance learning: The future of continuing professional development. *Community Practitioner: The Journal of the Community Practitioners' and Health Visitors' Association, 81*(10), 21–23.

[28] Madaus, J. (2011). The history of disability services in higher education. *New Directions for Higher Education, 154*, 5–15. doi: 10.1002/he.429

[29] Rusalem, H. (1962). The physically handicapped student and the college faculty. *College and University, 37*(2), 161–67.

[30] Roberts, J. B., Crittenden, L. A., Crittenden, J. C. (2011). Students with disabilities and online learning: A cross-institutional study of perceived satisfaction with accessibility compliance and services. *The Internet and Higher Education, 14*(4), 242–250. doi: 10.1016/j.iheduc.2011.05.004

[31] Madaus, J., Kowitt, J., & Lalor, A. (2012). The Higher Education Opportunity Act: Impact on students with disabilities. *Rehabilitation Research, Policy, and Education, 26*(1), 33–41.

[32] Tandy, C., & Meachum, M. (2009). Removing the barriers for students with disabilities: Accessible online and web enhanced courses. *Journal of Teaching in Social Work, 29*, 313–328. doi: 10.1080/08841230903022118

[33] Hollins, N., & Foley, A. (2013). The experiences of students with learning disabilities in a higher education virtual campus. *Educational Technology Research & Development, 61*(4), 607–624. doi: 10.1007/s11423-013-9302-9

[34] Edmunds, C. D. (2004). Providing access to students with disabilities in online distance education: Legal and technical concerns for higher education. *American Journal of Distance Education, 18*(1), 51–62. doi: 10.1207/s15389286ajde1801_5

[35] Seale, J. (2010). Editorial: Disability, technology, and e-learning: Challenging conceptions. *ALT-J Association for Learning Technology Journal, 14*(1), 1–8. doi: 10.1080/09687760500480025

[36] Simminolli, A., & Hinson, J. M. (2008). College students' with learning disabilities personal reactions to online learning. *Journal of College Reading & Learning, 38*(2), 49–62.

[37] Burgstahler, S., Corrigan, B., & McCarter, J. (2004). Making distance learning courses accessible to students and instructors with disabilities: A case study. *The Internet and Higher Education, 7*(3), 233–246. doi: 10.1016/j.iheduc.2004.06.004

[38] Kim-Rupnow, W. S., Dowrick, P. W., & Burke, L. S. (2001). Implications for improving access and outcomes for individuals with disabilities in postsecondary distance education. *American Journal of Distance Education, 15*(1), 25–40.

[39] Ravoi, A., & Barnum, K. (2003). Online course effectiveness: An analysis of student interactions and perceptions of learning. *Journal of Distance Education, 18*(1), 57–73.

[40] Keramidas, C. G., Ludlow, B. L., Collins, B. C., & Baird, C. M. (2007). Saving your sanity when teaching in an online environment: Lessons learned. *Rural Special Education Quarterly, 26*(1), 28–39.

[41] Leist, J., & Travis, J. (2010). Planning for online courses at rural community colleges. *New Directions for Community Colleges, 150*, 17–25.

[42] Menchaca, M. P., & Bekele, T. A. (2008). Learner and instructor identified success factors in distance education. *Distance Education, 29*(3), 231–252. doi: 10.1080/01587910802395771

[43] Nicolle, P. S., & Lou, Y. (2008). Technology adoption into teaching and learning by mainstream university faculty: A mixed methodology study revealing the "how, when, why, and why not". *Journal of Educational Research, 39*(3), 235–265. doi: 10.2190/EC.39.3.c

[44] Cjeda, B. D. (2007). Connecting to the larger world: Distance education in rural community colleges. *New Directions for Community Colleges, 137,* 87–98. doi: 10.1002/cc.273

[45] Carter, L., & Graham, R. D. (2012). The evolution of online education at a small Northern Ontario University: Theory and practice. *Journal of Distance Education, 26*(2), 1–7.

[46] Renes, S. (2014). Amplifying indigenous voices. *Hybrid Pedagogy.* Retrieved from http://www.hybridpedagogy.com/journal/amplifying-indigenous-voices/

[47] Priebe, L. C., Ross, T. L., & Low, K. W. (2008). Exploring the role of distance education in fostering equitable university access for first generation students: A phenomenological survey. *International Review of Research in Open and Distance Learning, 9*(1), 1–12.

[48] Sullivan, P. (2002). "It's easier to be yourself when you are invisible": Female college students discuss their online classroom experiences. *Innovative Higher Education, 27*(2), 129–144.

[49] Dykman, C. A., & Davis, C. K. (2008). Part one: The shift toward online education. *Journal of Information Systems, 19*(1), 11–16.

[50] Mapuva, J. (2009). Confronting challenges to e-learning in higher education institutions. *International Journal of Education & Development using Information & Communication Technology, 5*(3), 1–14.

[51] Craduck, L. (2012). The future of Australian e-Learning: It's all about access. *E-Journal of Business Education & Scholarship of Teaching, 6*(2), 1–11.

[52] Raturi, S., Hogan, R., & Thaman, K. H. (2012). Learners' access to tools and experience with technology at the University of the South Pacific: *Readiness for E-learning. Australasian Journal of Educational Technology, 27*(3), 411–427.

[53] U.S. Department of Commerce, National Telecommunications and Information Administration (NTIA). (1995). Falling through the net: A survey of the have nots in rural and urban America. Retrieved from http://www.ntia.doc.gov/ntiahome/fallingthru.html

[54] Hordzi, W. H. K. (2004). The challenges faced by University Of Education, Winneba distance education student-mothers during examinations. *IFE PsychologIA, 16*(2), 243–254. doi: 10.4314/ifep.v16i2.23814

[55] Perna, L. W. (2010). Understanding the working college student. *Academe, 9*(4), 30–32.

[56] Reay, D., Ball, S., & David, M. (2002). 'It's taking me a long time but I'll get there in the end': Mature students on access courses and higher education choice. *British Educational Research Journal, 28*(1), 5–19. doi: 10.1080/01411920120109711

[57] Vaccaro, A., & Lovell, C. (2010). Inspiration from home: Understanding family as key to adult women's self-investment. *Adult Education Quarterly, 60*(2), 161–176.

[58] Kimmel, S., Gaylor, K., Grubbs, R., & Hayes, B. (2012). Good times to hard times: An examination of adult learners' enrollment from 2004-2010. *Journal of Behavioral & Applied Management, 14*(1), 18–38.

[59] Artino, A. (2008). Motivational beliefs and perceptions of instructional quality: Predicting satisfaction with online training. *Journal of Computer Assisted Learning, 24*(3), 260–270. doi: 10.1111/j.1365-2729.2007.00258.x

[60] Smucny, D., & Stover, M. (2013). Enhancing teaching and learning for active-duty military students. *American Sociological Association Footnotes, 41*(3), 1–8.

[61] Hastie, M., Chun Hung, I., & Chen, N. S. (2010). A blended synchronous learning model for educational international collaboration. *Innovations in Education & Teaching International, 47*(1), 9–24. doi: 10.1080/14703290903525812

[62] Holland, D. (2010). Notes from the field: Lessons learned in building a framework for an international collaboration. *New Directions for Higher Education, 150*, 31–41. doi: 10.1002/he.388

[63] Rautenbach, J. V., & Black-Hughes, C. (2012). Bridging the hemispheres through the use of technology: International collaboration in social work training. *Journal of Social Work Education, 48*(4), 797–815. doi: 10.5175/JSWE.2012.201100114

[64] Ife, J. (1995, November). *Globalization from below: Social services and the new world order.* Paper presented at the Asia-Pacific Regional Social Services Conference, Christchurch, New Zealand.

[65] Leppisarsi, I., & Lee, O. (2012). Modelling digital natives' international collaboration: Finnish-Korean experiences of environmental education. *Journal of Educational Technology & Society, 15*(2), 244–256.

[66] Keengwe, J., Onchwari, G., & Onchwari, J. (2009). Teaching and student learning: Toward a learner-centered teaching model. *AACE Journal, 17*(1), 11–22.

[67] Moore, M. G. (2006). Editorial: Questions of culture. *American Journal of Distance Education, 20*(1), 1–5. doi: 10.1207/s15389286ajde2001_1

[68] Vosit-Stellar, J., Morse, A. B., & Mitrea, N. (2011). Evolution of an international collaboration: A unique experience across borders. *Clinical Journal of Oncology Nursing, 15*(5), 564–566.

[69] EBS (2008). *The East and the West.* Seoul, Korea: Educational Broadcasting System. Retrieved from https://www.youtube.com/watch?v=RnyaD1ZjS-s

[70] Boshier, R., Wilson, M., & Qayyum, A. (1998). Lifelong education and the world wide web: American hegemony or diverse utopia? *International Journal of Lifelong Learning, 18*(4), 275–285. doi: 10.1080/026013799293694

[71] Samuel, M. A., & Mariaye, H. (2014) De-colonising international collaboration: The University of KwaZulu-Natal-Mauritius Institute of Education Cohort PhD programme, *Compare: A Journal of Comparative and International Education, 44*(4), 501–521. doi: 10.1080/03057925.2013.795100

[72] Mitroff, I., & Linestone, H. (1993). The unbounded mind: Breaking the chains of traditional business thinking. New York, NY: Oxford University Press.

Permissions

List of Contributors

Martin Lesage, Gilles Raîche, Martin Riopel, Frédérick Fortin and Dalila Sebkhi
Faculty of Education, Education and Pedagogy Department, Université du Québec à Montréal (UQÀM), C.P., Montréal, Canada

Todorka Glushkova
Plovdiv University "Paisii Hilendarski", Bulgaria

Andrée Roy
Université de Moncton, Moncton, Canada

Charles Potter
Private Practice, Johannesburg, South Africa

Viliam Fedák and Pavel Záskalický
Department of Electrical Engineering and Mechatronics, Faculty of Electrical Engineering and Informatics, Technical University of Košice, Slovakia

Ahmad Rafi
Faculty of Creative Multimedia, Multimedia University, Cyberjaya, Selangor, Malaysia

Khairulanuar Samsudin and Hafizul Fahri Hanafi
Computing Department, Faculty of Art, Computing and Creative Industry, Sultan Idris University of Education, Tanjung Malim, Perak, Malaysia

Robert Repnik and Dominik Robič
Faculty of Natural Sciences and mathematics, University of Maribor, Maribor, Slovenia

Igor Pesek
Faculty of Natural Sciences and mathematics, University of Maribor, Maribor, Slovenia
Institute E-um, Ptuj, Slovenia

Susan L. Renes
School of Education, University of Alaska Fairbanks, Alaska

Index

CPSIA information can be obtained
at www.ICGtesting.com
Printed in the USA
BVHW061315240519
549249BV00005B/543/P